MAF

for

EVERYONE

20TH ANNIVERSARY EDITION WITH STUDY GUIDE

NEW TESTAMENT FOR EVERYONE
20TH ANNIVERSARY EDITION WITH STUDY GUIDE
N. T. Wright

Matthew for Everyone, Part 1
Matthew for Everyone, Part 2
Mark for Everyone
Luke for Everyone
John for Everyone, Part 1
John for Everyone, Part 2
Acts for Everyone, Part 1
Acts for Everyone, Part 2
Romans for Everyone, Part 1
Romans for Everyone, Part 2
1 Corinthians for Everyone
2 Corinthians for Everyone
Galatians and Thessalonians for Everyone
Ephesians, Philippians, Colossians and Philemon for Everyone
1 and 2 Timothy and Titus for Everyone
Hebrews for Everyone
James, Peter, John and Judah for Everyone
Revelation for Everyone

MARK

for

EVERYONE

20TH ANNIVERSARY EDITION WITH STUDY GUIDE

N. T.
WRIGHT

STUDY GUIDE BY MARK PRICE

WESTMINSTER
JOHN KNOX PRESS
LOUISVILLE • KENTUCKY

First published in Great Britain in 2001 by the
Society for Promoting Christian Knowledge
36 Causton Street
London SW1P 4ST
www.spckpublishing.co.uk

Copublished in 2004 by the Society for Promoting
Christian Knowledge, London, and Westminster John Knox Press,
100 Witherspoon Street, Louisville, KY 40202.

20th Anniversary Edition with Study Guide
Published in 2023
by Westminster John Knox Press
Louisville, Kentucky

23 24 25 26 27 28 29 30 31 32—10 9 8 7 6 5 4 3 2 1

Cover design by Allison Taylor

Library of Congress Cataloging-in-Publication Data

Names: Wright, N. T. (Nicholas Thomas), author. | Price, Mark, writer of
  supplementary textual content.
Title: Mark for everyone / N. T. Wright ; study guide by Mark Price.
Description: 20th anniversary edition with study guide. | Louisville,
  Kentucky : Westminster John Knox Press, 2023. | Series: New testament
  for everyone | "First published in Great Britain in 2001 by the Society
  for Promoting Christian Knowledge". | Summary: "Breaking down the gospel
  of Mark into brief, easy-to-study segments, Wright shows how the message
  of this ancient book speaks powerfully to the spiritual longings of
  contemporary readers. New Christians and longtime followers of Jesus
  alike will find inspiration and practical wisdom for their journey
  within these pages"-- Provided by publisher.
Identifiers: LCCN 2023020919 (print) | LCCN 2023020920 (ebook) | ISBN
  9780664266387 (paperback) | ISBN 9781646983223 (ebook)
Subjects: LCSH: Bible. Mark--Commentaries.
Classification: LCC BS2585.53 .W75 2023 (print) | LCC BS2585.53 (ebook) |
  DDC 226.3/07--dc23/eng/20230602
LC record available at https://lccn.loc.gov/2023020919
LC ebook record available at https://lccn.loc.gov/2023020920

Most Westminster John Knox Press books are available at special quantity
discounts when purchased in bulk by corporations, organizations and special-interest groups.
For more information, please e-mail SpecialSales@wjkbooks.com.

For
Sister Mary Magdalene SLG
with gratitude for the love, support and prayers
of over fifty years

CONTENTS

CONTENTS

CONTENTS

INTRODUCTION TO THE
ANNIVERSARY EDITION

It took me ten years, but I'm glad I did it. Writing a guide to the books of the New Testament felt at times like trying to climb all the Scottish mountains in quick succession. But the views from the tops were amazing, and discovering new pathways up and down was very rewarding as well. The real reward, though, has come in the messages I've received from around the world, telling me that the books have been helpful and encouraging, opening up new and unexpected vistas.

Perhaps I should say that this series wasn't designed to help with sermon preparation, though many preachers have confessed to me that they've used it that way. The books were meant, as their title suggests, for everyone, particularly for people who would never dream of picking up an academic commentary but who nevertheless want to dig a little deeper.

The New Testament seems intended to provoke all readers, at whatever stage, to fresh thought, understanding and practice. For that, we all need explanation, advice and encouragement. I'm glad these books seem to have had that effect, and I'm delighted that they are now available with study guides in these new editions.

N. T. Wright
2022

INTRODUCTION

On the very first occasion when someone stood up in public to tell people about Jesus, he made it very clear: this message is for *everyone*.

It was a great day – sometimes called the birthday of the church. The great wind of God's spirit had swept through Jesus' followers and filled them with a new joy and a sense of God's presence and power. Their leader, Peter, who only a few weeks before had been crying like a baby because he'd lied and cursed and denied even knowing Jesus, found himself on his feet explaining to a huge crowd that something had happened which had changed the world for ever. What God had done for him, Peter, he was beginning to do for the whole world: new life, forgiveness, new hope and power were opening up like spring flowers after a long winter. A new age had begun in which the living God was going to do new things in the world – beginning then and there with the individuals who were listening to him. 'This promise is for *you*,' he said, 'and for your children, and for everyone who is far away.' (Acts 2.39) It wasn't just for the person standing next to you. It was for everyone.

Within a remarkably short time this came true to such an extent that the young movement spread throughout much of the known world. And one way in which the *everyone* promise worked out was through the writings of the early Christian leaders. These short works – mostly letters and stories about Jesus – were widely circulated and eagerly read. They were never intended for either a religious or intellectual elite. From the very beginning they were meant for everyone.

That is as true today as it was then. Of course, it matters that some people give time and care to the historical evidence, the meaning of the original words (the early Christians wrote in Greek), and the exact and particular force of what different writers were saying about God, Jesus, the world and themselves. This series is based quite closely on that sort of work. But the point of it all is that the message can get out to everyone, especially to people who wouldn't normally read a book with footnotes and Greek words in it. That's the sort of person for whom these books are written. And that's why there's a glossary, in the back, of the key words that you can't really get along without, with a simple description of what they mean. Whenever you see a word in **bold type** in the text, you can go to the back and remind yourself what's going on.

There are of course many translations of the New Testament available today. The one I offer here is designed for the same kind of reader: one who mightn't necessarily understand the more formal, sometimes even ponderous, tones of some of the standard ones. I have of course tried to keep as close to the original as I can. But my main aim has been to be sure that the words can speak not just to some people, but to everyone.

Let me add a note about the translation the reader will find here of the Greek word *Christos*. Most translations simply say 'Christ', but most modern English speakers assume that that word is simply a proper name (as though 'Jesus' were Jesus 'Christian' name and 'Christ' were his 'surname'). For all sorts of reasons, I disagree; so I have experimented not only with 'Messiah' (which is what the word literally means) but sometimes, too, with 'King'.

This particular volume introduces you to the shortest and sharpest of the stories about Jesus. Many people think Mark's gospel was the first to be written, and certainly it has all the zip and punch of a quick, hasty story that's meant to grab you by the collar and make you face the truth about Jesus, about God and about yourself. So here it is: Mark for everyone!

Tom Wright

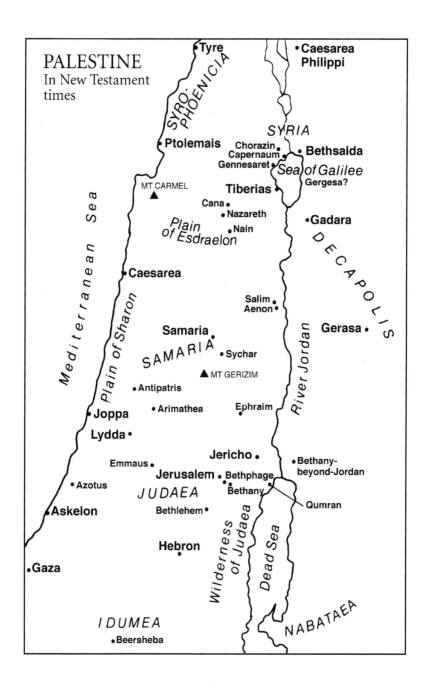

PALESTINE
In New Testament
times

Tyre

Caesarea Philippi

SYRO-PHOENICIA

SYRIA

Ptolemais

Chorazin
Capernaum
Gennesaret

Bethsaida

Sea of Galilee

Gergesa?

MT CARMEL

Tiberias

Cana
Nazareth
Nain

Gadara

Plain of Esdraelon

Mediterranean Sea

DECAPOLIS

Caesarea

Plain of Sharon

Salim
Aenon

Samaria

Gerasa

SAMARIA

Sychar

River Jordan

MT GERIZIM

Antipatris

Arimathea

Ephraim

Joppa

Lydda

Jericho

Bethany-beyond-Jordan

Emmaus

Jerusalem
Bethphage
Bethany

Azotus

JUDAEA

Qumran

Askelon

Bethlehem

Wilderness of Judaea

Dead Sea

Hebron

Gaza

IDUMEA

NABATAEA

Beersheba

MARK 1.1-8

The Preaching of John the Baptist

¹This is where the good news starts – the good news of Jesus the Messiah, God's son. ²Isaiah the prophet put it like this ('Look! I am sending my messenger ahead of me; he will clear the way for you!'): ³'A shout goes up in the desert: Make way for the Lord! Clear a straight path for him!' ⁴John the Baptizer appeared in the desert. He was announcing a baptism of repentance, to forgive sins. ⁵The whole of Judaea, and everyone who lived in Jerusalem, went out to him; they confessed their sins and were baptized by him in the river Jordan. ⁶John wore camel-hair clothes, with a leather belt round his waist. He used to eat locusts and wild honey. ⁷'Someone a lot stronger than me is coming close behind', John used to tell them. 'I don't deserve to squat down and undo his sandals. ⁸I've plunged you in the water; he's going to plunge you in the holy spirit.'

You are sound asleep and dreaming, when suddenly the door bursts open and a bright light shines full in your face. A voice, breaking in on your dream-world, shouts, 'Wake up! Get up! You'll be late!' And without more ado, the speaker splashes your face with cold water to make the point. Time to stop dreaming and face the most important day of your life.

That's what the opening of Mark's **gospel** is like. It's a great way to start, because what Mark is telling us is that that's what **John the Baptist** was like to the Jewish people of his day. John's ministry burst in upon the surprised Jewish world. Many had been looking for a sign from God, but they hadn't expected it to look like this. Many had wanted a **Messiah** to lead them against the Romans, but they weren't anticipating a prophet telling them to repent.

John was a voice, shouting across the dreams, and perhaps the nightmares, of the Judaism of Herod and Caiaphas, the Judaism that told again and again the story of freedom but had no idea what freedom would look like when it came. Some thought John was mad, that it was him who was dreaming; but here he was, splashing cold water all over them and telling them to get ready for the greatest moment in Jewish history, in world history.

The bright light he was shining in their faces was the story they all knew very well, but with a new twist. Every year, at Passover time, they recited the story of the **Exodus** from Egypt, telling over and over how God rescued Israel from Pharaoh, bringing them through the Red Sea

1

and away across the wilderness to their promised land. Along with the creation story, it's the most important story in the whole Old Testament, and John's hearers would have known it well. But instead of simply hearing the words and remembering the story, John was turning it into a drama, a play, and telling his hearers that they were the cast. They were to come through the water and be free. They were to leave behind 'Egypt' – the world of sin in which they were living, the world of rebelling against the living God. They, the Israel of the day, were looking in the wrong direction and going in the wrong direction. It was time to turn round and go the right way (that's what 'repentance' means). It was time to stop dreaming and wake up to God's reality.

The challenge had a sharp edge to it. Someone was coming, coming very soon, and John was getting people ready. If someone came into your town and told you that the President, or the Princess, or some other great person, was on their way to pay you a visit, you'd quickly rush around smartening things up. In Britain it's a standard joke that wherever the Queen goes she smells fresh paint. John was like the messenger going ahead of royalty, getting everywhere ready for the 'stronger one' who was coming after him. Israel as a whole needed smartening up. Each individual within Israel needed to smarten up. Someone was coming who would put even John in the shade.

Who did John think this 'someone' was? It's not clear, and perhaps it wasn't clear even to him. He may well have thought it would be YHWH himself, Israel's God in person. Or he may have thought it would be the Messiah. Or he may have thought it would somehow be both. But what this figure would do was quite clear. What John had done with water, the Coming One would do with spirit – the **holy spirit**.

This promise – it's a warning, too, of course, but basically it's a promise – picks up some more of the Jewish freedom images from the Old Testament. Mark points in the same direction with the two biblical quotations, from Malachi and Isaiah, that open the story. One of the great promises that Israel had cherished for centuries was that when YHWH finally made the Exodus story happen all over again, setting his people free once and for all, that would be the time when he would come to live personally with his people. He would be with them; he would be their God, and they would be his people. How would he do this? In the original Exodus story God's presence lived with Israel in the pillar of cloud and fire. This time it was to be similar but different. God's spirit would live with people, in people, becoming the air they breathe, the fire in their hearts. This is the promise they had lived on. John says it's now going to come true. But are they ready for it?

They certainly weren't ready – and perhaps John wasn't either – for what they got. Mark's opening verse tells us what to expect; all this is the beginning of the good news of Jesus the Messiah, God's son ('God's son', in the Judaism of the day, was a title for the Messiah). But things weren't that clear at the time. What they had was the voice and the water: they were now to get ready for the human figure who would make sense, but very disturbing sense, of it all.

The main thing Mark gets us to do in this opening passage is to sense the shock of the new thing God was doing. If you're sick, and unable to sleep much, sometimes the night seems to go on for ever. But then, just when you're dozing a bit, suddenly the alarm clock goes off: it really is morning. That's the mood here. It raises the question for us too: where are we asleep today, in our churches, our communities, our personal lives? What might it take to wake us up?

MARK 1.9–13

Jesus' Baptism

> [9]This is how it happened. Around that time, Jesus came from Nazareth in Galilee, and was baptized by John in the river Jordan. [10]That very moment, as he was coming out of the water, he saw the heavens open, and the spirit coming down like a dove onto him. [11]Then there came a voice out of the heavens: 'You are my son! You are the one I love! You make me very glad.'
>
> [12]All at once the spirit pushed him out into the desert. [13]He was in the desert forty days, and the satan tested him there. He was with the wild beasts, and angels waited on him.

A famous moviemaker had a huge legal wrangle with his long-time mentor and guide. The younger man simply couldn't handle criticism, and ended up rejecting the person who had helped him so much. When it was all over, a close friend summed up the real problem. 'It was all about an ungenerous father,' he explained, 'and a son looking for affirmation and love.'

It happens all the time, in families, businesses, all over. Many children grow up in our world who have never had a father say to them (either in words, in looks, or in hugs), 'You are my dear child', let alone, 'I'm pleased with you.' In the Western world, even those fathers who think this in their hearts are often too tongue-tied or embarrassed to tell their children how delighted they are with them. Many, alas, go by the completely opposite route: angry voices, bitter rejection, the slamming of doors.

The whole Christian **gospel** could be summed up in this point: that when the living God looks at us, at every baptized and believing Christian, he says to us what he said to Jesus on that day. He sees us, not as

3

we are in ourselves, but as we are in Jesus Christ. It sometimes seems impossible, especially to people who have never had this kind of support from their earthly parents, but it's true: God looks at us, and says, 'You are my dear, dear child; I'm delighted with you.' Try reading that sentence slowly, with your own name at the start, and reflect quietly on God saying that to you, both at your **baptism** and every day since.

How does this come about? It will take the whole story, particularly Jesus' death and **resurrection**, to explain. But this is what the Christian gospel is all about.

It is true for one simple but very profound reason: Jesus is the **Messiah**, and the Messiah represents his people. What is true of him is true of them. The word 'Messiah' means 'the anointed one'; and this story tells how Jesus was anointed with the **holy spirit**, marked out as God's son. The Messiah is called 'God's son' in a few biblical passages, including the one that the heavenly voice seems to be echoing here (Psalm 2.7). Though the early Christians realized quite quickly that Jesus was God's son in an even deeper sense, they clung on to his messiahship for dear life. It was because Jesus was and is Messiah that God said to them, as he does to us today, what he said to Jesus at his baptism. And without that word from God all we often hear, in our mind's ear, is doors being slammed.

Mark tells the story in quite solemn language, echoing the Old Testament: 'This is how it happened'; 'he saw the heavens open'. If we go back to the biblical roots we will realize what 'seeing heavens opened' means. It doesn't mean that Jesus saw a little door ajar miles up in the sky. '**Heaven**' in the Bible often means God's dimension behind ordinary reality. It's more as though an invisible curtain, right in front of us, was suddenly pulled back, so that instead of the trees and flowers and buildings, or in Jesus' case the river, the sandy desert and the crowds, we are standing in the presence of a different reality altogether.

A good deal of Christian **faith** is a matter of learning to live by this different reality even when we can't see it. Sometimes, at decisive and climactic moments, the curtain is drawn back and we see, or hear, what's really going on; but most of the time we walk by faith, not by sight. One of the things Mark is saying to us, in the way he's written his gospel, is that when we look at the whole life of Jesus that's how we are to understand it. Look at this story, he says, look at this life, and learn to see and hear in it the heavenly vision, the heavenly voice. Learn to hear these words addressed to yourself. Let them change you, mould you, make you somebody new, the person God wants you to be. Discover in this story the normally hidden heavenly dimension of God's world.

Any early Christian reading this passage would also, of course, believe that their own baptism into Jesus the Messiah was the moment when, for them, the curtain had been drawn back and these words had

4

been spoken to them. We need to find ways, in today's church, of bringing this to life with our own practice of baptism and teaching about it.

When we do this, we will be equipped, as Jesus was, to be sent out into the desert. Jesus is acting out the great drama of Israel's **Exodus** from Egypt, Israel's journey through the wilderness into the promised land. The road Jesus must tread, precisely because he is God's dear son, is the road that leads through the dry and dusty paths, through temptation and apparent failure. So it will be for us as well. If we start the journey imagining that our God is a bully, an angry threatening parent ready to yell at us, slam the door on us, or kick us out into the street because we haven't quite made the grade, we will fail at the first whisper of temptation. But if we remember the voice that spoke those powerful words of love we will find the way through.

Mark tells us that Jesus was 'with the wild beasts'. He doesn't say whether they're threatening, or whether this is a sign of new creation (with Jesus as the second Adam in a new garden of Eden?) or maybe both. But the angels were there, too. They were not to keep Jesus from being tested by **satan**, just as finally they would not keep him from Calvary itself, but to assure him that his beloved Father was watching over him, was there with him, was loving him, acting through him, pouring out his spirit all the time in and through him. Jesus went the way that all his people must go; and he could do it because he had heard the words of love, the words of life.

MARK 1.14–20

The Calling of the Disciples

¹⁴After John's arrest, Jesus came into Galilee, announcing God's good news.

¹⁵'The time is fulfilled!' he said; 'God's kingdom is arriving! Turn back, and believe the good news!'

¹⁶As he went along beside the sea of Galilee he saw Simon and his brother Andrew. They were fishermen, and were casting nets into the sea.

¹⁷'Follow me!' said Jesus to them. 'I'll have you fishing for people!'

¹⁸Straight away they left their nets and followed him. ¹⁹He went on a bit, and saw James, Zebedee's son, and John his brother. They were in the boat mending their nets, ²⁰and he called them then and there. They left their father Zebedee in the boat with the hired servants, and went off after him.

The poet John Betjeman describes in his verse autobiography how his father put pressure on him to follow him into the family business. The young John had no desire to do so; he wanted to be a poet. That's just a stupid dream, said his father; you've got to enter the family business, not only to make money, but for the family honour. You're the fourth generation. You've got to carry it on. The young man refused, and followed his own vocation, ending up as Poet Laureate, with a memorial in Westminster Abbey.

We have no idea how many generations the Zebedee family had been fishing on the sea of Galilee, but it was quite likely a lot more than four. In that country and culture, as in many countries and cultures to this day, a small family business can be handed on not only through generations but through centuries. It's safe and secure; people know what they're doing. If times are hard, the usual answer is simply to work a bit harder.

But then along came the young prophet from Nazareth, and told James and John, and their neighbours Peter and Andrew, to drop it all and follow him. And they did. Today I happened to take a walk in the evening sunlight by a Scottish harbour, and to my surprise I came upon a man, about my own age, sitting outside his harbourside front door mending a lobster pot. I asked myself how he would have responded if I had told him to give it all up and follow me – or even to give it all up and follow Jesus. (The town was, appropriately enough, St Andrews.) Only when you think a bit about the sort of life Peter, Andrew, James and John had had, and the totally unknown future Jesus was inviting them into, do you understand just how earth-shattering this little story was and is. Leave everything you've known, all your security, your family (and family solidarity was hugely important in that culture), and follow Jesus. Some people, maybe some people reading this, face that call today.

The way Mark tells the story sends echoes ringing back through the scriptures, the larger narrative of God's people. 'Leave your country and your father's house', said God to Abraham, 'and go the land I will show you.' Abraham, like Peter and the others, did what he was told, and went where he was sent. Mark is hinting to his readers that the old family business of the people of God is being left behind. God wants a new poetry to be written, and is calling a new people to write it.

And the name of the poem is 'the **kingdom** of God'. This was what all Israel had been waiting for. It wasn't a new piece of good advice. It wasn't a new political agenda. It wasn't a new type of spirituality. It might eventually lead to advice, agendas and certainly to prayer, but it was itself something more than all of these. It was the good (and extremely dangerous) news that the living God was on the move, was indeed now coming into his kingdom. And it demanded a definite response. It was 'God's **good news**'.

Notice how Jesus picks the moment to act. As long as **John** was announcing the kingdom, down by the Jordan, Jesus could bide his time. But when John is put into prison he knows it's time to act. Everything we know about Jesus suggests that he would have prayed and waited upon his Father for the sense that the moment had arrived. But God speaks through situations and events as well as through the still, small voice in the heart, and God was now saying that if this kingdom-movement was to go forwards rather than backwards, it was time for Jesus to go public with his own vocation. So he came to the Galilean villages as a wandering prophet, not a stationary one like John: a messenger urgently needing to tell people what was going on. And his message was that God's time had come. The moment had arrived.

If you were to walk down the street of any town or village with any Christian background and were to call out 'Repent and believe the **gospel**', people would think they knew what you meant: 'Give up your sins and become a Christian.' Of course, Jesus wanted people to stop sinning, but '**repentance**' for him meant two rather different things as well. First, it meant turning away from the social and political agendas which were driving Israel into a crazy, ruinous war. We can imagine someone saying that today in a country where ideologies are driving half the population into violent behaviour. Second, it meant calling Israel to turn back to a true loyalty to YHWH, their God. And, as anyone with a smattering of knowledge of the Bible would recognize, this was what had to happen before God would redeem Israel at last. The call to repent is part of the announcement that this is the time for the great moment of freedom, of God's rescue.

That's why it goes with the call to believe. Jesus' contemporaries trusted all sorts of things: their ancestry, their land, their **Temple**, their laws. Even their God – provided that this God did what they expected him to. Jesus was now calling them to trust the good news that their God was doing something new. To get in on the act, they had to cut loose from other ties and trust him and his message. That wasn't easy then and isn't easy now. But it's what Peter, Andrew, James and John did, and it's what all Christians are called to do today, tomorrow and on into God's future.

MARK 1.21–34

Exorcism and Healings

²¹They went to Capernaum. At once, on the sabbath, Jesus went into the synagogue and taught. ²²They were astonished at his teaching. He wasn't like the legal teachers; he said things on his own authority.

²³All at once, in their synagogue, there was a man with an unclean spirit.

²⁴'What business have you got with us, Jesus of Nazareth?' he yelled. 'Have you come to destroy us? I know who you are: you're God's Holy One!'

²⁵'Be quiet!' ordered Jesus. 'And come out of him!'

²⁶The unclean spirit convulsed the man, gave a great shout, and came out of him. ²⁷Everyone was astonished.

'What's this?' they started to say to each other. 'New teaching – with real authority! He even tells the unclean spirits what to do, and they do it!'

²⁸Word about Jesus spread at once, all over the surrounding district of Galilee.

²⁹They came out of the synagogue, and went at once (with James and John) into Simon and Andrew's house. ³⁰Simon's mother-in-law was in bed with a fever, and they told Jesus about her right away. ³¹He went in, took her by the hand, and raised her up. The fever left her, and she waited on them.

³²When the sun went down and evening came, they brought to Jesus everyone who was ill, including the demon-possessed. ³³The whole town was gathered around the door. ³⁴Jesus healed many people suffering from all kinds of diseases, and cast out many demons. He didn't allow the demons to speak, because they knew him.

Not long ago there was a great disaster at sea. A tourist boat, loaded with cars and holidaymakers, had failed to shut its doors properly; the water began to pour in; the boat began to sink, and panic set in. People were screaming as the happy, relaxed atmosphere of the ship turned in minutes into something worse than a horror movie.

All at once one man – not a member of the crew – took charge. In a clear voice he gave orders, telling people what to do. Relief mixed with the panic as people realized someone at least was in charge, and many managed to reach lifeboats they would otherwise have missed in the dark and the rush. The man himself made his way down to the people trapped in the hold. There he formed a human bridge: holding on with one hand to a ladder and with the other to part of the ship that was nearly submerged, he enabled still more to cross to safety. When the nightmare was over, the man himself was found to have drowned. He had literally given his life in using the authority he had assumed – the authority by which many had been saved.

Take that picture to a different sea coast, that of Galilee. A hundred yards inland, in the little town of Capernaum (the Bible sometimes calls these places 'cities', but we would think of them more as villages), was the synagogue. Here is a man, not one of the recognized teachers, who begins on his own authority to tell people what God's will is, how the **kingdom** is coming. The usual teachers – **priests** and **scribes**, the literate ones, with in some places **Pharisees** as well, the self-appointed scrupulous guardians of Jewish ancestral traditions – didn't teach like that. They always said 'as Moses said', or 'as **Rabbi** so-and-so said'. Jesus spoke with a quiet but compelling authority all of his own.

And with the same authority he spoke words of healing. Sometimes people for whom life had become a total nightmare – whose personalities seemed taken over by alien powers – confronted Jesus; indeed, they seem to have had a kind of inside track on recognizing him, knowing who he was and what he'd come to do. He'd come to stop the nightmare, to rescue people, both nations and individuals, from the destructive forces that enslaved them. So whether it was shrieking **demons**, a woman with a fever, or simply whatever diseases people happened to suffer from, Jesus dealt with them, all with the same gentle but deeply effective authority.

This is how Mark begins to tell us both about how Jesus became so popular so quickly and of how the course of his public career pointed inexorably to its dramatic conclusion. There is no doubt that Jesus quickly attracted huge crowds, and that his authoritative healings were the main reason. That in itself would have been threatening to the authorities; but, as we shall discover soon, there was more. Jesus had joined in a struggle against the forces of evil and destruction, forces that, like the dark, cruel sea pouring in on top of frightened and helpless travellers, seemed sometimes to be carrying all before them. Jesus came to be the human bridge across which people could climb to safety. And if, in the process, he himself paid with his own life the price of this saving authority, a human bridge with outstretched arms carrying people from death to life, that was simply part of the integrity of his action. The demons had their final shriek at him as he hung on the cross, challenging and mocking for the last time the validity of his authority. On the cross he completed the healing work he began that day in the synagogue.

When the church learns again how to speak and act with the same authority, we will find both the saving power of God unleashed once more and a similar heightened opposition from the forces of darkness. Similar, but not the same. The demons knew Jesus, and knew he had come to defeat them once and for all. They can still shriek, but since Calvary they no longer have authority. To believe this is the key to Christian testimony and saving action in the world that, despite its frequent panic and despair, has already been claimed by the loving authority of God in Jesus.

MARK 1.35-45

The Healing of a Man with a Skin Disease

[35]Very early – in the middle of the night, actually – Jesus got up and went out, off to a lonely place, and prayed. [36]Simon, and those with him, followed. [37]When they found him, they said, 'Everyone is looking for you!'

[38]'Let's go off to the other towns around here', Jesus replied, 'so that I can tell the news to people there too. That's why I came out.'

[39]So he went into their synagogues, throughout the whole of Galilee, telling the news and casting out demons.

[40]A man with a virulent skin disease came up to him. He knelt down and begged him, 'If you want to, you can make me clean!'

[41]Jesus was deeply moved. He reached out his hand and touched him, and said to him, 'I do want to: be clean!' [42]The disease left him at once, and he was clean.

[43]Jesus sent him away at once, with this stern warning: [44]'Mind you don't say anything to anyone! Just go and show yourself to the priest, and make the offering Moses commanded, to purify yourself and to give them a sign.'

[45]But the man went out and began to spread the news far and wide. He did this so effectively that Jesus couldn't any longer go publicly into a town. He stayed out in the open country, and people came to him from all around.

Oscar Wilde said he could resist everything except temptation. In rather the same way, some people can keep anything except a secret. However much you say 'You won't tell, will you?', and however much people say 'Oh no! Not a soul!' somehow the news leaks out, and we often have a good idea who it was who leaked it. It happens at the highest social levels, too. Governments, presidents and royal families are plagued by 'leaks' of information. Sometimes they simply learn to go with the flow and arrange some 'leaks' themselves, in the vain hope that this will keep people happy, not least in the media.

But why on earth did Jesus not want anything to leak out about his having healed a **leper**? If he was going around telling people the **good news** of the **kingdom**, surely more publicity was what he wanted? Why did he tell the poor man so fiercely (the word 'warned him sternly' is a very strong one in the original Greek) not to say anything? And are there any times when we, today, should be silent, however much we want to speak about Jesus and what he's done for us?

The answer seems to lie in what Jesus then told the leper to do. The sort of disease he had – the word 'leprosy' in those days covered a wide range of skin complaints, of which what we call 'leprosy' today is only one – was feared as highly infectious. That's why lepers had to live outside the towns, in special colonies.

Of course, if Jesus cured a blind person, then it was obvious that they could see. If he cured a cripple, anybody could tell that they were now able to walk. But if someone who had had leprosy showed up in their original town claiming to have been cured, people would be deeply suspicious. So Jesus told him to go through the official system. He should show himself to the priest; apart from the chief priests, who were based in Jerusalem, the priests lived all over Judaea and Galilee, acting as the religious and often scribal officials in local communities. And the next time the man was in Jerusalem, he would have to make the required sacrifice, thanking God officially, as it were, for his cure, and coming away with a proper public clean bill of health. The leper needed to keep the command of Moses, not in order to become clean, but in order to be seen to be clean.

Perhaps what Jesus was worried about, then, was news leaking out that he was doing things which seemed to challenge the authority of the **Temple** itself. As we shall soon see, there was more of this to come. It wasn't just that if news of spectacular healings got round, he soon wouldn't be able to move for the crowds (this is more or less what happened). It was that he might be attracting the wrong kind of notice. People would get angry. He was bypassing the system. And soon the question would be asked: is he really a loyal Jew? Can his message about the kingdom of God be real? Can we believe him? Isn't he dangerous? Hasn't he gone too far?

Behind the public activity and controversy lay Jesus' life of total dependence on the one he called Abba, Father. His praying habits were remarked on by his closest followers; this, obviously, was the source of his authority and power. On this occasion, after a day of intense excitement, with the news of God's kingdom going public with a bang, Jesus knew his need of a God-given sense of direction and inner strength, both to build on the apparent success of the previous day and to take things forward in the right way.

As we Christians pray today, especially when this prayer is costly and sacrificial, not merely a perfunctory few minutes now and then, the presence of this same Jesus is promised, by his **spirit**, to guide and encourage us. Part of this guidance will be the discernment to know when to speak and when to be silent, when what we are called to do should be kept secret and when it should be celebrated publicly. Sometimes, in some countries and in certain situations, some Christians will know, in prayer, that it is better not to attract too much attention to themselves. This isn't cowardice; it's wisdom. But if, as in Jesus' case, word leaks out anyway, we can remain confident, especially through prayer, that this same Jesus is with us as we face the cost of being kingdom-people, bringing the news and power of Jesus' healing love to the world.

MARK 2.1–12

The Healing of the Paralytic

[1]Jesus went back again to Capernaum, where, after a few days, word got round that he was at home. [2]A crowd gathered, so that people couldn't even get near the door as he was telling them the message.

[3]A party arrived: four people carrying a paralysed man, bringing him to Jesus. [4]They couldn't get through to him because of the crowd, so they opened up the roof above where he was. When they had dug through it, they used ropes to let down the stretcher on which the paralysed man was lying.

[5]Jesus saw their faith, and said to the paralysed man, 'Child, your sins are forgiven!'

[6]'How dare the fellow speak like this?' grumbled some of the legal experts among themselves. [7]'It's blasphemy! Who can forgive sins except God?'

[8]Jesus knew at once, in his spirit, that thoughts like this were in the air. 'Why do your hearts tell you to think that?' he asked. [9]'Answer me this', he went on. 'Is it easier to say to this cripple, "Your sins are forgiven", or to say, "Get up, pick up your stretcher, and walk"?

[10]'You want to know that the son of man has authority on earth to forgive sins?' He turned to the paralytic. [11]'I tell you,' he said, 'get up, take your stretcher, and go home.' [12]He got up, picked up the stretcher in a flash, and went out before them all.

Everyone was astonished, and they praised God. 'We've never seen anything like this!' they said.

Most people don't realize that this was probably Jesus' own house. He had moved to Capernaum from Nazareth; the point of the first two verses is that when Jesus returned from his short preaching trip around the neighbouring villages, he found crowds pressing around the door as though he were a movie star or well-known footballer. Jesus himself was the unlucky householder who had his roof ruined that day.

This opens up quite a new possibility for understanding what Jesus said to the paralysed man. How would you feel if someone made a big hole in your roof? But Jesus looks down and says, with a rueful smile: 'All right – I forgive you!' Something in his voice, though, made them all realize this was different. This forgiveness went deeper than mere domestic disputes. Jesus was speaking with a quiet authority which went down into the paralysed man's innermost being. Not surprisingly, those around felt uneasy. Only the priests could declare forgiveness, speaking in the name of God. If that's what the man needed, his friends should take him to the **Temple** in Jerusalem, not to a wandering preacher.

Mark's way of telling the tale makes it a signpost. It points on, through the twists and turns of the **gospel** story, to Jesus' trial before Caiaphas in chapter 14. The story is a tiny version of the whole gospel: Jesus teaching and healing, Jesus condemned for blasphemy, Jesus vindicated. The paralysed man's healing points forward to the new life that Jesus himself will have in the resurrection, and will share with everyone who wants it.

The key sentence, then, is the one in verse 10: 'The **son of man** has authority on earth to forgive sins.' 'The son of man', in Jesus' language, could simply mean 'I', or 'someone like me'. But taking 'the son of man' in Mark as a whole, Daniel 7 provides the clue to deeper meaning. There, 'one like a son of man' is the representative of God's true people. He is opposed by the forces of evil; but God vindicates him, rescues him, proves him to be in the right, and gives him *authority*. In Daniel, this authority enables him to dispense God's judgment. Here, in a fascinating twist, he has authority to dispense God's forgiveness. The saying points forward to Jesus' answer to Caiaphas (14.62).

In many cultures today, forgiveness is seen as a sign of weakness. Revenge, for them, is a moral duty. Sometimes whole families, whole communities, are torn apart this way; think of Northern Ireland, or the Balkans. 'It's the only language they understand', people say, as they plant another bomb or aim another rifle. Sometimes whole nations and governments engage in childish, but deadly, tit-for-tat retaliations. People who live that way tend to think that God lives that way too.

We shouldn't be surprised, then, that Jesus' unexpected declaration of forgiveness sent shock waves running through the house, the village, the nation, and finally through the world. It wasn't simply that he was committing a theological crime. The hole in his own roof was nothing compared with the hole he was tearing through an entire way of life. Forgiveness is the most powerful thing in the world, but because it is so costly we prefer to settle for second best. Jesus, already on his way to paying the full price, offered nothing less than the best.

Jesus' people have to be for the world what he was for Israel. We have to find ways of bringing healing and forgiveness to our communities. It can be done – think of the Truth and Reconciliation Commission in South Africa – but it is enormously costly. People will oppose it. But the new life that comes as a result is enough vindication, enough proof that the living God is at work.

Forgiveness can also, of course, change individuals. It can, as in this case, go down to the hidden roots of the personality, gently healing old, long-buried, hurts. Often people think healing and forgiveness is impossible. They find God distant or uncaring. But true faith won't be satisfied with that. This story is a picture of prayer. Don't stay on the edge of the crowd. Dig through God's roof and find yourself in his presence.

You will get more than you bargained for. It's not pleasant if you're helpless on a stretcher, but you don't have many responsibilities. Once you've met the living, forgiving God in Jesus, you'll find yourself on your feet, going out into the world in the power of God's love.

MARK 2.13–17

The Calling of Levi

¹³Once more Jesus went out beside the sea. All the crowd came to him, and he taught them.

¹⁴As he went along he saw Levi, son of Alphaeus, sitting at the toll booth. 'Follow me!' he said. And he got up and followed him.

¹⁵That's how Jesus came to be sitting at home with lots of tax-collectors and sinners. There they were, plenty of them, sitting with Jesus and his disciples; they had become his followers.

¹⁶When the legal experts from the Pharisees saw him eating with tax-collectors and sinners, they said to his disciples, 'Why does he eat with tax-collectors and sinners?'

¹⁷When Jesus heard it, he said to them, 'It's sick people who need the doctor, not healthy ones. I came to call the bad people, not the good ones.'

There are some jobs where you need a particularly thick skin.

In many modern Western countries, one of the worst is being a parking attendant or traffic warden. All day long it's your job to give people parking tickets, to fine them for leaving cars where they shouldn't. Over and over again angry motorists complain that it isn't fair, that they were only there for a couple of minutes, that the attendant is picking on them. I wonder what it feels like, day after day, to be shouted at for doing your job.

Suppose the parking attendant was working for a government you hated and wanted to get rid of. Suppose the parking laws had been introduced quite recently and people who'd parked their cars in the same spot for years suddenly found themselves fined for doing it. Pity the attendant in that situation.

Now put yourself in the shoes of Levi, son of Alphaeus. What was he doing collecting tolls at Capernaum? Who was he working for?

The chances are he was working for Herod Antipas. When Antipas's father, Herod the Great, had died in 4 BC, his large kingdom had been divided between three of his sons: Archelaus got Judaea in the south; Antipas got Galilee in the north, with some bits of the Jordan valley thrown in. Philip got the part we today call the Golan Heights, extending up into Syria. And the border between Antipas's territory and Philip's was the river Jordan as it ran south from Mount Hermon into the Sea of Galilee. The last town you'd go through travelling east from Antipas's land into Philip's, or the first you'd come to going west into Galilee, was Capernaum. Just as today you often have to pay a toll for the privilege of crossing a border, or even for using an airport or a motorway, so you had to pay a toll to cross from one part of the old kingdom into another.

Plenty of people could remember when you could make the journey for free. Now you had to pay. And who got shouted at, grumbled at and sworn at because of it? Levi, son of Alphaeus.

We don't know whether he'd chosen the job. Probably it was the only one he could find. We don't know whether he approved of the **Herodian** family, and Antipas in particular; most ordinary Jews disliked and resented them, but they were in power, the Romans were backing them, and there wasn't much anyone could do about it. But Levi, son of Alphaeus, had to sit there taking the anger and resentment into his own heart and **soul**.

And then one day Jesus came by. He didn't shout. He didn't swear. He didn't grumble. He did something totally unexpected. He said 'Follow me'. And Levi, we are told, no doubt with total astonishment all over his face, got up and followed him. Wouldn't you have done? It was perhaps the first time for ages that someone had treated him as a human being instead of a piece of dirt.

We shouldn't miss the deeper meaning of Jesus' call to Levi. Levi had been working for the man who thought of himself as King of the Jews. Now he was going to work for someone else with royal aspirations. Mark, telling the story, is leading us up to the point where Peter, speaking for the **Twelve**, will declare that Jesus is the **Messiah**, the King of the Jews (8.29).

But at the time people didn't see Jesus as a would-be king. They saw him as an odd combination: a doctor throwing a great party. Why a doctor? Because he went around healing people – not just people with physical ailments, but people like Levi who had become social outcasts because of the jobs they did or the lives they led. Why a party? Because Jesus' vision of the **kingdom** of God, like that of some ancient biblical prophets, was of a great feast to which everyone was invited. And people didn't like it. Would you want to go to a party with a lot of traffic wardens?

15

For Jesus to invite people like Levi to a feast in his own home – people known locally as 'sinners', an easy label to stick on those who didn't conform either to the strict religious requirements of the law or the strict political expectations of opposition to Herod and Rome – this was simply outrageous. He should know better. Mark is continuing to show how Jesus' early ministry aroused opposition at the social, cultural, political and above all religious levels. This is part of the long build-up of tension that will finally explode in Jerusalem.

But Jesus' answer to the sneering criticism went to the heart of the matter. He was being obedient to a calling, and that calling was to be a kind of doctor. There's no point in the doctor only keeping company with healthy people. The doctor must associate with the sick. Jesus' whole ministry was to bring health, not just to the physically sick, but to Israel as a whole and the world as a whole. That, however, would involve upsetting a lot of people for whom it was more comfortable to label people as 'outcasts' and ignore them from then on.

Jesus' actions and words ring out like a great bell into today's world, telling us what time it is (time for the doctor to see the patients), warning us to look at things from God's point of view (human respectability can so easily mask reality), encouraging us to extend his healing welcome, his transforming party, wherever it's needed.

MARK 2.18–22

Questions about Fasting

[18]John's disciples, and the Pharisees' disciples, were fasting. People came and said to Jesus, 'Look here: John's disciples are fasting, and so are the Pharisees' disciples; why aren't yours?'

[19]'How can the wedding guests fast', Jesus replied, 'if the bridegroom is there with them? As long as they've got the bridegroom with them, they can't fast.

[20]'Mind you, the time is coming when the bridegroom will be taken away from them. They'll fast then all right.

[21]'No one sews unshrunk cloth onto an old cloak. If they do, the new patch will tear the old cloth, and they'll end up with a worse hole. [22]Nor does anyone put new wine into old wineskins. If they do, the wine will burst the skins, and they'll lose the wine and the skins together. New wine needs new fresh skins.'

When I was a boy there was a craze for ginger-beer plants. An uncle gave us the starter kit, including the bacteria that, by a process I never understood, produced the secret ingredient that gave the homemade brew its fizz and taste. The problem was that the stuff was so powerful,

16

despite being non-alcoholic, that it always threatened to explode the bottles we put it in. The only safe place to keep it, we discovered, was the coal-shed, where, from time to time, we would discover shattered glass on the floor, and a trail in the coal dust where the liquid had drained away.

We don't have a coal-shed any more – and we don't brew ginger beer, if it comes to that. But the image remains with me when I read what Jesus says about new wine needing new skins. He is talking about the shatteringly new thing that was happening in and through his ministry. He was, after all, announcing the **kingdom** of God – saying that God was now becoming king in a whole new way, and performing actions to suit the words. Something quite different was coming to birth from anything that had happened before. Something powerful and explosive.

When people didn't understand it, he gave them three images about the new and the old. Like a set of telescope lenses, each image gives a slightly different focus, but when you put them all in a row you may be able to get the picture sharp and clear.

Take them in reverse order. Jesus ends with the one we've been thinking about: new wine in old bottles will result in broken bottles and wasted wine. (They used skins, not glass bottles, in Jesus' culture, but the point is the same.) What Jesus is doing can't be fitted in to the existing ways of thinking and living. If people try to do that they'll have the worst of both worlds. At the time, this meant that Jesus' powerful kingdom-ministry couldn't be fitted into the ways of thinking that his fellow first-century Galileans already had. They needed to think differently, to think bigger, to get new wineskins for the new wine he had to offer. Most people are threatened by that kind of challenge.

The middle image is about mending clothes (Jesus so often uses pictures taken from ordinary everyday life). A brand new piece of cloth won't do to patch a hole in an old coat. As it shrinks with time and weather, it will pull away from the hole and make a worse rent than before. This image doesn't work quite the same way as the wine and the skins: by itself it might suggest simply that you need an old piece of cloth for an old cloak, in other words that the old is good and the new bad. But the basic point Jesus is making is that new and old don't mix. People shouldn't be surprised when putting them together has unfortunate results.

The first picture Jesus gives is of a wedding, which takes us back to the question which sparked off the discussion in the first place. Imagine going to a wedding reception where everyone sat around and looked at the food but never touched a morsel of it. What sort of a celebration would that be? The day I am writing this, the London *Times* newspaper has published a string of letters about people giving things up for Lent, and about whether Sundays count as part of Lent or not. One man has written to say that, though he got married in Lent, he did it on a Sunday so that there wouldn't be any problem about having a feast. Sunday – the day of new **life**, of **resurrection** – overrides the command to be serious, to fast. For Jesus, his own presence is, in that sense, a perpetual Sunday. As long as he's there, it's always time for a party.

Jesus is doing two things together. He is comparing his own work – his public ministry, and his own presence with his followers – to a wedding celebration in which he is the bridegroom. And he is explaining why this means his followers are not keeping to the regular fast days that other devout Jews of the day were observing. Both of these need explaining a little.

Everybody likes a wedding. I don't think it's just because we like an excuse for a party, or because we like to see people happy. I think it's because weddings say something at a deep level about the goodness, the love and the lavish creativity of the God who made the world. So we shouldn't be surprised that some of the biblical writers, and some Jews nearer to Jesus' day, used the picture of a great wedding as a way of talking about the wonderful new world that God would eventually make, the world in which everyone would have more than enough and there would be peace and justice for all.

This was sometimes combined with another ancient Jewish idea: that Israel, as God's people, was God's bride – wayward, rebellious, sometimes running off with strangers, but eventually to be wooed and won back again. When Jesus describes his ministry to Israel in terms of the bridegroom at a wedding reception, there are disturbing new meanings in the air. New wine indeed for the old bottles to cope with.

And all because of a question about fasting. The main times when Jews of Jesus' day fasted were days that reminded them of the great disasters of old, like the time when the **Temple** was destroyed by the Babylonians in 587 BC. Surely Jesus, as a devout Jew, would want to keep holy days like that? No. Jesus was bringing the time of restoration, of new life, of the new start for which Israel had longed. Jesus was bringing into being the reality for which the Temple had been one of the great advance signposts: God's sovereign and saving presence in the midst of his people. This was a time for looking forwards to the great things God was beginning to do, not backwards to the times when Israel had been punished for her failures and infidelities.

Christians look back to the time of Jesus as the one-off moment when God did the great new thing that had long been promised. Everything is different as a result of what he did. But that doesn't stop us, sadly, from trying to combine the new things the **gospel** offers with the old things from the world all around us – or, indeed, the old and often unnecessary traditions from the church of former years. When God is doing new things, we should join the party, not grumble because the new wine is threatening to burst our poor old bottles. A good deal of day-to-day Christian wisdom consists in sorting out the new from the old.

MARK 2.23–28

Teachings on the Sabbath

²³One sabbath, Jesus was walking through the cornfields. His disciples made their way along, plucking corn as they went.

²⁴'Look here,' said the Pharisees to him, 'why are they doing something illegal on the sabbath?'

²⁵'Haven't you ever read what David did,' replied Jesus, 'when he was in difficulties, and he and his men got hungry? ²⁶He went into God's house (this was when Abiathar was high priest), and ate the "bread of the presence", which only the priests were allowed to eat – and he gave it to the people with him.

²⁷'The sabbath was made for humans,' he said, 'not humans for the sabbath; ²⁸so the son of man is master even of the sabbath.'

The twentieth century saw a great deal of secret police activity. The KGB in the Soviet Union, and the Stasi in East Germany, were legends in their own lifetime during the Communist period. Several countries in Central and South America, and some parts of Asia, have thriving secret police forces that are rightly feared by ordinary folk.

That's the picture we naturally think of when we find **Pharisees** spying on Jesus and his followers; and it's actually very misleading. The Pharisees were *not* in any sense an official secret police force, in Jesus' day or at any other time. They were an unofficial party, who had been active as a religious and political pressure group for nearly 200 years by Jesus' time. (Most political parties in modern Western democracies are much younger than that, at least in their present form.) The Pharisees were entirely self-chosen, and had no authority to make laws or enforce them. They did, though, have considerable influence on ordinary people, who respected their expertise in Israel's ancestral laws and traditions.

If they weren't like a secret police, then what were they like? Some were wise, devout, holy men. Some, though, behaved like nosey journalists in the modern world, setting themselves up as the self-appointed guardians of public morality and spying on people in the public eye. That's what seems to be going on here. They probably wouldn't have bothered to check on an ordinary group of people walking through cornfields on the **sabbath**. But Jesus and his followers weren't ordinary people. They were already marked out because of what Jesus was doing and the implicit claims he was making. They needed watching, to see if they were loyal Jews or not. Just as anyone who even looks as though they might run for office in some modern democracies will find the journalists taking a sudden interest in their everyday private behaviour, to see if there's any mud that might stick, so Jesus' growing reputation attracted similar attention.

Keeping the sabbath was, of course, one of the Ten Commandments, and it had been reinforced by the prophets and by subsequent Jewish teaching. It was one of the things that marked out the Jews, over the centuries, from their pagan neighbours – one of the things that reminded them that they were God's people. It wasn't an odd moral commandment which people observed to earn merit or favour with God; it was a sign that they belonged to the true God, the creator of the world, who had himself rested on the seventh day. Just as today, in some parts of Jerusalem, the successors of the Pharisees watch carefully to see that everybody in the area is observing the sabbath properly, so in Jesus' day some Pharisees checked up at least on would-be leaders and new movements.

Jesus' reply is a bit of a tease, but packs a strong punch. He doesn't deny that the **disciples** are out of line with traditional sabbath observance, but he pleads special circumstances and scriptural precedent. He puts himself on a par with King David in the period when David, already anointed by Samuel but not yet enthroned (because Saul was still king), was on the run, gathering support, waiting for his time to come. That's a pretty heavy claim: the implication is that Jesus is the true king, marked out by God (presumably in his **baptism**) but not yet recognized and enthroned. He therefore has the right, when he and his people are hungry, to bypass the normal regulations. In other words, this kind of sabbath-breaking, so far from being an act of casual or wanton civil disobedience, is a deliberate sign, like the refusal to fast: a sign that the King is here, that the kingdom is breaking in, that instead of waiting for the old creation to come to its point of rest the new creation is already bursting upon the old world.

All of this is summed up in the riddle at the end, which probably puzzled Jesus' hearers as much as it does people today. It is a combined comment about the sabbath and about Jesus' own authority. This is the second time we meet 'the **son of man**' in Mark; the setting seems to reinforce one particular meaning the phrase could have, namely the messianic figure which first-century Jews discovered in Daniel 7, whose arrival and enthronement signals the start of God's kingdom. Jesus doesn't mean that just any human being is 'Lord of the sabbath', but that the **Messiah**, the true representative human being, has authority over institutions that might otherwise repress human beings.

Jesus' action, and its explanation, were a coded messianic claim, a claim that in him the new day was dawning in which even Israel's God-given laws would be seen in a new light. How much more are the institutions and local customs of ordinary societies to be judged by the humanizing rule of the son of man!

MARK 3.1–6
Healing of the Man with the Withered Hand

¹Once more Jesus went to the synagogue. There was a man there with a withered hand. ²People were watching to see if Jesus would heal him on the sabbath, so that they could frame a charge against him.

³'Stand up', said Jesus to the man with the withered hand, 'and come out here.' And he said to them, ⁴'Is it lawful to do good on the sabbath, or to do evil? To save life or to kill?' They stayed quiet.

⁵He was deeply upset at their hard-heartedness, and looked round at them angrily. Then he said to the man, 'Stretch out your hand.' He stretched it out – and his hand was restored. ⁶The Pharisees went out right away and began to plot with the Herodians against Jesus, trying to find a way to destroy him.

It's difficult for me to remember what life was like when I was a boy. It's even harder for young people today to imagine what it was like in their own country 50 years ago. Almost everywhere has changed drastically. In England, one change is particularly noticeable. When I was young, everybody kept Sunday as a very special day. Just a few decades ago, in the average English town, there were no shops open on Sundays; there was no professional sport – yes, no football, no racing; everything was very, very quiet. Nothing like today.

A cartoon of the time sums up the attitude, and the problem. An anxious father, worried about what the neighbours may say, tells his little girl she mustn't play with her hoop in the street on Sunday. She should go into the back garden. 'Isn't it Sunday in the back garden?' asks the girl.

The irony, of course, is that whenever Jesus is faced with the question of **sabbath** observance he moves in the opposite direction. He appears to take a shockingly liberal line. This has been a problem for strict Sunday-observance enthusiasts, who for centuries have cheerfully transferred the Jewish commandment of observing the seventh day of the week and switched it to observing the first day – something the New

Testament never actually does (though it's clear the early Christians met for worship on the first day, the day they celebrated Jesus' **resurrection**). Today most Western Christians, frankly, are in a bit of a muddle on the issue. We all know that the old-style sabbath observance as a social phenomenon has gone for good. Even though we mostly believe that one day off from work in a week is a healthy ideal, it's not at all obvious how best, or most appropriately, to achieve it.

These thoughts and puzzles may crowd into our minds when we read about Jesus healing on the sabbath; but if we're going to see what it meant at the time we have to go back, not just to the 'sabbath' observance of our (or at least my) childhood, but to the world of first-century Palestine. For a Jew in Jesus' world, the sabbath had all that mixture of social pressure and legal sanction, but it meant much more as well. It was a badge of Jewishness for people who'd been persecuted and killed simply for being Jewish. It was a national flag that spoke of freedom to come, of hope for the great Day of Rest when God would finally liberate Israel from pagan oppression. It looked back to the creation of the world, and to the **Exodus** from Egypt, and it marked out those who kept it as God's special people, God's faithful people, God's hoping people. It was, after all, a commandment deeply embedded in the Jewish scriptures.

So why does Jesus appear to drive a coach and horses through it? Because it had become a weapon. It had become a sign of his fellow Jews' commitment to a fierce and exclusive nationalism. Along with other badges and flags, it spoke now not of Israel as the light of the world but of Israel as the children of light and the rest of the world as remaining in darkness. And this attitude, as so easily happens when religion and nationalism are wedded tightly together, spilled over into popular attitudes even towards fellow Jews. For many groups, it wasn't enough to be a loyal Jew; one had to be a better loyal Jew than the other lot. And in this no-win situation the whole point of the commandment – celebrating God's creation and redemption, past, present and future – had been lost sight of. The rule mattered more than the reality.

Jesus' verdict on that was that it constituted 'hard-heartedness' – one of the regular charges that the prophets levelled against law-*breaking* Israelites in days gone by. Like the wilderness generation under Moses, his contemporaries were unable to see and celebrate what God was actually doing in front of their noses. So he puts the question in its starkest terms, in words dripping with irony: is it legal to do good on the sabbath, or only to do evil? Is it legal to make people alive, or only to kill them? If the sabbath speaks of creation and redemption, the answer is obvious – and if the current interpretation of the rules says otherwise, so much the worse for the current interpretation of the rules.

Of course, it's not clear that what Jesus actually did – speaking a word of command, and leaving the man to stretch out his own hand, hardly a breach of sabbath observance – was breaking the official or even the unofficial interpretation of the sabbath. But his approach and attitude were clearly on a collision course with those of the self-appointed guardians of the ancestral traditions. In a move that antici-pates again the whole larger story Mark is telling, the unofficial leaders of Jewish opinion (the **Pharisees**) get together with their natural ene-mies (the supporters of Herod Antipas, whom the Pharisees normally regarded as a dangerous traitor to Judaism). Why did they do that?

The Pharisees had no power themselves. If they were going to attack Jesus, they needed to make unlikely alliances. Thus it would be at the end, when Caiaphas and Pilate together sent Jesus to his death; thus it would be not long afterwards, when the young Pharisee Saul of Tar-sus obtained authority from the chief **priests** to persecute the church. Thus it was in this instance, with local Galilean Pharisees making com-mon cause with the supporters of Herod Antipas, in a futile attempt to do away with Jesus.

Three questions emerge for today's church. First, have we fully appreciated the way in which God's kingdom burst in, through the work of Jesus, bringing a whole new domain in which new creation, and true redemption, had already arrived? Jesus wasn't just challeng-ing one or two residual bits of 'legalism'; he was at the cutting edge of God's new world. Second, are there ways in which the church today can get so blinded by its commitment to what appear necessary rules that it fails to see God's healing and restorative work breaking through? And, third, can we in any sense recapture the true spirit of the sabbath in a world where economic forces are frequently far more dehumanizing than the abused sabbath law ever was? How can we learn again what it means to live in a rhythm of work and rest, and to help one another in our wider society to do the same, without becoming legalists in the process?

MARK 3.7–19

The Twelve Are Appointed

[7]Jesus went off towards the sea with his disciples, and a large crowd from Galilee followed him. A great company, too, from Judaea, [8]Jeru-salem, Idumaea, Transjordan, and the region of Tyre and Sidon, heard what he was doing and came to him.

[9]There was a real danger that he might be crushed by the crowd, so he told his disciples to get a boat ready for him. [10]He healed large numbers, and sick people were pushing towards him to touch him.

23

¹¹Whenever unclean spirits saw him, they fell down in front of him and yelled out, 'You are the son of God!' ¹²He gave them strict orders not to reveal his identity.

¹³Jesus went up the mountain, and summoned the people he wanted, and they came to him. ¹⁴He appointed twelve (naming them 'apostles') to be with him and to be sent out as heralds, ¹⁵and to have authority to cast out demons. ¹⁶In appointing the Twelve, he named Simon 'Peter'; ¹⁷James, son of Zebedee, and his brother John, he named 'Boanerges', which means 'sons of thunder'. The others were ¹⁸Andrew, Philip, Bartholomew, Matthew, Thomas, James son of Alphaeus, Thaddaeus, Simon the Cananaean, ¹⁹and Judas Iscariot (the one who handed him over).

When I was a boy, the football team I support, Newcastle United, won the FA Cup, the world's oldest football trophy, three years out of five. Think what it was like in Newcastle when the players came back from the match at Wembley Stadium in London. The whole town turned out to watch and to cheer. Something similar happens when a film star comes to town. Or a rock star. The streets are full of people, and you wonder where they all came from.

It doesn't often happen that way today with people we think of as 'religious' leaders (though crowds do sometimes turn out when the Pope goes on tour). But we shouldn't just think of Jesus in what we today call 'religious' terms. The main reason people came flocking to him from all sides was because he was able to heal them. In a world where medical skill was, by our standards, extremely primitive, someone who appeared to be able to heal almost anyone of almost anything caused a stampede. Word went round from village to village and region to region. They didn't have radio, television or newspapers; but their bush telegraph was pretty effective. Suddenly the little town on the sea of Galilee was overrun with eager folk coming to be cured, or to bring sick relatives.

Mark doesn't let us forget, though, that as in everything Jesus did there was a darker and deeper side to it. Jesus' extraordinary healing powers were clearly operating on a spiritual level rather than through ordinary medical treatment; and once you engage with the spiritual level you are open to various evil forces as well as those of disease and death. Calling these forces 'unclean spirits' is a convenient way of saying two things about them. First, they are non-physical powers that operate upon, and sometimes within, a person. Second, they defile the one they inhabit, making such a person behave in ways that are untrue to their calling as a human being.

But these spirits know when they are in the presence of a power greater than themselves. They recognize in Jesus, not just a great healer, but a spiritual power and presence of an altogether different order from themselves. And so they yell out Jesus' real identity, which, so far as we know, the crowds hadn't yet imagined, and even the **disciples** had perhaps only begun to guess at. Jesus is 'the **son of God**', that is, the **Messiah**, the true King of Israel.

This is, of course, fighting talk. If word were to get about on that same bush telegraph that the healer was giving himself royal airs, or even that people were talking of him in that way, Herod Antipas might have something to say about it. So Jesus tells them to be quiet.

After the hurly-burly of the crowds, we watch a very different scene but with the same meaning. There's an old hymn that speaks of the '**sabbath** rest by Galilee' and the 'calm of hills above'; but the hills around the lake were not so much the place where people would go for peace and quiet, like day-trippers in the woods and mountains of Europe or America, as the places where people went to plot revolution. And what Jesus now does is among his most revolutionary gestures.

How many Members of Parliament, or of the Senate, or of an equivalent body, does your country have? Most people in most countries couldn't answer that question. Similarly, most English people (for instance) couldn't tell you how many counties there are in England. I suspect the same is true in most parts of the world. These numbers don't mean a great deal to us. They don't carry heavy significance.

But every Jew knew that there were **twelve** tribes in Israel – or, at least, that there had been. These twelve corresponded, more or less, to the twelve sons of the patriarch Jacob, whose stories are told in the book of Genesis. Ten of the tribes had been lost seven centuries earlier when the Assyrians invaded and carried them off. But the prophets had spoken of a coming restoration, and a great many Jews were longing for it. The time would come, they believed, when their God would turn everything around and make them a great nation once again.

So when Jesus called twelve of his followers apart from the crowds and gave them special status and a special commission, nobody who heard of it could miss what he was doing. He was saying, more clearly than any words could have done: this isn't simply a great healing mission. This isn't even simply a time of spiritual renewal. This is the restoration we've all been waiting for. It's happening at every level: spiritual, physical, social and – inevitably – political. Anyone launching a restoration movement was doing so in the face of the current rulers, and the current pressure groups. Jesus went up into the hills for the same reason that others did at the time: to shape his followers into a truly revolutionary group, and to do so away from the prying eyes of the authorities.

Here, too, there was a darker and deeper side. One of the twelve, Mark tells us, would turn out to be a traitor. But that, too, would be taken up within Jesus' revolutionary purpose. His **kingdom** was not the usual sort, and it would not come by the usual methods.

What would today's churches have to do to bring people out on the streets as though their team had just won the Cup?

MARK 3.20–30

Jesus and Beelzebul

²⁰He went into the house. A crowd gathered again, so that they couldn't even have a meal. ²¹When his family heard it, they came to restrain him. 'He's out of his mind', they said.

²²Experts who had come from Jerusalem were saying, 'He is possessed by Beelzebul! He casts out demons by the prince of demons!'

²³Jesus summoned them and spoke to them in pictures. 'How can the Accuser cast out the Accuser? ²⁴If a kingdom splits into two factions, it can't last; ²⁵if a household splits into two factions, it can't last. ²⁶So if the Accuser revolts against himself and splits into two, he can't last – his time is up! ²⁷But remember: no one can get into a strong man's house and steal his property unless first they tie up the strong man; then they can plunder his house.

²⁸'I'm telling you the truth: people will be forgiven all sins, and all blasphemies of whatever sort. ²⁹But people who blaspheme the holy spirit will never find forgiveness. They will be guilty of an eternal sin.' ³⁰That was his response to their claim that he had an unclean spirit.

From the safety of my armchair, I watched the mass demonstration on the TV news. It started peacefully, at least on the surface. Banners and placards gave out a strong message, but the crowd seemed relaxed enough. The police were standing well back, watching for trouble but quite cheerful. Some of them joked with the marchers as they went by.

Nobody knew how it happened, but suddenly everything changed. There was a scuffle and a scrap, and a whole section of the crowd stopped marching and started shouting at the police. Some threw bottles. The police charged the demonstrators, swinging batons at random. The battle quickly spread up and down the street. Shops were smashed, hundreds were arrested.

The close-up TV shots, and the recordings of what people were saying at the time, made it clear what had happened. The police had decided that the demonstrators were 'scum'. The demonstrators had decided that the police were 'pigs'. Once they had labelled them like that they could do what they liked. They were no longer dealing with humans, but with animals, and dirty ones at that. Raise the stakes, stick a label on people, and then it doesn't matter what you do and who you hurt.

That's what seems to be going on as word about Jesus spreads to Jerusalem. After all, if Jesus' own family begin to think he's mad, what is the wider public to make of him – particularly that part of the wider public that concerns itself with the ancestral traditions of Israel? This passage is in fact a powerful witness to the remarkable things Jesus was doing. The early church certainly didn't make up the story about people saying he was mad, or in league with the devil. Equally, people only say that kind of thing when the stakes are raised, when something is happening for which there is no other explanation – in this case, when a power is at work to heal people who themselves seem to be in the grip of demonic forces.

Mark, of course, wants us to understand precisely what is going on. **John the Baptist** said that Jesus was 'someone stronger than me' (1.7). When Jesus now speaks about tying up the strong man and plundering his house, we are meant to understand that Jesus is now acting as the Stronger One, who has won an initial victory over the enemy (the temptation after the **baptism**) and is now able to make inroads into his territory.

The **scribes**, of course, don't like what he's doing because it doesn't fit into their categories. Jesus isn't accredited. He must therefore be sidelined. He must be labelled in such a way that people will no longer take him seriously. He must, they say, be in league with the arch-demon, Beelzebul. Maybe he's even possessed by Beelzebul. That would explain it; and it would also justify them doing anything they wanted to control him, to contain him, perhaps to silence him for ever. Again, Mark allows the dark shadow of the cross to fall on the page even at this early stage in the story.

Jesus doesn't respond in kind. He doesn't lash back with an instant label for the scribes. He merely points out the flaw in their thinking. If the **accuser** (the word in Hebrew is 'the **satan**', which was becoming a proper name by this time, but without losing its original meaning) were to cast out the satan, he (or it) is fighting against himself. If civil war breaks out in a kingdom, it's the end of the kingdom; if members of a household start fighting among themselves, it's the end of the family unit. So if the devil is fighting the devil, the devil's kingdom is obviously coming to an end. Thus, even if the scribes' analysis of the situation is correct, the kingdom of the satan is toppling. In other words, Jesus' basic claim, that in his work God's **kingdom** is arriving, is true, even if their 'labelling' of him is accurate.

But of course the label is wrong. Jesus offers a different account of what's going on. The Stronger One has arrived, and the Strong One finds his house being burgled. Jesus' healings, and particularly his exorcisms, are signs that God's kingdom is indeed arriving, the kingdom in which people who have been held captive will at last be set free.

Jesus does, though, add a warning, which has often been misunderstood. What is this 'unforgivable sin' in verse 29?

His critics had painted themselves into a corner. Once you label what is in fact the work of the **holy spirit** as the work of the devil, there's no way back. It's like holding a conspiracy theory: all the evidence you see will simply confirm your belief. You will be blind to the truth. It isn't that God gets specially angry with one sin in particular. It's rather that if you decide firmly that the doctor who is offering to perform a life-saving operation on you is in fact a sadistic murderer, you will never give your consent to the operation.

There is no middle way, for the world today as for Israel then. Jesus isn't just a 'mildly interesting historical figure', as some in today's world would like him to be (another label, please note, designed to neutralize Jesus and keep him out of harm's way). He is either the one who brought God's kingdom, or a dangerous madman. Those who preach and live by Jesus' message must be on the alert for opposition of all sorts, sometimes subtle, sometimes threatening. And they must learn, too, how to respond.

MARK 3.31–35

Jesus' Family

³¹Jesus' mother and brothers appeared. They waited outside the house, and sent in a message, asking for him.

³²'Look!' said the crowd sitting around Jesus. 'Your mother, your brothers, and your sisters are outside! They're searching for you!'

³³'Who is my mother?' replied Jesus. 'Who are my brothers?'

³⁴He looked around him at the people sitting there in a ring. 'Here is my mother!' he said. 'Here are my brothers! ³⁵Anybody who does God's will is my brother! And my sister! And my mother!'

My older daughter called this morning, to thank us for the Easter present we'd sent her. It will be the first Easter she hasn't been with us, which will be strange. The six of us have usually been together at Easter, just as at Christmas. If we were Americans, we'd probably add 'and Thanksgiving'.

But those are about the only times, apart from family weddings and funerals, that one expects a growing family to come back home. They have their lives to live; they have to be where their jobs, or their studying or their new relationships will take them. Families in the Western world don't imagine that they will all live in the same neighbourhood. Sometimes when I talk to friends in North America you'd think the family had deliberately decided to live as far apart as possible: a son in Florida, a daughter in Vancouver, another son in Boston, and so on.

For Westerners, then, Jesus' words, though perhaps mildly shocking, don't mean that much. As we grow up we develop a circle of friends who know us much better, who spend much more time with us, than our parents and siblings. We regard that as normal.

But in Jesus' world it was scandalous – as it would still be in some places. The family bond was tight and long-lasting. As with many non-Western cultures today, it was normal for children to live close to their parents, maybe even in the same house. The family unit would often be a business unit as well, sharing everything in common. What's more, for Jews the close family bond was part of the God-given fabric of thinking and living. Loyalty to the family was the local and specific outworking of loyalty to Israel as the people of God. Break the link, and you've undermined a major pillar in the way Jews in the first century (and in the twentieth, come to that) think and feel about the world and themselves.

But as Mark has already shown us, Jesus was quite capable of challenging the symbols that lay at the heart of the Jewish sense of identity. Family solidarity was up there with **sabbath** observance, the food laws, and other signs of Jewish identity. It meant one was being loyal to the ancestral heritage, and thereby to the God of Abraham, Isaac and Jacob.

Despite what pious Christian traditions have sometimes said about Mary, Jesus' mother, at this stage at least she clearly didn't have any idea what he was up to. She had brought the rest of the family down to Capernaum from Nazareth to find him and take him away, to stop him behaving in such an outrageous fashion, bringing dishonour to the family name. They thought he was mad (see verse 21).

Jesus just makes matters worse. He slices through the whole traditional structure in one clean cut. He has a different vocation, a different mission, and it involves breaking hallowed family ties. God is doing the unthinkable: he is starting a new family, a new holy people, and is doing so without regard for ordinary human family bonds. Unless you read verses 34 and 35 as deeply shocking, you haven't got the message.

How easy it is to slide back again into a sense of belonging, of group identity, that comes from something other than loyalty to Jesus. We substitute longstanding friendship, membership in the same group, tribe, family, club, party, social class or whatever it may be. But the call to be 'around' Jesus, to listen to him, even if 'those outside' think us crazy, is what matters. The church in every generation, and in every place, needs to remember this and act on it.

Mark has here set up a picture of 'those inside' and 'those outside' which is going to be very important in the next chapter. The **gospel**, and allegiance to Jesus, produce a division, often an unexpected and unwelcome one, in every group or society where they make their way. Mark's call to his readers then and now is to stick with Jesus whatever the cost.

MARK 4.1–20

The Parable of the Sower

[1]Once again Jesus began to teach beside the sea. A huge crowd gathered; so he got into a boat and stationed himself on the sea, with all the crowd on the shore looking out to sea. [2]He taught them lots of things in parables. This is how his teaching went.

[3]'Listen!' he said. 'Once upon a time there was a sower who went out sowing. [4]As he was sowing, some seed fell beside the path, and the birds came and ate it up. [5]Other seed fell on the rock, where it didn't have much soil. There was no depth to the ground, so it shot up at once; [6]but when the sun came up it was scorched, and withered away, because it hadn't got any root. [7]Other seed fell in among thorns; the thorns grew up and choked it, and it didn't give any crop. [8]And other seeds fell into good soil, and gave a harvest, which grew up and increased, and bore a yield, in some cases thirtyfold, in some sixtyfold, and in some a hundredfold.'

[9]And he added, 'If you've got ears, then listen!'

[10]When they were alone, the people who were around Jesus, with the Twelve, asked him about the parables.

[11]'The mystery of God's kingdom is given to you,' he replied, 'but for the people outside it's all in parables, [12]so that "they may look and look but never see, and hear and hear but never understand; otherwise they would turn and be forgiven".

[13]'Don't you understand the parable?' he said to them. 'How are you going to understand all the parables?

[14]'The sower sows the word. [15]The ones by the path are people who hear the word, but immediately the Accuser comes and takes away the word that has been sown in them. [16]The ones sown on the rock are those who hear the word and accept it with excitement, [17]but don't have any root in themselves. They are short-term enthusiasts. When the word brings them trouble or hostility they quickly become disillusioned. [18]The others – the ones sown among thorns – are those who hear the word, [19]and the worries of the present age, and the deceit of riches, and desire for other kinds of things, come in and choke the word, so that it produces no fruit. [20]But the ones sown on good soil are the people who hear the word and receive it, and produce fruit, some thirtyfold, some sixtyfold, some a hundredfold.'

I once knew a young man who was suffering from severe depression. Eventually he went to a psychiatrist and told her, not only how bad he was feeling, but what he'd been dreaming about, night after night. He was inside a house which was on fire. A close friend was setting light to it and pouring petrol on the flames. He was terrified, but he always managed to get out in the end.

The psychiatrist had no difficulty in explaining. In a dream, the house stands for your whole self. The friend is a part of your own personality that's important to you, but in this case is causing trouble. The story tells you what, at a level below conscious thought, you really know about what's happening: in this case, that though this time is very unpleasant you will eventually emerge safe and sound.

The ancient world knew about dreams and their interpretation. The Old Testament has plenty of them. Jesus' **parables** are in some ways like dreams in search of meanings. Certainly this one is.

Alternatively, think of a political cartoon in a newspaper. Cartoons often use animals to represent countries or politicians. A lion might stand for the UK, a bear for Russia, or an eagle for the USA. Your own country, and its neighbours, will have their regular symbols; so will many political parties. If you know the symbols, you'll understand what's going on. But if you don't know you won't get the message. Sometimes when I'm abroad I find the newspapers frustrating because I don't know the code and can't understand the cartoons.

The ancient world knew about using symbols, not least animals, to tell coded stories about nations and kingdoms. There are stories like that in the Old Testament. Jesus' parables are a bit like that too. Certainly this one is.

The codes, the images in Jesus' dream-like stories, are often taken from his biblical background. A sower sowing seed is not just a familiar picture from everyday farming life. It's a picture of God sowing Israel again in her own land after the long years of **exile**; of God restoring the fortunes of his people, making the family farm fruitful again after the thorns and thistles have had it their own way for too long. There is even a hint of the restoration of the garden of Eden. 'The grass withers', said the prophet Isaiah, 'and the flower fades; but the word of our God will stand for ever' (40.8). Or again (Isaiah 55.10–11), God's word will be like rain or snow, producing good harvests. This is a story about the word that produces fruit, even though grass withers and flowers fade.

The problem – and this seems to be the main reason Jesus taught in parables – is that Jesus' vision of how God was sowing his word was, as we would say today, politically incorrect. People were expecting a great moment of renewal. They believed that Israel would be rescued lock, stock and barrel; God's **kingdom** would explode onto the world stage

31

in a blaze of glory. No, declares Jesus: it's more like a farmer sowing seed, much of which apparently goes to waste because the soil isn't fit for it, can't sustain it.

For those who understand the dream language, the code, this was and is bad news. It isn't just a comment on the way in which people in general sometimes listen to preachers and sometimes don't. (It would be a pretty dull sermon that simply commented on the way people listened to sermons.) It's a specific comment, a political cartoon, on what was happening as Jesus himself was announcing and inaugurating God's kingdom.

As we've already seen, some people were getting on board, while others were standing aloof. Now we see other reactions as well. Some hear and forget; some are enthusiastic but short-term; some have too much else in their minds and hearts. Yes, there are some who are fruitful, very fruitful indeed (any farmer would be delighted with a hundredfold yield); but Jesus is giving a coded warning that belonging to the kingdom isn't automatic. The kingdom is coming all right, but not in the way they have imagined.

Everything Jesus does creates a division within the Israel of his day. The parables not only explain this, but are themselves part of the process. They work, they function, as a sharply focused version of Jesus' entire ministry. Hence the comment in the middle. Jesus is not only telling them the dream, but giving them the interpretation. He is not only sketching the cartoon, but explaining the code. But those outside, who are fascinated by the story and the picture, can't understand it.

Why not? Doesn't Jesus want everybody to get the message? Yes and no. What he is saying is such dynamite that it can't be said straightforwardly, out on the street. Any kingdom-movement was dangerous enough (if Herod, or the Roman authorities, heard about it, they'd be worried); but if word got out that Jesus' kingdom-vision was radically unlike what most people wanted and expected, the ordinary people would be furious too. It was doubly dangerous. Put the cartoon into plain prose and somebody might sue.

It's a 'mystery' (verse 11): not just a puzzle, but a divine secret which Jesus is revealing. But as with all divine revelation, you can only understand it if you believe, if you trust.

For us today, the parable says a lot about how the message of Jesus worked among his hearers, and about what that message was (the dramatic and subversive renewal of Israel and the world). But it also challenges our own preaching of the kingdom. Is what we're saying so subversive, so unexpected, that we would be well advised to clothe it in dream language, or in code? If you were to draw a cartoon instead of preaching a sermon, what would it look like? Who would you expect to be offended if they cracked the code?

MARK 4.21-25

A Lamp on Its Stand

> [21]Jesus said to them, 'When you bring a lamp into a room, do you put it under a bucket, or under a bed? Of course not! It goes on a lamp-stand. [22]No: nothing is secret except what's meant to be revealed, and nothing is covered up except what's meant to be uncovered. [23]If you have ears, then listen!
>
> [24]'Be careful with what you hear,' he went on. 'The scales you use will be used for you, and more so. [25]If you have something, you'll be given more; but if you have nothing, even what you have will be taken away.'

Yesterday I took part in a procession. It started outside St Margaret's Church, Westminster, and as Big Ben struck the hour we began to move, singing hymns, around the green and into the great west doors of Westminster Abbey. I like singing hymns, and though I was at the back of the procession and a long way away from the choir, I went on singing even though nobody much could hear me.

Or so I thought. What I didn't know was that the microphone which had been fitted to me for the service we were going into was already switched on. The people inside the Abbey could hear me singing a long solo through the public address system. Had I known, I would have shut up like a clam.

Had Jesus been speaking today, he might have said, 'When you put on a microphone, do you then cover it with a handkerchief so you can't be heard? Of course not! Whatever is said (or sung) in secret will be broadcast to everybody!' In other words: I am telling you these things now, in secret; but the reason for announcing the **kingdom**, for bringing God's light into the world, is so that everyone will see it.

This is both a promise and a warning. The promise: don't worry, this kingdom-message will be public knowledge soon enough. The warning: make sure you're listening now, because you will need to know.

The next little saying is even more cryptic. In its traditional translation ('the measure you give will be the measure you get'), it has inspired all sorts of reflections, including a whole Shakespeare play about the meaning of justice. Here Jesus seems to be telling his followers that the level to which they pay attention to what he's teaching them will be the level at which they will receive the benefits of the kingdom.

33

This isn't quite like saying 'You'll get out of this what you put in', since of course when everything depends on the grace of God it's never a matter simply of people trying a bit harder and so getting a better return on their moral investment. It's rather, again, a promise and a warning, both of which are amplified in the final little saying. If they grasp what Jesus is saying and go deeper and deeper into it, they will get more and more from it. But if they remain at the superficial level, like the incomprehending crowds, they will lose even that sense of God doing something new in their midst which they have at present.

On the day I am writing this, a radio station telephoned me. Would it be true, they asked, to say that fewer people in the Western world know the basic Christian story than was true 30 years ago?

Certainly, I replied, in Britain and Western Europe. I'm not sure it's true in America, and it certainly isn't true in Africa and south-east Asia, where the churches are growing rapidly. But where, as in Britain and much of Europe, it's widely assumed that Christianity has had its day, is old-fashioned and out of date, those who still call themselves Christians need to take the warning of these verses very much to heart. We have to pay closer heed to what we have been taught, to the kingdom-message, the Jesus-message, the story of our salvation. If we loosen our grip on it, we may lose it altogether.

On the other hand, if we go deeper into what we already basically know, we will find there is more, and more, and more to learn, to feed on, to grow into. And we will find that the things we whisper to one another in small groups, in apparently dwindling churches, will one day be shouted from the housetops. God's microphone is in place, and we may not realize who will be listening if we start to sing.

MARK 4.26–34

More Seed Parables

[26]'This is what God's kingdom is like', said Jesus. 'Once upon a time a man sowed seed on the ground. [27]Every night he went to bed; every day he got up; and the seed sprouted and grew without him knowing how it did it. [28]The ground produces crops by itself: first the stalk, then the ear, then the complete corn in the ear. [29]But when the crop is ready, in goes the sickle at once, because harvest has arrived.'

[30]'What shall we say God's kingdom is like?' he said. 'What picture shall we give of it? [31]It's like a grain of mustard seed. When it's sown on the ground, it's the smallest of all the seeds on the earth. [32]But when it's sown, it springs up and becomes the biggest of all shrubs. It grows large branches, so that "the birds of the air make their nests" within its shade.'

> [33]He used to tell them a lot of parables like this, speaking the word as much as they were able to hear. [34]He never spoke except in parables. But he explained everything to his own disciples in private.

I have always enjoyed listening to good choirs. I have even, on rare occasions, sung in one or two, in fear and trembling lest my amateur ability should reveal itself by a wrong note, a fluffed entry, or – that dread moment for all irregular singers – keeping the sound going a second too long after everyone else has fallen silent.

When you audition for a choir, often the conductor will ask you to pick notes out of a chord. Here is a chord of three, four or five notes; you can hear it all together, but can you hear the notes individually, and sing each in turn? It's often quite a test.

Something like that is involved in learning to read Jesus' **parables**. We can all see the surface meaning of the story: in this case, the secret growth of a seed, or the small seed that produces a big bush. But can you see the individual notes that go to make up these chords? I suspect that Jesus' first hearers had a bit of a struggle with it, too; that's why Mark says that he explained everything to his **disciples** in private. As we've already seen, Jesus wasn't being deliberately difficult for the sake of it. His message was so explosive that this was the only way he could say it.

Take the first chord – the story about the seed that grows in secret. It's so simple as to seem quite innocuous. The seed grows secretly, doing its own thing unobserved in the earth, and eventually there appear the stalk, the ear of corn and the swelling corn inside the ear. Then, of course, comes harvest. Seems straightforward enough.

But listen to the two notes inside this chord that give it its peculiar and dangerous undertone. Begin at the end. 'In goes the sickle at once, because harvest has arrived.' That's a quotation from the prophet Joel (3.13). We find it near the end of his short book, which is all about the coming Day of the Lord, the time when, after terrible devastation coming on God's people, God will restore their fortunes, pour out his spirit upon them, and reap a harvest of judgment against the nations round about. That's the vision of the coming Day that many of Jesus' contemporaries were cherishing. Jesus is telling them that God's promised moment is indeed coming – but it won't look like what they were expecting. God is not simply vindicating Israel and condemning those outside. When judgment comes, it will look rather different. But come it will.

The other note that helps to explain the difference is in the apparently innocent description of how the seed starts to germinate and grow. The farmer, Jesus says, goes to bed and gets up, goes to bed and gets up, night and day . . . but still doesn't know how the seed sprouts and grows. The answer, of course, is that the seed is doing what the man is doing. It is sleeping in the soil and then getting up. This is how God's present creation works: night and day, seedtime and harvest, the cycle of the day and the year mirroring one another within God's promised stable order (see Genesis 1.4–13; 8.22).

But what's the significance of this within the coming of the **kingdom**? Answer: the seed is laid in the earth and then arises. The word for 'get up' is one of the regular words for the **resurrection**. And the resurrection, by this stage in Jewish thinking, wasn't about how individuals would find 'life after death'. It was about how God would dramatically restore Israel's fortunes, even raising the saints of old to share in the new blessing.

The first parable here, then, is about the fact that, though Jesus' ministry in Galilee doesn't look like the sort of kingdom-of-God-movement people were expecting, it was in fact the seedtime for God's long-promised and long-awaited harvest. People wouldn't be able to see how God's promised plant would grow from this seed; but grow it would, and harvest would come. The story is a warning against looking down on the small beginnings, in Jesus' Galilean ministry, of the great work that God was to do. It can function as a warning, too, against looking down on the small beginnings – a moment of vocation, two or three people meeting to pray and plan – that often, today, herald the start of some great new initiative that God has in mind.

The second parable, too, has a couple of notes inside its chord that give it its peculiar flavour. The first one comes in the question Jesus asks: What shall we say God's kingdom is like? What picture shall we give of it?

In one of the best-known passages in the Jewish Bible, the fortieth chapter of Isaiah, the prophet asks a very similar question about God himself: To what will you liken God, or what likeness compare with him (Isaiah 40.18)? It's not just an accidental echo. The passage is all about a fresh vision of God, the creator, coming to rescue his people, coming to restore Israel after her time of devastation. Israel mustn't think her God is incapable, powerless, on a level with the pagan idols that promise much and do nothing.

So here, nobody should look at Jesus in Galilee, surrounded by a local crowd, and say, 'How can this possibly be the beginning of the kingdom of God?' The mustard seed is the smallest at the start, but in the end it grows into a large shrub. That's Jesus' picture of what God's way of working, God's way of growing the kingdom, is like.

And at the end it will be a royal kingdom like those spoken of in scripture. The other echo, the other note in the chord, comes at the end of the story: the birds of the air make their nests in its shade. Ezekiel and Daniel both use this as an image of a great kingdom, growing like a tree until those around can shelter under it (Ezekiel 17.23; 31.6; Daniel 4.12, 21). Don't worry, Jesus is saying. Remember who your God is and what he's promised. Realize that this small beginning is the start of God's intended kingdom – the kingdom that will eventually offer shade to the whole world.

Jesus' hearers, of course, probably knew their scriptures better than most of us do. They might be able to pick out the notes in the chord and at least begin to make some sense of it all. The challenge for us, as readers of Jesus' parables in a very different world, is to think out what we have to do to be kingdom-workers, kingdom-explainers, in our own day. How can we strike fresh chords so that people will be teased into picking out the notes, and perhaps even into joining in the song?

MARK 4.35-41

Jesus Calms the Storm

³⁵That day, when it was evening, Jesus said to them, 'Let's go over to the other side.'

³⁶They left the crowd, and took him with them in the boat he'd been in. There were other boats with him too.

³⁷A big windstorm blew up. The waves beat on the boat, and it quickly began to fill. ³⁸Jesus, however, was asleep on a cushion in the stern. They woke him up.

'Teacher!' they said to him, 'We're going down! Don't you care?'

³⁹He got up, scolded the wind, and said to the sea, 'Silence! Shut up!' The wind died, and there was a flat calm. ⁴⁰Then he said to them, 'Why are you scared? Don't you believe yet?'

⁴¹Great fear stole over them. 'Who *is* this?' they said to each other. 'Even the wind and the sea do what he says!'

It isn't only boats that are in danger on the Sea of Galilee. To this day, the car parks on the western shore have signs warning drivers of what happens in high winds. The sea can get very rough very quickly, and big waves can swamp cars parked on what looked like a safe beach. I have in my study a photograph of the lake, which I took from the top of the Golan Heights on a calm and sunny day; but when the wind suddenly gets up you wouldn't want to hang around outside with a camera. A boat on the lake suddenly gets tossed around like a child's toy.

This tale, though, isn't just about danger and rescue. Behind stories like this, Mark's readers would probably have heard older echoes. Think

37

of Jonah. Instead of doing what God told him, he was sailing away in the wrong direction; a great storm arose, which was only calmed when, at his prompting, the sailors threw him overboard. Or think of the Israelites, coming out of Egypt when God made a way through the sea. Think even further back, to the stories of creation, when God's order, God's new world, emerged from the dark primal sea. The Psalms several times speak of the creator God who rules the raging of the sea, telling its rough and threatening waves to quieten down (e.g. 65.7; 89.9; 93.3–4; 107.23–30).

Put these pictures together, and what do you have? Apart from fishermen, the Jews were not a seafaring people; they left that to their Phoenician neighbours to the north. The sea came to symbolize, for them, the dark power of evil, threatening to destroy God's good creation, God's people, God's purposes. In books like Daniel, the sea is where the monsters come from.

So when Jesus rescues the **disciples** from a storm, we are witnessing something which says, in concrete terms, what the **parables** earlier in the chapter were saying in word-pictures. God's sovereign power is being unleashed; that is, God's **kingdom** is at hand. It isn't like people thought it would be, but this is the real thing. It's the same power that made the world in the first place. And this power is now living in Jesus, and acting through him. Just as in Daniel 7 the monsters who've come up from the sea are finally put to flight by 'one like a **son of man**', so here Jesus assumes the role of God's agent in defeating the forces of chaos. He isn't a Jonah, running away from God's command, so the disciples don't have to throw him overboard. He is doing exactly what the living God wants.

The forces of evil are roused, angry and threatening, but Jesus is so confident of God's presence and power that he can fall asleep on a pillow. The disciples are cross: doesn't he care that the boat is about to go to the bottom and take them with it? Jesus quizzically reverses the question, putting them on the spot in a way which Mark is using to build us up towards chapter 8: don't you yet have **faith**?

When you read a good book you often only see the point of earlier bits when you get to the later bits. (Indeed, one of the definitions of a good book is that it needs reading at least twice!) Anyone who already knew Mark's whole story might well read this paragraph and see in it, like someone looking the wrong way through a pair of binoculars, a tiny version of the whole thing. Here is Jesus with the disciples, going about their business; here are the forces of evil (madmen shrieking in the synagogue, angry men plotting, powerful men capturing Jesus and putting him to death); here is Jesus, not now asleep on a pillow but slumped on the cross. We hear his voice: Why are you afraid? Don't you believe? And on the third day the storm is still, the tomb is empty, and great fear comes upon them all. Who then *is* this?

Imagine this as a blockbuster movie – it would need a big screen to do it justice – and audition for a part. Make it *your* story. Actually, if you sign on with Jesus for the kingdom of God, it will become your story whether you realize it, whether you like it, or not. Wind and storms will come your way. The power of evil was broken on the cross and in the empty tomb, but like people who have lost their cause and are now angry, that power has a shrill malevolence about it. Christians – the church as a whole, local churches here and there, individual Christians – can get hurt or even killed as a result.

Mark's first readers probably knew that better than most of us. They would have identified easily with the frightened men in the boat. That's Mark's invitation to all of us: OK, go on, wake Jesus up, pray to him in your fear and anger. And don't be surprised when he turns to you, as the storm subsides in the background, and asks when you're going to get some real faith.

MARK 5.1–20

The Healing of the Demoniac

¹So they came over the sea to the land of the Gerasenes. ²When they got out of the boat, they were suddenly confronted by a man with an unclean spirit. ³He was emerging from a graveyard, which was where he lived. Nobody had been able to tie him up, not even with a chain; ⁴he had often been bound with shackles and chains, but he used to tear up the chains and snap the shackles. No one had the strength to tame him. ⁵On and on, night and day, he used to shout out in the graveyard and on the hillside, and slash himself with stones.

⁶When he saw Jesus a long way away, he ran and threw himself down in front of him.

⁷'Why you and me, Jesus?' he shouted at the top of his voice. 'Why you and me, son of the High God? By God, stop torturing me!' – ⁸this last, because Jesus was saying to him, 'Unclean spirit, come out of him!'

⁹'What's your name?' Jesus asked him.

'Legion', he replied. 'That's my name – there are lots of us!' ¹⁰And he implored Jesus not to send them out of the country.

¹¹It so happened that right there, near the hillside, was a sizeable herd of pigs. They were grazing.

¹²'Send us to the pigs', begged the spirits, 'so that we can enter them.'

¹³So Jesus gave them permission. The unclean spirits came out and went into the pigs. The herd rushed down the steep slope into the sea – about two thousand of them! – and were drowned.

[14]The herdsmen fled. They told it in the town, they told it in the countryside, and people came to see what had happened. [15]They came to Jesus; and there they saw the man who had been demon-possessed, who had had the 'legion', seated, clothed and stone-cold sober. They were afraid. [16]The people who had seen it all told them what had happened to the man – and to the pigs. [17]And they began to beg Jesus to leave their district.

[18]Jesus was getting back into the boat, when the man asked if he could go with him. [19]Jesus wouldn't let him.

'Go back home', he said. 'Go to your people and tell them what the Lord has done for you. Tell them how he had pity on you.'

[20]He went off, and began to announce in the Ten Towns what Jesus had done for him. Everyone was astonished.

The east side of the Sea of Galilee, rising steeply up to the Golan Heights, is still disputed territory, 2,000 years on from this story. For many years, it belonged to Syria; the Israelis took it in the war of 1967; it's a bargaining counter in the long-drawn-out peace process, and successive politicians all try to do something about it. It would be nice to think that by the time you read this book everything will be agreed, but I fear the story looks like going on for some while yet.

The politics of Jesus' day were every bit as complicated as those of our own. After the death of Herod the Great in 4 BC, when the country was divided up between his sons, Philip got the bit to the north-east of the Sea of Galilee. But the bit to the south-east, where this story takes place, had never really been Jewish territory. It was called the 'Decapolis', which means 'Ten Towns', even though different writers even in the ancient world could never agree which ten they were talking about. In the same way, the **scribes** who copied the manuscripts of Mark couldn't agree about whether this incident took place near Gerasa, Gergasa or Gadara – hence the variations which you'll find in different translations of verse 1.

The point for our purposes is clear: it wasn't Jewish land, and the people weren't Jews. Why, if they had been, would they have been keeping pigs? Everyone knew the Jews regarded them as unclean. That's the first thing to get straight.

While we're on about uncleanness, graveyards were also considered places of contamination. For a Jew, contact with the dead, or with graves, made you unclean. The man who rushes out to meet Jesus is about as unclean as you could get.

For the century or so before Jesus' time the whole area had been overrun by the Romans. The legions had marched in and taken over, as they did everywhere from Britain to Egypt. Whoever got in their way was crushed. A few people – local politicians, tax-collectors, call girls – did all right out of the Romans. Most people saw them as The Enemy. As **satan** incarnate.

And some people found that they were gripped by that evil force internally as well as externally. Two thousand years hasn't given us much more insight into the strange condition they called demon-possession, though there is plenty of evidence for such phenomena in our world too. (Just because some people become paranoid and insist on seeing **demons** behind every bush, causing every problem in life, that doesn't mean there aren't malevolent forces out there that can get a grip on people – perhaps especially when a society crumbles under alien powers.) It seems as though this poor fellow had become, from one point of view, totally obsessed by the powers that had taken over his country; from another point of view, totally possessed by the troop of phantom invaders that had taken over his humanity. They had given him a super-human strength (there is evidence for this sort of thing today, too), but had left him a human wreck: naked, isolated, self-destructive.

Why Jesus went to that bit of territory we'll never know. But what he did was not only dramatic; it was deeply symbolic. Many in the area, Jews and non-Jews alike, must have longed to see the Romans pushed back into the Mediterranean Sea. If they read books like Daniel, they would (as we saw earlier) understand the sea as the place where the monsters came from – and the monsters were like cartoon characters standing for the big hitters on the world's political scene. Rome was the Monster of all monsters. Rome was unclean. Rome was a nation of pigs. The best place for Rome was back in the sea.

So what was going to happen when the man who was announcing God's **kingdom**, God's sovereign rule over all human rule, came face to face with someone obsessed, and 'possessed', by Rome and her unclean legions? God's kingdom is to bring healing, restoring justice to Israel and the world. If unclean beings are fouling up human lives, the answer is plain. Into the sea with them.

But it's not as easy as that. Again Mark is telling us to look at the bigger story. At the climax of Mark's story Jesus himself will end up naked, isolated, outside the town among the tombs, shouting incomprehensible things as he is torn apart on the cross by the standard Roman torture, his flesh torn to ribbons by the small stones in the Roman lash. And that, Mark is saying, will be how the demons are dealt with. That is how healing takes place. Jesus is coming to share the plight of the people, to let the enemy do its worst to him, to take the full force of evil on himself and let the others go free.

This story shows that underneath the pain and injustice of political enslavement there is a spiritual battle. Leave that out, and you simply

41

go round the endless cycle of violence and counter-violence. Mark sees Jesus' kingdom-movement, which reached its climax in his death, as the means by which all earthly powers are brought to heel, even though the messengers of the kingdom may suffer in the process. Those who follow Jesus are now to put into practice the victory he achieved.

The big picture must never exclude the little picture. The focus of Mark's big canvas is on one man in deep human distress and need, and on Jesus meeting that need and healing that distress. Wherever humans are in pain today – in other words, in every community in the world – the gentle healing message of Jesus needs to be applied, identifying with those in pain to bring God's healing where it's needed. Notice how, precisely as part of that healing, Jesus doesn't let the man stay with him. He isn't to become, in that sense, dependent on Jesus. He is to stand on his own feet, depending on Jesus in a different way: he is to find a new life, back in his own community, telling in non-Jewish areas what Jesus had done. Some time before St Paul coined the phrase, this unnamed but beloved man seems to have become the first **apostle** to the **Gentiles**.

MARK 5.21–34

Jairus's Daughter and the Woman with Chronic Bleeding

[21]Jesus crossed over once more in the boat to the other side. There a large crowd gathered around him, and he was by the seashore.

[22]One of the synagogue presidents, a man named Jairus, arrived. When he saw Jesus he fell down at his feet.

[23]'My daughter's going to die! My daughter's going to die!' he pleaded. 'Please come – lay your hands on her – rescue her and let her live!'

[24]Jesus went off with him. A large crowd followed, and pressed in on him.

[25]A woman who had had internal bleeding for twelve years heard about Jesus. [26](She'd had a rough time at the hands of one doctor after another; she'd spent all she had on treatment, and had got worse rather than better.) [27]She came up in the crowd behind him and touched his clothes. [28]'If I can just touch his clothes,' she said to herself, 'I'll be rescued.' [29]At once her flow of blood dried up. She knew, in her body, that her illness was cured.

[30]Jesus knew at once, inside himself, that power had gone out of him. He turned around in the crowd and said, 'Who touched my clothes?'

[31]'You see this crowd crushing you,' said the disciples, 'and you say "Who touched me?"'

³²He looked round to see who had done it. ³³The woman came up; she was afraid and trembling, but she knew what had happened to her. She fell down in front of him and told him the whole truth. ³⁴'My daughter,' Jesus said to her, 'your faith has rescued you. Go in peace. Be healed from your illness.'

We really should take this passage with the next one, since in Mark's mind they are all part of the same story. But both are so full of interest that it's worth holding them apart for the moment, provided we remember how closely they belong together.

What Mark has done is to place one tale inside the other, in what is sometimes called a Markan sandwich. (We'll see him do this again in, for example, 11.12–25.) The flavour of the outer story adds zest to the inner one; the taste of the inner one is meant in turn to permeate the outer one. The outer story is about Jairus, one of the local synagogue presidents, and particularly his 12-year-old daughter; the inner story is about a much older woman, who for the same twelve years has suffered severe internal bleeding.

Both stories are about fear and **faith**, and the power of Jesus to take people from one to the other. Both, singly and together, are worth spending time 'inside', in the sense of meditating on them, imagining you are in the crowd watching it all happen, then – if you dare! – identifying with the various characters at the centre of the drama. That's a wonderful way to turn scripture into prayer – and today, as in Jesus' day, to turn fear into faith.

Let's start the process by identifying with Jairus, the synagogue president (it sounds a grand title, but in a town of at most a few hundred, with two or three such officers, it wasn't that prestigious). Since the time when Jesus moved from Nazareth to Capernaum, he can't always have been an easy person to have in the village congregation. Local experts in Jewish law were upset at some of the things he was doing; murmurs around the place suggested that if Herod Antipas got to hear of a new **kingdom-of-God** movement there would be trouble. Jairus might well have felt he could do without someone likely to land the town in the spotlight for all the wrong reasons. At best, he'd probably want to keep a safe distance. Let others go after this Jesus; sooner or later we'll see if anything comes of his efforts, and for the moment it's better to preserve something like neutrality.

Until disaster strikes. Jairus's daughter, who features as the young heroine in the animated movie *The Miracle Maker*, is twelve years old – almost old enough, in that culture, to be getting married. And now she's very, very sick, apparently about to die. Without letting sentimental imagination run away with us, we can see easily enough the agonized

43

household, the distraught father, hope slipping away like sand through a sieve, and then word arriving that the strange teacher has just come back from across the lake. Jairus pockets his pride and forgets his fears – why worry about religious controversy or political danger when your daughter's dying? – and rushes off to Jesus, throwing himself down at his feet (most undignified! What will they whisper about him next **sabbath?**). He gasps out his request. And Jesus goes with him, the eager crowd of course in tow.

Mark now breaks off. The story of the older woman not only keeps us in suspense, as we wait to find out what happens to Jairus and his daughter (we can imagine Jairus hopping from one foot to the other while the conversation takes place); it provides depth and extra meaning.

Jesus is on his way to a house where, as we already suspect, he will find a corpse. Thoughts of sorrow would mingle with the threat of impurity, since contact with a dead body is one of the chief sources of impurity in Jewish law. Here, on the other hand, is a woman who has chronic internal bleeding; one of the other main causes of impurity was bodily discharges and those who had them (especially women). Jairus has asked Jesus to come to his house so that his daughter may be rescued, or 'saved'; the woman says to herself, 'If I can only touch his clothes, I'll be rescued.' 'Your faith has saved you', says Jesus to the woman. 'Don't be afraid – only believe', he says to Jairus (verse 36). Clearly Mark intends us to see the stories knocking sparks off each other.

The woman's perpetual uncleanness (with all its consequences in her family and social life) explains her fear both of openly requesting help and then of being discovered after she's received it. But one of the most remarkable things about the story is the way in which Jesus knows at once that power has gone out of him. (This, and the funny little exchange with the **disciples** that follows – like someone asking 'who touched me' in a rugby scrum – look to me like the sure sign of an eyewitness.)

Healing by touch, not least when the healer wasn't expecting it, is such a strange phenomenon that we probably can't probe much further about how such things work. But they highlight for us the intimate nature of the contact between the individual and Jesus that Mark expects and hopes his readers to develop for themselves. When life crowds in with all its pressures, there is still room for us to creep up behind Jesus – if that's all we feel we can do – and reach out to touch him, in that odd mixture of fear and faith that characterizes so much Christian discipleship.

Then the other odd thing: was it Jesus' power that rescued the woman, or her own faith? Clearly it was Jesus' power; but he says, 'Your faith has rescued you.' The answer must be that faith, though itself powerless, is the channel through which Jesus' power can work (compare 6.5). He is not a magician, doing conjuring tricks by some secret power for an amazed but uninvolved audience. He is (though the onlookers don't yet realize this) God's son, the one through whom the living God is remaking Israel, humans, the world. And faith, however much fear and trembling may accompany it, is the first sign of that remaking, that renewal, that new life. Where are you in this story?

MARK 5.35–43

The Raising of Jairus's Daughter

[35]As he said this, some people arrived from the synagogue president's house.

'Your daughter's dead', they said. 'Why bother the teacher any more?' [36]Jesus overheard the message. 'Don't be afraid!' he said to the synagogue president. 'Just believe!'

[37]He didn't let anyone go with him except Peter, James and James's brother John. [38]They arrived at the synagogue president's house, and saw a commotion, with a lot of weeping and wailing. [39]Jesus went inside.

'Why are you making such a fuss?' he said. 'Why all this weeping? The child isn't dead; she's asleep.' [40]And they laughed at him.

He put them all out. Then he took the child's father and mother, and his companions, and they went in to where the child was. [41]He took hold of her hand, and said to her, '*Talitha koum*', which means 'Time to get up, little girl!' [42]At once the girl got up and walked about. (She was twelve years old.) They were astonished out of their wits. [43]Then he commanded them over and over not to let anyone know about it, and told them to give her something to eat.

Right on cue, as the suspense heightens, messengers come to tell Jairus that his daughter has now died. He shouldn't bother Jesus any longer. Telling Jairus not to be afraid, and just to believe, in that setting must have sounded like telling someone to paddle across the Pacific in a canoe. (Today's newspaper tells me that someone has just done something rather like that. But most of us wouldn't even dream of trying.) But so many extraordinary things were happening in Capernaum just then that Jairus, numb with grief and horror as he must have been, may also have discovered a spark of **faith** which enabled him to walk with Jesus the short distance (Capernaum was only a small town) to his own front door.

They would soon know they were getting near. As in many countries of the world to this day, particularly where grief is a regular visitor to the average house in the absence of modern Western medicine, there were well-established rituals for beginning the grieving process. Professional mourners would come in weeping and wailing, sometimes with flute accompaniment (Matthew mentions the latter at this point). They made it possible for family members to give vent to their feelings without restraint or embarrassment. As we know today, bottling up grief is extremely unhealthy; better to get on with it, to let it come.

But Jesus isn't having any of it. Having kept the crowds at bay (how did he manage that, we may wonder?) he takes his three closest followers, Peter, James and John, and they go together into the house. 'She's not dead', he declares; 'she's asleep!' Often in the ancient world, and particularly in Judaism and Christianity, sleep was used as a metaphor for death, and indeed sometimes (as in John 11.11) Jesus says 'asleep' when he means 'dead'. Mark is perhaps hoping that his readers will hear, from the previous chapter, the story of the seed and the plant. It goes to sleep and rises up . . . and now that's what will happen to this girl, as a further sign that the **kingdom** of God is breaking in upon Israel in the unlikely form of a young prophet doing extraordinary things in one little town by the lake. A further sign, too, of how the story will end, with astonished people coming to see the place where a dead body once lay but now lies no longer.

They laughed at him, as they have laughed at Jesus' followers from that day to this; but Jesus got on with what had to be done. The crowd is left behind; six people only go into the room where the dead girl is lying. This time it is Jesus who reaches out his hand; this time he says a word of command, one of the few things to have come to us in the original Aramaic: *Talitha koum*, 'Time to get up, little girl!' Up she got, and walked round the room. And again the eyewitness touch: give her something to eat.

The passage leaves us with all sorts of questions. To begin with, why has Mark told us the Aramaic words that Jesus spoke? It is virtually certain that, though Jesus and his followers would be able to speak and understand Greek, their normal everyday language would be Aramaic. So what's special about these words? Why leave them untranslated, along with only a handful of others (like 'Abba' in the Gethsemane scene, 14.36)? The best answer is probably that the scene, and the crucial words, made such a deep impression on Peter and the others that whenever they told the story afterwards, even in Greek to non-Jewish audiences, they kept the crucial words as they were. It wasn't a magic formula, a kind of 'abracadabra'; they were the ordinary words you might use to wake up a sleeping child. But part of the point of the **gospel** story, and of this whole section of Mark, is precisely that the life-giving power of God is breaking into, and working through, the ordinary details of life.

A further question: why did Jesus apparently only raise Jairus's daughter, the widow's son at Nain (Luke 7.11–17), and Lazarus (John 11.1–44)? There must have been plenty of other recently dead people whose grieving relatives came to him or his followers for help. Some people, indeed, have objected to these stories not just on the grounds that they're incredible (though actually stories of people being restored to life, however unusual, are known both in the Old Testament and in non-Jewish traditions), but that they're unfair: if God did it once or twice, why not to everybody? This is sometimes even raised as an objection to Christian belief in Jesus' **resurrection**; why should God treat Jesus as a special case? If God can do that sort of thing, why doesn't he prevent awful things like the Holocaust from happening in our own day?

This question misses the whole point of the larger story that Mark is telling us. Just as Jesus wasn't coming to be a one-man liberation movement in the traditional revolutionary sense, so he wasn't coming to be a one-man emergency medical centre. He was indeed starting a revolution, and he was indeed bringing God's healing power, but his aim went deeper; these things were signs of the real revolution, the real healing, that God was to accomplish through his death and resurrection. Signposts are important, but they aren't the destination. For that we must read on.

This question, though, is related to the point which Mark rubs in here as so often: Jesus tells them strictly not to tell anyone (we've already seen this in 1.34, with the **demons**, and we'll see it again in 7.36 and 8.30). The point seems to be that what Jesus is doing, as well as what he's saying (hence the **parables**), is dangerous and subversive. If Herod knew that someone with this authority over death itself was on the loose, at the head of a kingdom-of-God movement, he'd be very worried. If the religious leaders in the **Temple**, or the self-appointed **legal experts**, knew that someone was acting in this way, outside the official channels, and claiming to be thereby launching a kingdom-movement, they would do their best to stifle it.

Only if we see Jesus' movement in all its dimensions, including the political one, will we understand that behind the intense and intimate human dramas of each story there lies a larger, and darker, theme to which Mark is repeatedly drawing our attention. Jesus is on his way to confronting evil at its very heart. He will meet Death itself, which threatens God's whole beautiful creation, and defeat it in a way as unexpected as these two healings. This time, though, there will be no command to silence.

MARK 6.1–6

A Prophet in His Own Town

¹Jesus went away from there, and came to his home region. His disciples followed him. ²On the sabbath, he began to teach in the synagogue. When they heard him, lots of people were astonished.

'Where does he get it all from?' they said. 'What's this wisdom he's been given? How does he get this kind of power in his hands? ³Isn't he the builder, Mary's son? Isn't he the brother of James, Joses, Judah and Simon? And aren't his sisters here with us?' They took offence at him.

⁴'Prophets have honour everywhere', said Jesus, 'except in their own country, their own family, and their own home.'

⁵He couldn't do anything remarkable there, except that he laid hands on a few sick people and cured them. ⁶Their unbelief dumbfounded him.

He went round the villages, teaching.

Most preachers can remember the first time they stood up to preach in front of their own parents. It's not the same as with other things people do. If you're a musician, they probably heard you practising when you were little; if you're a footballer, they saw you playing in the garden. But preaching is something dangerously public that emerges from something intensely private. Parents, and others who have known you when you were growing up, are inclined to be embarrassed both at the revelation of something so deeply personal and at its being waved around in front of the neighbours. Everybody is vulnerable at a moment like that.

Multiply that up a bit to allow for the fact that Jesus' message was different. He wasn't just another synagogue preacher, telling people how to obey God's law, offering God's hope for the future, explaining from the prophets something about when the **kingdom** might come. He was saying, apparently on his own authority, that the kingdom *was* coming, then and there. Where he was, the kingdom was. And if there was any doubt on the matter, he was doing things that demonstrated it.

But in Nazareth there *was* doubt, and Jesus didn't do very much in consequence. This is the odd thing. They had heard what he'd done in Capernaum and around the lakeshore; now they were teasing, mocking, challenging him to do the same back home where everyone knew him.

I think, though, that there was more to it than just putting the 'local boy made good' in his place. The kind of kingdom Jesus was talking about was not the sort of kingdom his contemporaries wanted to hear about. When the good folk of Nazareth had such an excuse for rejecting him, they took it with both hands. They didn't need to believe such a dangerous message; they could dismiss it as 'Oh, he's just the local handyman'. As if that made any difference. Actually, like Mary mistaking Jesus for the gardener in John 20, there may be a hidden irony here: Jesus is indeed the one who can fix things, the one who is putting up a building, the one people should go to to get things sorted out.

Once again we see the mysterious connection between healing and **faith**. Lack of faith, it seems, seriously hinders Jesus' power; an important lesson for all who try to preach or live the kingdom. If even Jesus was thwarted by the unbelief of those around, we shouldn't be surprised if sometimes we don't seem able to do what we thought we should (though it would be dangerously easy to use this as an excuse, to blame our own incompetence on others). And as so often in Mark, there is a pointer here towards the time when Jesus came to the city the **Messiah** might think of as home, to the **Temple** where a Messiah ought to go, and was once again rejected, this time with fatal consequences. Already at this stage of the story we are being pointed on to see where it will all lead.

This glimpse of Jesus' family reminds us that he had many blood-relatives who continued to be important in the life of the early church. Indeed, two of his great-nephews (grandsons, presumably, of one of the brothers or sisters mentioned here) were hauled up before the Emperor Domitian in the 90s of the first century on a charge of being part of a royal family. They got off by showing Domitian their hands; they were farm labourers. But clearly this kind of notoriety was something the family was not wanting or considering during Jesus' public career. Jesus seems to have come from a large family, most of whom had names associated in Jewish tradition with zealous godly revolution against paganism.

The most famous of these brothers is James, to whom Jesus appeared after the **resurrection** (1 Corinthians 15.7) and who became the great leader in the Jerusalem church, the anchorman of early Christianity while Peter and Paul were off on their travels around the world. It's good to be reminded that at this stage (as in 3.31–35) he was simply a puzzled, and perhaps angry, younger brother. The individual human dramas behind the larger story of the **gospel** are worth pondering, to learn the manifold ways in which God has worked in different hearts and lives.

Christians today need to keep in mind both the big picture of what God is doing in our world and our time, and the many smaller pictures of the individual humans, perhaps at the moment in rebellion against the gospel, who by God's grace will become people of faith and prayer. James, at this stage, shared the general unbelief of Nazareth. Within 30 years his name would be known throughout the land, and across the world, as synonymous with faithful and persistent teaching and prayer – and loyalty to his older brother, Jesus the Messiah.

MARK 6.7–13

The Twelve Sent Out

[7]Jesus called the Twelve, and began to send them out in pairs, giving them authority over unclean spirits. [8]These were his instructions: they were not to take anything for the road, just one staff; no bread, no bag, no cash in the belt; [9]to wear sandals, and not to wear a second tunic.

[10]'Whenever you go into a house,' he told them, 'stay there until you leave the district. [11]If any place doesn't welcome you, or won't listen to you, go away and wipe the dust from your feet as evidence against them.'

[12]They went off and announced that people should repent. [13]They cast out several demons; and they anointed many sick people with oil, and cured them.

'No time for coffee this morning,' I told my teenage son today. 'You've got a train to catch. You need to be at that meeting.'

He had emerged, sleepily, half an hour before his train left; it takes at least 20 minutes to get to the station. Pull on a pair of shoes, grab a bag, here's some money, off you go. I hope he makes it.

Jesus didn't even let them take a bag, or money. These are emergency instructions for a swift and dangerous mission, not a programme for the continuing life of the church after Easter. There have been a few brave souls who have tried to live like this in later times, but the church has usually, and in my view rightly, recognized that these commands are specific to Jesus' own day and the setting of his mission in first-century Palestine.

There is, though, some similarity between what the **disciples** must have looked like as they went on their way and the appearance of some wandering philosophers, of whom we have scattered reports, who went about the ancient world begging, teaching people – often in stark and shocking ways – that the present world with all its pomp and show was a sham and a nonsense and they shouldn't pay any more attention to it. These were the Cynics, so called because of the Greek word *cyon*, meaning 'dog' (in a world where dogs were more likely to be vermin than family pets). They had the reputation of barking at the rich and respectable. Some people, seeing a pair of Jesus' disciples coming into a village, might have thought at first they were that sort of people.

They would soon have learnt otherwise. The similarity between the Cynics and Jesus' disciples wasn't more than skin deep. Cynics didn't cast out **demons**; Mark makes this the main thing the disciples were to do. Nor was that simply a way of healing distressed souls. It was, as we've already seen, a sign that God's **kingdom** was breaking in at last.

That's why it was so urgent, and why they had to take minimum extra bits and pieces, rely on local hospitality, and focus entirely on the task in hand. They were kingdom-heralds, outriders warning people that something was about to happen (the Cynics didn't think anything new was going to happen, just that the present world was an unredeemable mess), and that everyone should get ready for it. Getting ready would mean repenting: not just feeling sorry for particular sins, but changing one's entire outlook and aims. Jesus' agenda left no room for compromise, and no time to waste.

Jesus anticipated that some places wouldn't welcome the message. There are always some who would rather stay sick than face the bracing challenge of a new way of life, a new outlook. But the disciples are to respond with a solemn symbolic action, wiping the dust of the place off their feet. How easy it would be, we naturally think, for this to become an act of pique or petulance. Yet in the context of Jesus' mission nothing else would do. There was no time to waste. Mark's breathless **gospel** focuses here on the disciples' breathless mission: and if people won't have it, there's no time to lose. On to the next place, and woe to those who have missed their chance.

Jesus' sharing of his urgent mission with the **Twelve** was not, then, simply an example of a good leader choosing to delegate, to give his followers experience and get the work done more quickly – though no doubt that is all true as well. It was a deeply symbolic act of witness to the Israel of his day as to what time it was in God's urgent timetable. History – Israel's history, the world's history – was rushing towards its climax, its showdown. Off go the Twelve, symbolic of God's renewed people, driving out evil before them, awakening memories of old prophecies of the sick being healed as the kingdom came. Jesus, it seems, was doing three things: he was gathering support, he was giving as many as possible a final chance to repent before the great moment came, and he was preparing the ground for the very different work that would take place in the aftermath of the great catastrophe.

If we are to make this passage our own today, therefore, it won't do either to suppose that we have to copy exactly Jesus' instructions to his followers, which were for a specific time, place and purpose, or to imagine that we can set the whole thing aside as irrelevant. Though the greatest crisis came and went with Jesus' death and **resurrection**, the church and the world have faced all sorts of crises at various stages ever since. Part of Christian discipleship is the spiritual sensitivity and discernment to know when there is an emergency on, and what steps to take. There have been many times in recent years, in many places around the globe, when the church's task has been, like the Twelve, to go urgently around, with minimum hindrances or distractions, warning people that the world is heading rapidly in the wrong direction, and doing things which show clearly that evil has been defeated through Jesus and can be defeated again today.

In my judgment, the Jubilee 2000 movement, seeking to remit the massive and unpayable debts of third-world countries, is one such movement. But there are others. Learning to hear a passage like this and to respond obediently involves learning to listen to the prophetic call of God, and to the pain of the present world, and to live at the point of intersection between the two. And when the call comes, there's no time to lose.

By the way: yes, he made it. Just.

MARK 6.14–16

The Speculations of Herod

¹⁴Jesus' name became well known, and reached the ears of King Herod.

'It's John the Baptist', he said, 'risen from the dead! That's why these powers are at work in him.'

¹⁵Other people said, 'It's Elijah!'

Others said, 'He's a prophet, like one of the old prophets.'

¹⁶'No', said Herod when he heard this. 'It's John. I cut off his head, and he's been raised.'

Private life is a modern invention. Until quite recently, most people lived in small communities where everyone knew everyone else's business. Until a few hundred years ago, everybody heard what was going on in the world by talking to neighbours and strangers, gossiping in marketplaces, and passing on stories of anything curious or striking. Only the royal, and the very rich, could afford something approaching privacy; and they achieved it, often enough, by employing deaf-mute slaves. Even then, word would often leak out as to what the king was doing . . .

That's the background for understanding what Herod heard about Jesus, and for that matter what the early Christians knew about Herod. In Britain to this day, rumours about royalty are passed to and fro between gossip columnists and fashion magazines; if a member of the royal family comes to town (or, in countries without royalty, if the President comes to town) local people will talk for weeks about who she spoke to, what she said, what she wore, and so on. How much more in a culture like first-century Palestine, without newsprint, radio or television.

And how much more when something truly remarkable was afoot. Everybody must have heard about the young prophet who was going about doing extraordinary things. Rumours were running round: maybe this was Elijah, who according to Jewish tradition would return to get things ready for the final judgment. (In scripture, he hadn't really died, but was instead scooped up to **heaven** direct, so it was appropriate that he might come back, and Malachi 4.5 had said he would do just that.) Or maybe it was one of the other great prophets of old. Jesus was behaving as a prophet; he spoke of himself as a prophet; it wasn't surprising that they thought of him like that.

Herod, though, had a more precise suggestion, which is all the more interesting in the light of subsequent events. He proposed that Jesus might be **John the Baptist**, back from the dead: that would explain, he thought, why he had these remarkable powers. If he'd been down to death and back again anything might be possible; John hadn't performed powerful healings, so it wasn't a matter of things returning to the way they had been before, but rather of something new and dramatic which needed accounting for. Maybe, then, thought Herod, he'd come back from the dead. Herod probably didn't have a well-worked-out theory about **resurrection**. It was an idea around at the time, but he was using it without any precision.

It shows, though, both that Jesus was indeed doing remarkable things, forcing people to unlikely explanations, and that, as we might expect with the **kingdom of God**, the kingdoms of the world were forced to take notice of it and, it seems, to take evasive action. It puts the question to us, if we desire or design to be kingdom-agents in our own world, on this further side of Jesus' actual resurrection: what should we be doing, that the powers of the world would hear about it and scratch their heads in puzzlement? And are we prepared for the result?

Mark is quite clear what will happen to people who announce, and inaugurate, God's kingdom. The present story of John, including Herod's garbled and muddled thinking, points forward to the greater story that is yet to come. Herod is wrong, but not completely wrong; for in Jesus the resurrection power of God is indeed at work – not because he's John, back from the dead, but because he is the one through whom, not very long from now, death will indeed be overcome. The mighty works he is doing at the moment, taking on the kingdom of darkness and beating it, will reach their climax in his personal decisive confrontation with that kingdom. But first he, like John, must suffer a cruel and unjust death.

Christians in many parts of today's world still face torture and death for their **faith**. They may take comfort, and the rest of us may be strengthened in our prayers for them, from the strange story of Jesus, Herod and John. The God who called and equipped John and Jesus, and who through them confronted Herod and by implication all other rulers, remains sovereign. Those who watch what's going on may draw all the wrong conclusions. But God knows what the right ones are. This God will vindicate and reward those who remain faithful to their calling in the face of intimidation, persecution and death itself.

MARK 6.17–29

Herod and John the Baptist

[17]What had happened was this. Herod had married Herodias, his brother Philip's wife. [18]John regularly told Herod it wasn't right for him to take his brother's wife; so Herod gave the word, arrested him and tied him up in prison. [19]Herodias kept up a grudge against him and wanted to kill him, but couldn't; [20]Herod knew that John was a just and holy man, and he was afraid of him. So he protected him, and used to listen to him regularly. What he heard disturbed him greatly, and yet he enjoyed listening to him.

[21]And then, one day, the moment came. There was a great party. It was Herod's birthday, and he gave a feast for his leading retainers, militia officers, and the great and good of Galilee. [22]Herodias's daughter came in and danced, and Herod and his guests were delighted.

'Tell me what you'd like', said the king to the girl, 'and I'll give it you!'

[23]He swore to her, over and over again, 'Whatever you ask me, I'll give it you – right up to half my kingdom!'

[24]She went out, and said to her mother, 'What shall I ask for?'

'The head of John the Baptist', she replied.

[25]So she went back at once to the king, all eager, and made her request: 'I want you to give me, right now, on a dish – the head of John the Baptist!'

[26]The king was distraught. But his oaths on the one hand, and his guests on the other, meant he hadn't the guts to refuse her. [27]So he sent a jailer straight away with orders to bring John's head. He went and beheaded him in the prison, [28]brought the head on a dish, and gave it to the girl. The girl gave it to her mother.

[29]When John's followers heard about it, they came and took his body, and buried it in a tomb.

What sells newspapers? Three things, and if they're combined, so much the better. Royalty: almost any story about a member of a royal family will sell, not only in Britain or Norway or wherever it began, but around the rest of the world. Sex: nothing like a scandal, especially if it's to do with people in high places. Religion: though God has slipped down the ratings in recent years, people are still aware that there are unanswered questions out there, and someone who seems to be an authentic spokesperson for God is newsworthy.

Put this package together, locate it in first-century Galilee, and you have the story of Herod and **John the Baptist**. There's nothing private about this story. It would have been round the palace within minutes, round the neighbourhood by morning, and round all Galilee within a day or two. If it had happened today it would be all over the newspapers. It's sordid, shabby and shameful – exactly the sort of thing that everybody likes to hear, however much they pretend otherwise. The scandalous goings-on at Herod's birthday party, with his step-daughter performing an erotic dance, his rash (and no doubt drunken) promise, and his command to execute the prophet to whom all Galilee and Judaea had gone for **baptism** – you can just hear the whispers, the rumours, the shaking of heads, the mutterings that no good would come of it. Within a decade, Herod had been banished to faraway Gaul, left to die in disgrace in a distant land. Within a generation, John's story had been written up by Mark, honouring him as a fearless witness to the **kingdom of God.**

Why did John make such a fuss over Herod Antipas's taking of his brother's wife? Not simply, I think, because such a thing was immoral, against the law, and setting a bad example to the Jewish public into the bargain. Herod, following his father, cherished a great ambition: to have the Jews recognize him as their true king. Though with hindsight we can see there was never a chance of this, he must have thought it at least possible. He was completing his father's great project of rebuilding the **Temple** in Jerusalem, and this had been closely associated with royalty ever since Solomon built the first temple a thousand years before.

John the Baptist, though, was launching a very different kind of kingdom-movement. His baptism, offering forgiveness of sins, was effectively upstaging the Temple itself. His promise, of a Coming One who was about to appear, spoke of a figure very different from Herod. And as though to rub in the point, he told his followers that Herod's aspirations were out of line. Would God's anointed really behave in such a fashion? A **Messiah** marrying his brother's wife?

No wonder Herod – and particularly Herodias, the woman at the centre of the scandal – were annoyed. Yet Herod had enough Jewish sensibility about him to listen to John again and again, torn between his anxiety at what John was saying and a strange compulsion to go on listening. But then came the day, with the party, the guests, the wine, the famous dance, the rash promises and the executioner's grim trip to the dungeon. The kingdoms of the world are indeed to become the kingdom of God, but those who speak of this in advance are likely to suffer the anger of those who feel their power slipping away from them. The casual, accidental nature of the event gives an extra dimension to the tragedy, a belittling of the noble and lonely prophet.

If royalty, sex and religion form such an explosive mixture, we shouldn't be surprised at the chequered history of court intrigue, scandal and disaster that have dogged the steps of the church ever since royalty became interested in Christianity in the fourth century. But there have always been kingdom-prophets to declare God's judgment on human pride and folly, and to suffer the consequences. Mark, in telling this story, is not only looking on to the death of Jesus himself, a political football between the Roman governor, the Jewish high **priest**, and the expectations of the fickle crowd. He is looking further, to the little communities of Christians he knew, wherever they were, facing persecution and hardship for their determination to stick with the kingdom-message whatever the authorities might do.

We aren't told what John said as the executioner came for him. This isn't a story, like many other Jewish stories of righteous men brutally killed, of a martyr who took the opportunity for a speech affirming his message and warning of God's vengeance. But Mark leaves his readers in no doubt. John was a righteous and holy man, and the kingdom of which he had spoken, and the forgiveness he had offered, were the reality that would win the day. Even in so solemn and ugly a story there can be found real encouragement to faithful witness and constant hope.

MARK 6.30–44

The Feeding of the Five Thousand

[30]The apostles came back to Jesus and told him all they had done and taught. [31]'All right,' he said, 'it's time for a break. Come away, just you, and we'll go somewhere lonely and private.' (Crowds of people were coming and going and they didn't even have time to eat.)

[32]So they went off privately in the boat to a deserted spot. [33]And . . . crowds saw them going, realized what was happening, hurried on foot from all the towns, and arrived there first. [34]When Jesus got out of the boat he saw the huge crowd, and was deeply sorry for them, because they were like a flock without a shepherd. So he started to teach them many things.

[35]It was already getting late when his disciples came to him and said, 'Look: there's nothing here. It's getting late. [36]Send them away. They need to go off into the countryside and the villages and buy themselves some food.'

[37]'Why don't you give them something?' Jesus replied.

'Are you suggesting', they asked, 'that we should go and spend two hundred dinars and get food for this lot?'

[38]'Well,' said Jesus, 'how many loaves have you got? Go and see.'

They found out, and said, 'Five, and a couple of fish.'

[39]Jesus told them to sit everyone down, group by group, on the green grass. [40]So they sat down in companies, by hundreds and by fifties. [41]Then he took the five loaves and the two fishes, looked up to heaven, blessed the bread, broke it, and gave it to his disciples to give to the crowd. Then he divided the two fish for them all. [42]Everyone ate, and had plenty. [43]They picked up the leftovers, and there were twelve baskets of broken pieces, and of the fish.

[44]The number of men who had eaten was five thousand.

Some break. Just when we think Jesus is anticipating modern therapeutic ideals – taking a good rest after a combination of an exhausting piece of work and sudden bad news – it all goes horribly wrong. The short boat trip is the only time he and the **disciples** have to themselves. By the time they get to the shore everyone else has got there first.

We can guess the disciples' reaction. But they couldn't have guessed what Jesus would say, or what he would do next. In retrospect, they realized that his primary feeling when faced with this great crowd, so eager for something even though they didn't know what, was deep human compassion. He was sorry for them. And – this is Mark's comment, reflecting the growing post-Easter awareness of what had been in Jesus' mind – he saw them as leaderless, kingless folk. 'Sheep without a shepherd' is a regular biblical way of describing the people of Israel when they have no leader, no king (Numbers 27.17; 1 Kings 22.17; Ezekiel 34.5; Zechariah 10.2).

Think back through the story Mark has just told us. Herod is off in his palace, probably far to the south of the Sea of Galilee, carousing with his cronies, winking at pretty girls, beheading prophets. His henchmen on the ground are grasping bullies. Here are his people, desperate for leadership. And here is a young prophet to whom they flock. Is he the king-in-waiting? That's the echo we must hear behind this story.

A few notes so we get the detail right before being swept away by the main event. The grass is green; if you've been to Galilee, you will know that this means the story is set in the springtime. Grass grows quickly in spring, but once the rains stop in May it gets scorched with the fierce sun. This takes place, then, around Passover time. Mark will have been aware of this, and of the way in which the words he uses to describe what Jesus did with the bread fit so neatly into the pattern the early church came to use for its own regular bread-breaking new-Passover meal: he took, blessed, broke and gave it.

Equally, the men sit down (we assume there were women and children there, but the numbers in the story refer specifically to males) in groups of a hundred or of fifty. Although the words for 'company' and 'group' are not specifically military, there is perhaps just a hint of formal organization about the way things are done; they presumably didn't need to be arranged in numbered groups. Anyone watching might already be asking: Who does this man think he is?

What followed would only intensify that question. Jesus first teases the disciples, then astonishes them, and us. Many still find the tale quite incredible, but the vivid detail, the different sources that speak of it, and the wider setting of all that we know about Jesus, make it easier to suppose he did something like this than that anyone within a generation would make up such a striking story when everybody could have told them it didn't happen. But what did it mean? What *does* it mean?

What we are seeing here is a sign of *new creation*. Something was going on, there in Jesus' public career, which was unleashing an explosive force into the world. It wasn't what we (or they) would call magic, the manipulation of the natural world to suit one's own ends. It was the power of a totally obedient life, a life given up to the **kingdom of God**, to God's sovereign and saving rule breaking in at last to a world for so long under enemy occupation. We are probably meant to make the connection between Jesus' compassion for the crowds and his action with the bread and the fish. God's kingdom is not simply a matter of power, but also of overflowing love, and the two here go inextricably together.

Perhaps the most obvious question that presses upon us today as we read this story is: it was all very well for the five thousand, but what about us today? Wasn't it a bit odd for Jesus to feed them (they could after all have gone and bought food) but not to feed the millions in our own world who wait with big, round eyes, and big, round stomachs at food distribution centres (if they're lucky), making guest appearances on our television screens and charity posters, and in our consciences? What about them? If God could do it then, why doesn't he do it now?

One obvious answer is what Jesus said to the disciples: you give them something to eat. But the question deserves more than that. It comes out of an assumption which itself needs challenging. What we call Jesus' '**miracles**' were not done as acts of supernatural power, in order to show that there was a God who had such power, who was operating through Jesus, and who could (if he chose) solve all problems with a snap of the conjurer's fingers. The mighty acts of Jesus were not that sort of thing at all. They were about the breaking in of God's kingdom in and through Jesus, a complex event which would reach its full climax in his death and **resurrection**. From that point there would go out into all the world the power of new creation; but it would always have to struggle against the still-resistant forces of evil.

If, then, we repeat Jesus' command ('You give them something to eat') that doesn't just mean 'work a bit harder at famine relief', though that would certainly help. It will also mean that those who discover the living God in and through Jesus must be prepared to face up to the evil structures and powers that still dominate and control so much of God's world, and to challenge them in the name of Jesus and with the power of his victory on the cross. It isn't just a matter of 'he did supernatural things, so why shouldn't we?' It's a matter of the full achievement of Jesus, of which these strange acts were just a part and a signpost, being brought to bear, through prayer and faithful action, on the world that still waits for the kingdom.

William Wilberforce did it with slavery (it took him an entire lifetime, too); who will do it with world poverty and starvation?

MARK 6.45–56

Jesus Walks on Water

[45]At once Jesus made his disciples get into the boat and set sail across towards Bethsaida, while he dismissed the crowd. [46]He took his leave of them and went off up the mountain to pray.

[47]When evening came, the boat was in the middle of the sea, and he was alone on the shore. [48]He saw they were having to work hard at rowing, because the wind was against them; and he came to them, in the small hours of the night, walking on the sea. He intended to go past them, [49]but they saw him walking on the sea and thought it was an apparition. They yelled out; [50]all of them saw him, and they were scared stiff.

At once he spoke to them.

'Cheer up,' he said, 'it's me. Don't be afraid.'

[51]He came up to them and got into the boat, and the wind stopped. They were overwhelmed with astonishment. [52]They hadn't understood about the loaves, because their hearts were hardened.

[53]They made landfall at Gennesaret, and tied up the boat. [54]People recognized Jesus as soon as they got out of the boat, [55]and scurried about the whole region to bring sick people on stretchers to wherever they heard that he was. [56]And wherever he went, in villages, towns or in the open country, they placed the sick in the marketplaces and begged him to let them touch even the hem of his garment. And all who touched it were healed.

I listened last night to an organ recital, given by one of the world's leading organists on a truly great instrument. Bach, Reger, Bruckner – wonderful composers, wonderful music, a magical evening. But there was one piece I had never heard before. By a modern composer, it built up a wall of sound, with chords and trills and little bits of melody all woven together, coming at the ear in wave after wave of exciting and dramatic music. Every time you thought, 'There – that's where we were going', there was more. It was quite overwhelming.

Then, just as you thought you might not be able to take it much longer, from within the wall of sound something different began to emerge. A slow chorale melody appeared quietly, like a cat that had been sleeping unnoticed in a corner of the room but that now uncoiled itself, stood up, stretched elegantly and started to walk about. The melody grew and swelled, blending with the previous sound but steadily taking command. Eventually the whole piece came together in a blaze of tune and sound, leaving us drained but happy.

In these recent sections of his **gospel**, Mark has been building up what we could think of as a wall of sound. The gospel sets off at a run (remember all those 'immediately's in the first two chapters, and quite a few since). Jesus is always healing and teaching, healing and teaching. The stakes are raised: **demons** are driven out, storms are stilled. Then the feeding of the five thousand. And now this: walking on the water. Then more healings. And more. When is it going to end? What's going to happen? Where is it all heading?

But at this point, within the steady build-up of astonishing events, we hear a dark theme emerge, a chorale tune in a minor key, which is now going to run alongside the other events until it achieves an initial resolution in chapter 8. 'They hadn't understood about the loaves', says Mark of the **disciples**, 'because their hearts were hardened.' It's the first time he's said something like that about the disciples, but we haven't heard the last of it by any means.

Nor is this simply a remark about the disciples themselves. It's a hint to us, the readers. What have *we* learnt from the story of the loaves? Clearly, Mark is hoping, something that will make us less than totally astonished to see Jesus walking on the water – though how he can suppose anyone of any period of history could avoid being startled by that is a moot point. But what he seems to be stressing is Jesus' sovereignty over the natural world. If they had reflected on the loaves and fishes, they might have realized (Mark seems to be saying) that water wouldn't be too much of a problem either – though Jesus never does anything like this again.

The chorale melody that we are beginning to hear, then, has two basic parts to it: the question of who precisely Jesus is, and the puzzle that the disciples don't seem to be learning their lesson, despite being first-hand observers of it all. And through the wall of sound provided by the apparently endless stream of sick people coming to be healed, and the restless running around of those who bring them, Mark is inviting us to ask the question for ourselves, and to ask, in addition, whether we are like the disciples, watching events happen but not drawing the right conclusions, or whether our hearts have been softened, or perhaps opened, to believe the extraordinary thing that is occurring before our eyes.

Because what Mark is beginning to tell us about Jesus is like nothing else before or since. And we mustn't jump to easy conclusions, either. For generations people have supposed that walking on water is offered as evidence of Jesus' 'divinity' (as opposed to being hungry, sad or thirsty, which is supposedly evidence of his 'humanity'). It's not as straightforward as that.

When Mark draws the veil aside in chapter 8 (we may allow ourselves to peep ahead for a moment), the conclusion is not that Jesus is divine, but that he is **Messiah**. True, Mark will point beyond that to deeper truths as well; but at the moment this is where the story is going. Somehow the remarkable things Jesus is doing point, in Mark's mind at least, to the truth that Jesus is the truly human one, Israel's Lord who is to be the world's Lord, anticipating in his rule over wind and wave, over bread and fish, the sovereignty that Israel believed the Messiah would have over the whole world. When the New Testament writers want to tell us that Jesus is in some sense divine, this is not something set apart from hunger, thirst, fear, sorrow and death itself, but found mysteriously in the middle of them all. What we see now is his genuine humanness: this is the authority that humans were supposed to have over the natural world, and lost – for ever, it had seemed – with sin and death.

We are right, then, to be astonished; but not to do what so many in the last two hundred years have done, and elevate that astonishment into a critical principle, ruling out from our world (and that of Jesus) anything that breaks what we think of as laws of nature. Nor is this a plea to allow for 'supernature' or 'supernaturalism', as though there were simply a different force which might invade our world from outside. Rather, we are invited to see something more mysterious by far: a dimension *of* our world which is normally hidden, which had indeed died, but which Jesus brings to new life. Mark is offering Jesus to our startled imagination as the world's rightful king, long exiled, now returning. He is, in Paul's language, the last Adam. From his time with the beasts in the wilderness (1.13), he is now striding the garden, putting things to rights.

If we can't or won't see this – and it makes us at least blink and rub our eyes – Mark indicates that we are in good company. I don't think

61

his remark about the disciples being hard-hearted is a major criticism of them; what else might one expect? He is simply warning that to grasp all this will need more than suspension of disbelief, as though one were in the theatre for the evening. It will take a complete change of heart. Fortunately, as he will explain in due course, that is what (among other things) Jesus has come to bring. It is in our thinking, our imagining, our praying as well as in our bodily health that we are invited to come, like the frantic crowds, and touch the hem of Jesus' garment, looking for salvation.

MARK 7.1–13

God's Law and Human Tradition

[1]The Pharisees gathered round Jesus, together with some legal experts from Jerusalem. [2]They saw that some of his disciples were eating their food with unclean (that is, unwashed) hands.

[3](The Pharisees, you see – and indeed all the Jews – don't eat unless they first carefully wash their hands. This is to maintain the tradition of the elders. [4]When they come in from the market, they never eat without washing. There are many other traditions which they observe: washings of cups, pots and bronze dishes.)

[5]Anyway, the Pharisees and legal experts asked Jesus, 'Why don't your disciples follow the tradition of the elders? Why do they eat their food with unwashed hands?'

[6] 'Isaiah summed you up just right', Jesus replied. 'What hypocrites, you are! What he said was this:

With their lips this people honours me,
but with their hearts they turn away from me;
[7]all in vain they think to worship me,
all they teach is human commands.

[8]'You abandon God's commands, and keep human tradition!

[9]'So,' he went on, 'you have a fine way of setting aside God's command so as to maintain your tradition. [10]Here's an example: Moses said, "Honour your father and your mother", and, "Anyone who slanders father or mother should die." [11]But you say, "If someone says to their father or mother, 'What you might get from me – it's Korban!'" (which means, 'given-to-God'), [12]you don't let them do anything else for their father or mother! [13]The net result is that you invalidate God's word through this tradition which you hand on. And there are lots more things like that which you do.'

I read a book about jokes the other day (not just a book of jokes, you understand, though there were plenty of them, but a philosophical book *about* jokes; humour is, as you might say, a very funny thing). One of the crucial things about jokes, the author was explaining, is that the less explanation you have to give the better. What makes telling and hearing a joke fun, as well as funny, is that teller and hearer discover they share a little bit of private world together, the bit you have to understand, without it being mentioned, in order to get the point of the joke. Some of the best jokes are Jewish jokes (the book was written by a Jewish philosopher), but it is part of the deal that you have to know the Jewish world on the inside to get the point.

One of the difficulties with Mark 7 is that unless you're inside the Jewish world you won't get the point. Mark already knows this, which is why he's explained to his readers something which, if they were Jewish, they wouldn't have needed to have spelled out like this. (This passage, about ritual washing of hands, pots and so on, is in fact one of the reasons why scholars conclude that his audience was primarily **Gentile**.) Suddenly Mark's stories about healing have stopped for a minute, and we have a debate instead, focusing on a controversy about the interpretation and practice of Judaism by Jesus and his followers. And for this, even if it spoils the story for those who live in that world, we need some explanations.

Mark gives us the first one: ritual washing of hands before food, and of cooking vessels, was one key part of a highly complex and developed system of purity regulations. These were eventually codified and written down about two hundred years after Jesus' day, but they were already well known, in the form of oral traditions, by his time. Of course, all societies have purity laws of one sort or another; Western children today are taught quite strictly when and how to wash their hands to prevent infection and disease, and woe betide any restaurant owner or delicatessen manager whose staff don't observe a very strict code of hygiene. So what's the problem? Why would anyone grumble about purity laws?

The problem comes in three layers, like a joke within a joke with an extra twist at the end. We need to take it slowly and look at each in turn.

First, we need to distinguish the surface issue from the underlying one. The question Jesus was asked was about purity; but the first answer he gave was about people obeying human traditions rather than God's word; and he gave a particular, and complicated, example. We'll come back to purity in the next section, so let's for the moment concentrate on tradition.

Part of the difficulty here is that many Christians have grown up knowing that there is a long-standing debate in the Western churches about the relative place and value of 'scripture' and 'tradition'. We are in danger, if we're not careful, of hearing this story with this debate in mind – like somebody who goes to a lecture on Irish literature but whose only previous knowledge of Ireland comes from hearing English people telling 'Irish' jokes (which usually assume, scandalously, that the Irish are ignorant). The debate in the churches has usually been between Catholics (placing a high value on tradition) and Protestants (placing a high value on scripture), often in relation to various practices of the church and to theological doctrines such as justification. That's the sort of thing people often think of as soon as they hear a question raised about 'scripture' and 'tradition'.

The debate between Jesus and the **Pharisees**, however, was between two different ways of understanding what it meant to be a good Jew in the first century. This wasn't just about doctrine or (what we would call) 'ethics', but about political agendas as well. Of course there are parallels and overlaps between our meanings and Jesus', but it's important to go back to the first century at this point and not get stuck in the sixteenth, or in times even closer to our own.

The charge Jesus levels against the Pharisees and **legal experts** is that, by teaching as fundamental law what is in fact only human custom rather than divine revelation, they are guilty of hypocrisy, play-acting. They are claiming to be teachers of God's truth and law, but in fact they are only teaching human traditions.

The question comes up, obviously, because the earlier question was about the tradition of purity. But to make his point, Jesus instances a clever way in which a tradition, or custom, was being used to enable people to get round their financial obligations to their parents. Like a cunning tax accountant finding a loophole in the law which enables someone to get away without paying any tax at all, the legal experts have found a way in which someone, by declaring their property to belong to God, can be free of all further obligation to their parents. Hypocrisy indeed: it was God who commanded the duty to parents in the first place, and officially 'giving the money to God' actually makes a mockery of the God they are claiming to honour.

The wider issue for Jesus and the Pharisees was: who speaks for God today? Who is offering a way of life which honours the God who spoke through scripture (something Jesus assumes throughout)? The Pharisees had built up, over nearly two centuries by Jesus' day, an agenda which was (in our terms) both political and religious. The two went together. The traditions they had developed meant that scripture was being interpreted and applied in particular directions, supporting particular programmes, not least the move towards revolt against Rome. The way the biblical purity laws were being applied worked in the same direction. That was where you might get if you went all the way with the 'traditions' that the hard-line Pharisees were urging people to accept.

Jesus, then, wasn't simply supporting an abstract idea, 'scripture', against another one, 'tradition'. He was challenging, by his whole kingdom-movement, the very basis on which the Pharisees had built up their edifice. If the **kingdom** was indeed coming in the work he was doing – by healing, by feasting with outcasts, by rolling back the kingdom of darkness – then the way that the layers of Pharisaic tradition had been pointing for long enough was quite simply ruled out from the start.

Jesus' knock-down argument for what he was doing was that it was the fulfilment of scripture. Go his way, and you got scripture thrown in. Go the Pharisees' way, and scripture – supposedly the basis for tradition, but actually often undermined by it – would lose out.

Thinking our way through the complexities of first-century debates is always tough (though anyone who wants to read the New Testament seriously has to get used to it). It's like learning jokes in a new language. But it alerts us not only to similar debates in our own day, but to a bigger principle. Often when people get angry, and start asking questions as to why someone's doing something, it's because there is a larger agenda at stake. Often it has political dimensions to it which don't appear on the surface. Part of being a Christian is to learn the art of spiritual discernment. And part of that art is learning to understand scripture, and to test human traditions against it.

MARK 7.14–23

Clean and Unclean

[14]Jesus summoned the crowd again.

'Listen to me, all of you,' he said, 'and get this straight. [15]What goes into you from outside can't make you unclean. What makes you unclean is what comes out from inside.'

[17]When they got back into the house, away from the crowd, his disciples asked him about the parable.

[18]'You didn't get it either?' he asked. 'Don't you see that whatever goes into someone from outside can't make them unclean? [19]It doesn't go into the heart; it only goes into the stomach, and then carries on, out down the drain.' (Result: all foods are clean.)

[20]'What makes someone unclean', he went on, 'is what comes out of them. [21]Evil intentions come from inside, out of people's hearts – sexual immorality, theft, murder, [22]adultery, greed, wickedness, treachery, debauchery, envy, slander, pride, stupidity. [23]These evil things all come from inside. They are what make someone unclean.'

Back to jokes again. Have you ever told a joke and seen a row of blank stares? They didn't get it? What can you do? Explain it? Surely that'll take all the fun out of it. Yes, but a **parable** isn't a joke. This one in particular was no laughing matter. Some of the most famous martyr stories in Jesus' world were about Jewish people who had been tortured and killed for refusing to eat unclean food, particularly pork. And Jesus has grasped something, a deep truth about the way humans are, which means that as part of his **kingdom**-message he must take a different line. A radically different line. It's not going to go down well. You might as well try to tell the leaders of the old South Africa that all races are equal in the sight of God. It's not something they're going to want to hear.

That's why Jesus had to use parables, not only here but on many other occasions. It was the only way he could say some of the most devastating things he wanted to say. If you're trying to tell your own world that it's going the wrong way, that its heroes fought for the wrong cause and its martyrs died in the wrong ditch, you'll be careful how you do it. It's got to be cryptic. The **Pharisees** needed to be answered (clearly the dispute was not private; Jesus had to make some kind of statement), but Jesus was not about to hand them an obvious propaganda victory.

But he had expected his **disciples** to get the point. Again they are slow on the uptake. They share the general puzzlement: talk of 'what goes into you' and 'what comes out of you' seems to lead only one way, to a kind of lavatory humour which might have been appropriate in Greek comic plays but probably not as part of Jesus' kingdom-announcement. What could he have meant?

Only when they get back in the house does Jesus explain, just as he did in Mark 4 with the parable of the sower. He hadn't been talking about physical things that come out of people; they, like food that goes in, are irrelevant for the purposes of purity. He is talking about what comes out of the heart. The purity laws, he's suggesting, point to the real need of humans for a deeper purity, a purity of motive. Eating meat, from crocodile to kangaroo, from pig to porcupine, won't affect that. Those who get stuck on regulations about food, and never progress to the real point, are quite literally missing the heart of the matter. By focusing on outward purity, they are avoiding the much deeper challenge of the **gospel**, the challenge to the human heart. (We today still use 'the heart' as a way of speaking about such things, even though we know that the actual heart pumps blood, not motivations; most cultures have a way of talking about where motives come from, and this will do as well as any.)

At this point a lot of contemporary readers get thrown off the scent. Popular religion and philosophy, from at least the time of Plato, have often suggested that the physical world is bad and the spiritual world is good. We expect Jesus to say that sort of thing. So when he says that food doesn't matter and the heart does, what we are ready to hear is 'externals – physical things – don't matter; what matters are the internal, spiritual things'. And so, since what he says looks like that at first glance, we assume he's said what we expected him to say. And since we can fit that view into several other things most people today believe, the passage doesn't disturb us.

But we would be wrong. The passage should disturb us. Jesus is precisely *not* saying that external and physical things are irrelevant or bad and internal or spiritual things are good. He is not saying that if we get in touch with our deepest feelings, or learn to listen to what our heart is truly telling us, we will find our real identity and thereby discover happiness, fulfilment or whatever. He is insisting that good and bad external and physical actions come from internal and spiritual sources, and that therefore the poisoned wells of human motivation are the real problem to which the purity laws are pointing. We cannot isolate one part of our human make-up and blame it for evil. We can't suggest that 'getting in touch with our truest feelings' will sort us out. What if the feelings that most truly express who we currently are turn out to be murderous, adulterous, envious and the rest? The fact that they are there, in our hearts, does not mean they are thereby validated. On the contrary, it means we have a problem, a problem that runs right through us. There is a crack in the building which isn't just a bit of damaged stonework on the exterior; the whole structure is faulty. Keeping physical purity laws can be a way of papering over the crack; so can 'getting in touch with your feelings'. If there is evil, it infects the whole. That's what purity and impurity are really all about.

Interestingly, Jesus says nothing at this stage about his proposed cure for the disease he has diagnosed. We are left to infer it. As in a later passage (10.5), however, the assumption Mark clearly wants us to make is this: *Jesus is offering a cure for the problems of the heart*, for the springs of motivation that result in wicked thoughts and deeds. If he isn't doing this, he is mocking his followers, and us too, showing us what's wrong but never hinting at the solution. But of course, the kingdom of God is the solution. But . . . what precisely does that mean? As Mark allows this question to surface in our minds, he also tells us: read on and you'll find out.

So what was at stake between Jesus' agenda and that of the Pharisees? As we have learnt through a lot of recent study, purity regulations in a society or culture regularly reflect the concerns which that society or culture has about its own boundaries. If the society feels the threat of invasion, it will reinforce its purity codes, as a way of insisting to itself, and anyone else who may notice, that it really is what it should be. The lesson is obvious. The Jews in the Middle East had for centuries been surrounded and infiltrated by paganism, both as cultural force and as military might. What could be more natural than to reinforce the purity codes which said, in the powerful language of cultural symbol, 'We are Jews! We are different! We don't live like you do!'

But what if the kingdom of God meant throwing open the doors of God's people to anyone and everyone who would repent and believe? What would happen to the symbols then? Mark's next story indicates that for him at least this was precisely what was happening. This was Jesus' ultimate agenda, and this was why he had to oppose the way the purity laws were being applied.

Mark's little comment ('Result: all foods are clean') is his aside to his own community. It draws attention to the fact – which for at least a generation the church needed to be reminded of – that the old Jewish laws about clean and unclean foods, laws which divided Jew from **Gentile** even though they were in theory now one in Christian **faith**, were irrelevant. Paul's letters show us how this issue remained an explosive one within the early church. Mark is very much aware of the need to address it as well.

Was Jesus therefore, despite what he had just said, setting aside scripture, which is where the laws about clean and unclean food come from? Yes and no. Yes: the Bible says don't eat pork (and lots of other things), and Mark at least thinks Jesus is saying this doesn't apply any more. No: Jesus' basic point is that purity laws, including food laws, don't actually touch the real human problem, and that that is what the kingdom of God addresses. But behind this is the strong sense, already here in Jesus, and hammered out in the early church, that what happened in Jesus brought the old scriptures, the whole **covenant** with Israel, to a new completion, a new fulfilment. The scriptures spoke of purity, and set up codes as signposts to it; Jesus was offering the reality. When you arrive at the destination you don't need the signposts any more, not because they were worthless but precisely because they were correct.

Learning to read the Old Testament this way wasn't easy in the early church, and it isn't easy today. The starting point is to realize that the Jewish scriptures aren't to be seen as a timeless code of behaviour, but as the story which leads to Jesus. This doesn't mean we can casually set aside bits we don't like or understand. When things are set aside, as the purity laws are here, it's not because they're irrelevant but because the deeper truth to which they pointed has now arrived. Everything the scriptures were getting at reached a peak in Jesus Christ; from now on everything is different. Figuring out that difference, and still remaining loyal to scripture, is one of the key arts of being a Christian, then and now.

MARK 7.24–30

The Syrophoenician Woman

²⁴Jesus got up, left that place, and went to the region of Tyre. When he went into a house, he didn't want anyone to know, but it wasn't possible for him to remain hidden. ²⁵On the contrary: news of him at once reached a woman who had a young daughter with an unclean spirit. She came and threw herself down at his feet. ²⁶She was Greek, a Syrophoenician by race; and she asked him to cast the demon out of her daughter.

²⁷'First let the children eat what they want', Jesus replied. 'It's not right to take the children's bread and throw it to the dogs.'

²⁸'Well, Master,' she said, 'even the dogs under the table eat the crumbs that the children drop.'

²⁹'Well said!' replied Jesus. 'Off you go; the demon has left your daughter.'

³⁰So she went home, and found the child lying on the bed, and the demon gone.

Not just another healing, more a political incident. This very odd story has all the trappings of a dangerous event for Jesus, and Mark helps us to understand it by the way he's linked it to what went before. We've just heard a fresh view of cleanness and uncleanness; now here is a girl with an unclean spirit. We've just heard Jesus say something which, when decoded, undermines the protective fence that first-century Jews maintained around their own identity; now here he is, in a decidedly **Gentile** town, trying to lie low for a while and then doing, with a healing **miracle**, what he'd just done with his cryptic sayings.

This explains the very odd exchange between Jesus and the woman. The tone of voice throughout, though urgent and (on the woman's part) desperate, is nevertheless that of teasing banter. Some have tried, with feminist agendas in mind, to make out that the woman put Jesus straight, correcting and indeed rebuking his restricted viewpoint, but this is hardly what Mark intended. She accepts, after all, the apparent insult (Jews often thought of Gentiles as 'dogs', and what Gentiles said about Jews was usually just as uncomplimentary), and turns it to her own advantage. Had she (or Mark, telling the story) wanted to challenge or correct Jesus this was hardly the way to go about it.

The point at issue, rather, is that Jesus was conscious during his ministry, and the early church was conscious thereafter, that his personal vocation was not to spread the **gospel** to the Gentile world, but to tell the Jewish people themselves that their long-awaited deliverance was at hand, and indeed to bring it about by completing his vocation in Jerusalem. (The same point comes through in, for example, Matthew

10.5–6 and Romans 15.8–9.) He believed, as any Jew of that period might, that if and when Israel was redeemed, that would be the time for the rest of the world to be brought under the saving (and judging) rule of Israel's God, the world's creator. The Gentiles would be brought in soon enough; for the moment it was vital that he not be distracted from his primary task. He had come north, out of Jewish territory, not to preach and heal but to lie low for a while after doing and saying some quite risky things.

Jesus isn't, then, denying that Gentiles have a claim on the love and mercy of the one true God. He is careful not to be drawn away to an extension of his work into other areas, which would divert him from the difficult and dangerous tasks to which he was called. Publicity in Tyre (some distance up the coast from Galilee) would have sent all the wrong signals; Jesus' work wasn't primarily that of an itinerant medical missionary, but of inaugurating God's **kingdom**.

The story is therefore a sharp reminder to us that Jesus wasn't simply called to go around being helpful to everyone. He had specific (and controversial) things to do and a limited time to do them. If we remake Jesus in the cosy image of a universal problem-solver, we will miss the towering importance of his unique assignment. If he must not be distracted from the **messianic** vocation that will lead him to the cross, nor must we, readers of the gospel and followers of Jesus, be distracted from focusing on that too by our natural, and indeed God-given, desire to spread the healing message of the gospel as widely as possible.

Nevertheless, what Jesus did was seen by the **disciples**, and written up by Mark, as a sign that he had meant what he'd said about cleanness and uncleanness. The old barriers, the old taboos, were being swept away. The dogs under the table were already sharing the children's bread; pretty soon they would cease to be dogs, and become children alongside the others. Mark, we may be sure, has one eye at least on his own community, in which Gentiles had come to share in the kingdom-blessings promised to Israel. Precisely because we must understand Jesus' words as referring to a temporary, short-term urgency in which Israel needed to hear the gospel before it was too late, we must also see that this short-term situation came to an end with the crucifixion, never to return. As Jesus dies, Mark has a Roman centurion affirm that he was truly the **son of God** (15.39). From that moment on, what was anticipated in the Syrophoenician woman became universally true. The King of the Jews had become the saviour of the world.

MARK 7.31–37

A Deaf and Mute Man Is Healed

³¹Jesus went away from the region of Tyre, through Sidon, round towards the sea of Galilee, and into the region of the Ten Towns. ³²They brought to him a man who was deaf and had a speech impediment, and asked that he would lay his hand on him.

³³Jesus took the man off in private, away from the crowd. He put his fingers into his ears, spat, and touched his tongue. ³⁴Then he looked up to heaven, groaned, and said to him, '*Ephphatha*' (that is, 'Be opened'). ³⁵Immediately the man's ears were opened, and his tongue was untied, and he spoke clearly.

³⁶Jesus gave them orders not to tell anyone. But the more he ordered them, the more they spread the news. ³⁷They were totally astonished.

'Everything he does is marvellous!' they said. 'He even makes the deaf hear and the mute speak!'

I received a leaked memo the other day on my fax machine. It wasn't a very serious leak – something that would be in the papers in a couple of days anyway – but it gave me a strange feeling. It goes on all the time in political circles, of course, where reputations are made and broken with one careless remark that gets out to the newspapers, and where calculated leaks are made to destabilize political opponents. But it doesn't normally happen to me.

Jesus wanted to keep some things secret until the right moment, but the news didn't just leak out – it poured out, as people simply couldn't stop talking about what they'd seen him do. But this is a puzzle. Why would Jesus do things like this if he didn't want people to talk about them?

When you start thinking about secrets – people keeping silent, or speaking out – you realize that this little story has quite a lot of that sort of thing going on. The man himself is deaf, and can hardly speak (when Jesus heals him, Mark uses a graphic phrase which suggests that his tongue had been tied up in knots and was suddenly untied); but then he speaks plainly. From silence to speech in one quick move. Jesus takes him off privately, but it can't remain hidden. He tells the people around not to spread it, but they can't stop talking. Secrets and speech, secrets and speech; that's what the story is all about. Why?

As we've already seen, Jesus was doing things which raised dangerous ideas and suspicions. The self-appointed **legal experts** were already angry with him; word of his doings had already got back to Herod Antipas. In a world where rumour was a fast and effective means of

71

getting news about, and where to be talked of as a prophet was to court disaster (look what had happened to the last one), rumours of the prophet Jesus were everywhere. And yet his mission, to bring God's **kingdom** in power, overthrowing the tyrannous rule of the enemy, had to go forward.

At this point we can only speculate, but Mark seems to invite us to do just that. Perhaps Jesus was hoping for a bit more time before he had to draw things to a head. Perhaps he was intending to travel around for some while yet, gathering more support, giving more of his beloved but obstinate Galileans a chance to hear his message and to turn their ideas around. But things were already difficult; Mark's story to this point has been full of times when Jesus had hoped to be alone, to escape the crowds, only to find that they were there waiting for him wherever he went. Now he must have realized that only a few more remarkable cures would bring such notoriety that the authorities would be bound to close in on him. He couldn't stop his kingdom-bringing work, but he couldn't stop people talking about it either.

Mark is thus preparing us for what's to come in the next chapter, when Jesus does indeed bring things to a head in a conversation with the **disciples**, which results in a new phase of his ministry. But in the meantime he's also reminding us of the significance of these healings. 'He even makes the deaf hear, and the mute speak'; Mark's readers might well have known what Jesus' Galilean onlookers had in mind, namely the prophecy of Isaiah (35.5–6): blind eyes will be opened, deaf ears unstopped, and silent tongues start to sing.

This was a prophecy of the renewal of Israel after the long, sad years of **exile**. God's people would be rescued from pagan oppression, and creation itself would celebrate. Healing then, and perhaps healing now (though we don't always realize it), can never be simply a matter of correcting a few faults in the machine called the human body. It always was and is, and perhaps supremely so in Jesus' actions, a sign of God's love breaking in to the painful and death-laden present world. It was and is a pointer to the great Healing that will occur when the secret is out, when Jesus is finally revealed to the whole world, and our present stammering praise is turned into full-hearted song.

When Mark urges his readers to follow Jesus, he envisages, not a boring life of conventional religion, but things happening that would make people astonished. If we're still too deaf to hear what he's saying, the problem is perhaps with us rather than with the message.

MARK 8.1-10

The Feeding of the Four Thousand

[1]Once again, about that time, a large crowd gathered with nothing to eat.

Jesus called the disciples.

[2]'I'm really sorry for the people', he said. 'They've been with me three days now, and they haven't got anything to eat. [3]If I send them home hungry, they'll collapse on the way. Some of them have come from miles off.'

[4]'Where could you get food for all this lot, out here in the wilderness?' answered his disciples.

[5]'How many loaves have you got?' he asked. 'Seven', they replied.

[6]He told the crowd to sit down on the ground. Then he took the seven loaves, gave thanks, broke them and gave them to his disciples to share around, and they gave them to the crowd. [7]They had a few small fish, which he also blessed and told them to distribute. [8]They ate; they were satisfied; and they took up seven baskets of leftover bits. [9]There were about four thousand people. And he sent them away.

[10]At once Jesus got into the boat with his disciples and went to the region of Dalmanoutha.

Two more loaves, a thousand less people, and five fewer baskets remaining. It's almost like a dream; we've heard the story before, it seems, two chapters earlier, and yet it's different. The **disciples** seem to be living in a dream, too; whatever it is that's happening, it's so much bigger and so very different from what they had been expecting or hoping for that they simply couldn't take it all in.

Of course, clever and subtle minds have probed closely to see if maybe Mark is trying to tell us something more than simply 'Jesus did it again'. Perhaps, some have said, the 5,000, with the 12 baskets left over, represent Jesus' ministry to the Jewish world (with its 12 tribes), while the 4,000, with the seven baskets left over, represent his promise to the wider **Gentile** world (with, in Jewish folklore, 70 nations). Coming after the events of chapter 7, and probably located in Gentile territory, there may be a hint here that this second feeding involves a wider group than simply Jesus' Jewish audience.

It's only a hint, though, and frankly it's difficult to be sure that Mark himself meant it. In any case, Mark describes Jesus going not only around Galilee – which was itself certainly not exclusively Jewish territory – but also north to Tyre and, frequently, east to the Decapolis, predominantly Gentile territory but certainly with many Jewish inhabitants too. He doesn't seem to worry too much, when describing crowds, about whether Jesus' followers were Jewish or not. The main difference to which he draws attention is the length of time the crowd has been with Jesus (three days) and the fact that, unlike the earlier incident, there are no villages nearby where they could go to get food. The situation is altogether more urgent.

Mark is setting the scene for the theme we shall look at in the next section, namely the failure of the disciples fully to understand what was going on. But this is hardly a matter of great blame. Nothing like this had ever happened before; we can excuse them (and Mark is certainly happy to) for being a bit slow on the uptake. He seems to be emphasizing that the feedings, along with the healings, are ways in which Jesus' identity, as the true **Messiah**, was being unveiled; but since no first-century Jews known to us were expecting a Messiah who would multiply loaves and fishes we can, once more, hardly blame them for that.

So what can we learn today from this strange story, and its earlier lookalike companion?

It would be easy to reflect on the ways in which, throughout Christian experience, Jesus continues to have compassion on those who follow him, to be aware of and sensitive to their needs, and to meet those needs, often in unexpected ways. 'In everything, by prayer and supplication, let your requests be made known to God', wrote St Paul (Philippians 4.6). Such prayer receives strong and warm encouragement from knowing that the risen Jesus certainly cares for his people at least as much, in his glorified state, as he had done when sharing our earthly existence. Unlike Matthew and Luke, Mark doesn't include in his **gospel** a version of the Lord's Prayer; but the Jesus he shows us is precisely one who would encourage us to pray not only that God's **kingdom** would come on earth as in **heaven**, but also that God would give us this day our daily bread. Many Christians fail to appreciate and appropriate this personal concern that their Lord has for them. One does not hear of people being rebuked for asking too much, or too frequently.

At the same time, it is noticeable that in both stories Jesus not only feeds the crowds; he involves his disciples in the feeding. The closer we are to Jesus, the more likely it is that he will call us to share in his work of compassion, healing and feeding, bringing his kingdom-work to an ever wider circle. Unlike magicians in the ancient world, performing tricks to gain money or personal kudos, Jesus is concerned to bring his disciples into the work in which he is engaged. The Christian life, as a disciplined rhythm of following Jesus, involves not only being fed but becoming in turn one through whom Jesus' love can be extended to the world.

Of course our resources will seem, and feel, totally inadequate. That is Jesus' problem, not ours; and these stories indicate well enough that he will cope with it. Our task, as has been said often enough but still needs to be heard and acted upon, is not to bemoan how few loaves and fishes we have for the crowd, but to offer them to Jesus, to do whatever he wants with them; and then to be ready to distribute them, to our own surprise, at his command.

MARK 8.11–21

The Leaven of the Pharisees and Herod

[11]The Pharisees came out and began to dispute with Jesus. They were asking him for a sign from heaven, to test him out.

[12]Jesus groaned deeply in his spirit. 'Why is this generation looking for a sign?' he said. 'I'm telling you the truth: no sign will be given to this generation.' [13]He left them again, got into the boat, and crossed over to the other side.

[14]They had forgotten to get any bread, and had only one loaf with them in the boat.

[15]'Beware!' said Jesus sternly to them, 'Watch out for leaven – the Pharisees' leaven, and Herod's leaven too!'

[16]'It must be something to do with us not having any bread', they said to each other.

[17]'Why are you grumbling about not bringing bread?' said Jesus, who knew what they were thinking. 'Don't you get it? Don't you understand? Have your hearts gone hard?

[18]Can't you see with your two good eyes?
Can't you hear with your two good ears?

And don't you remember? [19]When I broke the five loaves for the five thousand, how many baskets full of broken bits were left over?'

'Twelve', they said.

[20]'And the seven loaves for the four thousand – how many baskets full of bits were left over?'

'Seven', they replied.

[21]'You still don't get it?'

Think of your schooldays. What was your worst subject – the one you always dreaded, the one you longed to give up? Now try (if the memory isn't too painful) to remember what it was like sitting in a desk with the teacher trying to explain something to you for the twentieth or thirtieth time. Teachers have a particular type of sorrowful look when they have said something as clearly as they can, over and over again, and the pupil still doesn't get it. I think Jesus had that look on his face at the end of this conversation in the boat.

What's more, he knew it was important that they learn the lesson sooner rather than later. Things were hotting up. Right on cue, the **Pharisees** appear and ask for a sign – as though what Jesus had just been doing wasn't a substantial sign in itself. What sort of a sign are they wanting? What does Jesus read into it?

Jesus seems to regard their request for a sign as being itself a kind of sign – a sign to him that 'this generation', that is, the main stream of life and thought among his Jewish contemporaries, was determined not to hear the message he was announcing, determined to go their own way, to struggle for the **kingdom** on their own terms rather than his. He was staking his own vocation on the signs of God's kingdom that he was performing, and if they couldn't or wouldn't see it that must mean that their notion of the kingdom was radically different from his – and, if he was right, from God's as well. This clash of kingdom-visions, of course, continues right to the end, reaching its climax in Jesus' crucifixion.

That's why Jesus warns the **disciples** against the 'leaven' of the Pharisees and of Herod. The Jews used leaven to make ordinary bread, but at Passover time they were forbidden it, to remind them of when they were in such a hurry to leave their slavery in Egypt that they only had time to make unleavened bread. Now Jesus speaks of 'leaven', not to warn the disciples about the wrong sort of bread, but to put them on their guard against the wrong sort of kingdom-vision. The Pharisees are diluting the vision: they want God to set up a kingdom for the benefit of Jews who can observe the law with great strictness, not for the benefit of the wider company Jesus has in mind. Herod and his entourage are diluting the vision: they want God to establish their royal family as the true Kings of Israel. Neither of these comes near the mark, though 'this generation' are led astray by both. Jesus' kingdom-vision is very different, and his extraordinary feedings are signs of what it's about and assurances to the disciples that it really is happening.

It's urgent that they get the message. Jesus can see the signs of growing hostility; it is vital that the disciples realize, soon now, what he's doing and why, because the time will shortly come when they will have to go to Jerusalem with a mission, not of feeding hungry people, but of challenging the heart of the system. And the disciples will only be able and willing to come with him if they realize that he isn't just a healer, that he isn't just a prophet, but that he is something more, something that puts the Pharisees and even royal Herod into (at least) second place. Like a good teacher, Jesus won't give them the answer directly. There's no point in the mathematics teacher simply telling the students the right answer to the problem. They have to be able to work it out for themselves. Jesus is pointing to the evidence; why can't they yet draw the conclusion?

In the middle of it all, Jesus quotes from the prophet Jeremiah (5.21). This isn't just a poetic way of saying 'I can't believe how blind you are'. It's a way of saying 'You're in danger of going the way of the Israelites in Jeremiah's day!' What was the problem in those days? Much like the problem Jesus saw with the Pharisees and with Herod. People were so caught up with their own concerns, and so unconcerned about injustice and wickedness in their society, that God had no alternative but to abandon them to their fate at the hands of foreigners. If they effectively worship other gods, those other gods (and their devotees) will have power over them. That, as we shall see, lies near the heart of Jesus' warnings against his contemporaries.

When you watch white-water canoeing it looks exciting and dangerous – and it is. But when you actually do it, one of the most exciting moments comes just before the fast and furious action begins. You paddle along a smooth, flat river; all you can see ahead is a V-shaped end to the water. That's where you have to aim. One moment you can, if you choose, paddle to the side and avoid the rapids. The next moment you know it's too late. You're going down the rapids whether you like it or not.

What Mark is describing here is a moment like that. It's the moment when Jesus realizes that he's going down the rapids, starting right now. The confrontation between his kingdom-mission and its rivals is coming up fast. He is anxious that the disciples should understand what's happening.

It all raises the question for us: if we are beginning to understand what Jesus' mission was all about, and to make it the foundation of our **faith** and hope, do we understand what he is doing right now, not only in our own lives, but in our world? What would make Jesus 'groan deeply' today? What is it about us that would make him say, like a frustrated teacher, 'You still don't get it?'

MARK 8.22–30

Peter's Declaration of Jesus' Messiahship

²²They arrived at Bethsaida. A blind man was brought to Jesus, and they begged him to touch him. ²³He took his hand, led him off outside the village, and put spittle on his eyes. Then he laid his hands on him, and asked, 'Can you see anything?'

²⁴'I can see people,' said the man, peering around, 'but they look like trees walking about.'

²⁵Then Jesus laid his hands on him once more. This time he looked hard, and his sight came back: he could see everything clearly. ²⁶Jesus sent him back home.

'Don't even go into the village', he said.

²⁷Jesus and his disciples came to the villages of Caesarea Philippi. On the way he asked his disciples, 'Who are people saying that I am?'

²⁸'John the Baptist,' they said, 'or, some say, Elijah; or, others say, one of the prophets.'

²⁹'What about you?' asked Jesus. 'Who do you say I am?'

Peter spoke up. 'You're the Messiah', he said.

³⁰He gave them strict orders not to tell anyone about him.

It's quite a walk from Bethsaida to Caesarea Philippi. Even in a car, on modern roads, the trip takes an hour or two. Bethsaida is near the north shore of the Sea of Galilee; Caesarea Philippi is away up north, on the slopes of Mount Hermon, by the source of the River Jordan. Climb a little higher, and on a clear day you can see right down the Jordan valley. Why did Jesus take the **disciples** all that way, a good distance from the normal to-and-fro around the lake, to have this conversation?

We'd better think hard about this, because this passage is really the centre-point, the turning-point, of Mark's **gospel**. This, too, is a mountain slope; a clear day's thinking at this point will give you a view not only back through the gospel story we've already read, but on, down that same Jordan valley, to where the road, and the story, turn uphill to the final confrontation in Jerusalem.

Mark has put together the story of the blind man receiving his sight and of the blind disciples gaining their insight, in order, of course, to highlight what's going on in the second story by means of the parallel with the first. Jesus takes the blind man away from the village; he takes the disciples away from the lake and the crowds. At the end, he insists in both cases on secrecy. He's reached the point where it's vital that word doesn't leak out. If his **kingdom**-mission is becoming more explicitly a **Messiah**-mission, this really is dangerous. He must do what he has to do swiftly and secretly.

In between, both stories tell of a two-stage process of illumination. The blind man sees people, but they look like trees walking about; the crowds see Jesus, but they think he's just a prophet. (If you want to get a good picture of how Jesus appeared to his contemporaries, forget 'gentle Jesus, meek and mild' and read the stories of **John the Baptist**, Elijah and the other great prophets: fearless men of God who spoke out against evil and injustice, and brought hope to God's puzzled and suffering people.) Then, as it were with a second touch, Jesus faces the disciples themselves with the question. Now at last their eyes are opened. They have understood about the loaves, and all the other signs. 'You're the Messiah!' Peter speaks for them all.

It's vital for us to be clear at this point. Calling Jesus 'Messiah' doesn't mean calling him 'divine', let alone 'the second person of the Trinity'. Mark believes Jesus was and is divine, and will eventually show us why; but this moment in the gospel story is about something else. It's about the politically dangerous and theologically risky claim that Jesus is the true King of Israel, the final heir to the throne of David, the one before whom Herod Antipas and all other would-be Jewish princelings are just shabby little impostors. The disciples weren't expecting a divine redeemer; they were longing for a king. And they thought they'd found one.

Nor was it only Herod who might be suspicious. In Jesus' day there was a prominent temple in Caesarea Philippi to the newest pagan 'god' – the Roman Emperor himself. A Messiah announcing God's kingdom was a challenge to Rome itself.

As we'll see in the next passage, Jesus immediately starts on the next phase in his teaching programme, and the disciples turn out to be just as slow on the uptake as they were with the first part. But let's pause and reflect on what they, and we, have learnt thus far.

Jesus is a prophet, announcing the kingdom of God: the long-awaited moment when God would rule Israel, and ultimately the world, with the justice and mercy of which the scriptures had spoken and for which Israel had longed. All mere human rule, with its mixtures of justice and oppression, mercy and corruption, would fade before it. What Jesus has been doing – notably, for Mark, the healings, the battles with evil, and the extraordinary feedings, stilling of storms, and so on – are signs that this is indeed the moment when the true God is beginning to exercise this power. Finally the disciples have taken a further step: Jesus is not just *announcing* the kingdom. He thinks he's the king.

By no means all Jews wanted or expected a Messiah. But those who did were clear (not least from their readings of scripture) that he had to do three things. He had to rebuild, or cleanse, the **Temple**. He had to defeat the enemy that was threatening God's people. And he had to bring God's justice – that rich, restoring, purging, healing power – to bear both in Israel and out into the world. No doubt these ideas were believed and expressed in different ways by different people. But there was a central agenda. The Messiah would be God's agent in bringing in the kingdom, in sorting out the mess and muddle Israel was in, in putting the **Gentiles** in their place.

Jesus had already been redefining that set of tasks. He hadn't been gathering a military force. He hadn't been announcing a programme to topple the **Sadducees** – the **high priests** and their associates. He had been going around doing things that spoke powerfully but cryptically of a strange new agenda: God's healing energy sweeping through the land, bringing about a new state of affairs, arousing passionate opposition as well as passionate loyalty. And he'd been saying things, by way of explanation, which were often so cryptic that even his friends were puzzled by them. Now finally they have grasped the initial point at least. He is giving the dream of a Messiah a face-lift. He has in mind a new way of being God's appointed, and anointed, king.

Just how new that way is will now emerge. But for the moment we need to examine our own answers to the question. Who do we say Jesus is? Would we like to think of him as simply a great human teacher? Would we prefer him as a Superman figure, able to 'zap' all the world's problems into shape? Are we prepared to have the easy answers of our culture challenged by the actual Jesus, by his redefined notion of messiahship, and by the call, coming up in the next section, to follow him in his risky vocation?

MARK 8.31—9.1

Jesus Predicts His Death

³¹Jesus now began to teach them something new.

'There's big trouble in store for the son of man', he said. 'The elders, the chief priests and the scribes are going to reject him. He will be killed – and after three days he'll be raised.' ³²He said all this quite explicitly.

At this, Peter took him aside and started to scold him. ³³But he turned round, saw the disciples, and scolded Peter.

'Get behind me, Accuser!' he said. 'You're thinking human thoughts, not God's thoughts.'

³⁴He called the crowd to him, with his disciples. 'If any of you want to come the way I'm going,' he said, 'you must say "no" to your own selves, pick up your cross, and follow me. ³⁵Yes: if you want to save your life, you'll lose it; but if you lose your life because of me and the message you'll save it. ³⁶After all, what use is it to win the world and lose your life? ³⁷What can you give in exchange for your life? ³⁸If you're ashamed of me and my words in this cheating and sinning generation, the son of man will be ashamed of you when he "comes in the glory of his father with the holy angels".

¹'I'm telling you the truth,' he said; 'some people standing here won't experience death before they see God's kingdom come in power.'

I watched from a window as the riot police got ready. They looked like sportsmen preparing for a match, putting on pads and helmets, gloves and special outer clothes. Only this wasn't a game. It was real. They didn't know, quite literally, what was going to be thrown at them. They appeared quite calm, but they must have been tense inside. They were being called to go off to meet danger, including possible injury or even death. Many people in our world, such as fire crews and those who work in lifeboats, face similar situations every day.

Jesus' friends and followers were used to danger. It was a perilous time; anyone growing up in Galilee just then knew about revolutions, about holy people hoping God would act and deliver them, and ending up getting crucified instead. Any new leader, any prophet, any teacher with something fresh to say, might go that way. They must have known that by following Jesus they were taking risks. The death of Jesus' mentor, **John the Baptist**, will simply have confirmed that.

But this was different. This was something new. Mark says Jesus 'began to teach them' this, implying that it was quite a new point that could only be begun once they'd declared that he was the **Messiah** – like a schoolteacher who can only begin the next stage of mathematics when the pupils have learnt to add and subtract, or a language teacher who can only start on great poetry when the pupils have got the hang of how the language works. And the new lesson wasn't just that there might be danger ahead; the new lesson was that Jesus had to walk straight into it. Nor would it simply be a risky gamble that might just pay off. It would be certain death. This was what he had to do.

You might as well have had a football captain tell the team that he was intending to let the opposition score ten goals right away. This wasn't what Peter and the rest had in mind. They may not have thought of Jesus as a military leader, but they certainly didn't think of him going straight to his death. As Charlie Brown once said, winning ain't everything but losing ain't anything; and Jesus seemed to be saying he was going to lose. Worse, he was inviting them to come and lose alongside him.

This is the heart of what's going on here, and it explains both the tricky language Jesus uses (tricky for them to puzzle out at first hearing, tricky for us to reconstruct what he meant) and the strong negative reaction of Peter, so soon after telling Jesus that he and the rest thought he was the Messiah. Messiahs don't get killed by the authorities. A Messiah who did that would be shown up precisely as a false Messiah.

So why did Jesus say that's what had to happen?

Mark will explain this to us bit by bit over the coming chapters. But already there is a hint, an allusion. 'The **son of man**' must have all this happen to him, declares Jesus; only so will 'the son of man come in the glory of his Father with the holy angels'. Only so will the **kingdom** of God come – and some standing there, he says, will see this happen.

This dense and cryptic way of talking is like someone today who peppers their speech with quotations from Shakespeare which only make sense when you think about what's going on in the play at the time. (Why would anyone do that? Well, perhaps because they knew it was difficult to say it any other way. Sometimes poetry, perhaps quite old poetry, is the only way to say something really important.) Jesus is half quoting, half hinting at, themes from the prophetic books of Daniel and Zechariah. 'The son of man' in Daniel 7 represents God's people as they are suffering at the hands of pagan enemies. He will eventually be vindicated, after his suffering, as God sets up the kingdom at last. Jesus is both warning his followers that this is how he understands his vocation and destiny as Israel's representative (i.e. the Messiah), and that they must be prepared to follow in his steps.

So important is this message that opposition to the plan, wherever it comes from, must be seen as satanic, from the **Accuser**. Even Peter, Jesus' right-hand man, is capable of thinking like a mere mortal, not looking at things from God's point of view. This is a challenge to all of us, as the church in every generation struggles not only to think but to live from God's point of view in a world where such a thing is madness. This is the point at which God's kingdom, coming 'on earth as it is in **heaven**', will challenge and overturn all normal human assumptions about power and glory, about what is really important in life and in the world.

Jesus thinks, it seems, that the kingdom will come during the lifetime of some people present. It has been fashionable to take Mark 9.1 as a classic example of misplaced hope, with Jesus and the early Christians looking for the end of the space-time world and the establishment of a totally different existence. But that's not what Jewish language like this means. The coming of God's kingdom with power has a lot more to do with the radical defeat of deep-rooted evil than with the destruction of the good world that God made and loves. Jesus seems to think that evil will be defeated, and the kingdom will come, precisely through his own suffering and death.

Why he thought that, and what it means for those who follow him, will become clear as we proceed. But this passage makes it clear that following him is the only way to go. Following Jesus is, more or less, Mark's definition of what being a Christian means; and Jesus is not leading us on a pleasant afternoon hike, but on a walk into danger and risk. Or did we suppose that the kingdom of God would mean merely a few minor adjustments in our ordinary lives?

MARK 9.2-13

The Transfiguration

²A week later, Jesus took Peter, James and John away by themselves, and went up a high mountain. There he was transformed before their eyes. ³His clothes shone with a whiteness that no laundry on earth could match. ⁴Elijah appeared to them, and Moses too, and they were talking with Jesus.

⁵'Teacher,' said Peter as he saw this, 'it's great to be here! Let's make three shelters, one for you, one for Moses and one for Elijah!' ⁶(He didn't know what to say; they were terrified.)

⁷Then a cloud overshadowed them, and a voice came out of the cloud: 'This is my son, the one I love. Listen to him!'

⁸Then, quite suddenly, they looked round and saw nobody there any more, only Jesus with them.

⁹As they came down the mountain, Jesus instructed them not to talk to anyone about what they had seen, 'until', he said, 'the son of man has been raised from the dead.' ¹⁰They held on to this saying among themselves, puzzling about what this 'rising from the dead' might mean.

¹¹'Why then', they asked him, 'do the legal experts say "Elijah must come first"?'

¹²'Elijah does come first,' he replied, 'and his job is to put everything straight. But what do you think it means that "the son of man must suffer many things and be treated with contempt"? ¹³Actually, listen to this: Elijah has already come, and they did to him whatever they wanted. That's what scripture said about him.'

Science teachers never tire, so I'm told, of the moment when a child first looks into a microscope. What up until then had seemed a boring little speck of dirt can suddenly become full of pattern, colour and interest. The child will never look at things the same way again; everything now has the potential to be more than it seems.

The same thing happens elsewhere. Telescopes transform the night sky into a world of awe and power. A good actor can turn an apparently insignificant line into a profound and moving statement of beauty and truth.

Take those quite common experiences and move them up a few notches on the scale of fact and experience. The story of Jesus' 'transformation' or 'transfiguration' describes what seems to have been an actual event, but an event in which the deepest significance of everyday reality suddenly and overwhelmingly confronted Peter, James and John.

It's easy enough (and they themselves must have known this) to dismiss such an experience as a hallucination, albeit a very odd one. Jewish scriptures and traditions tell of various events like this, when the veil of ordinariness that normally prevents us from seeing the 'inside' of a situation is drawn back, and a fuller reality is disclosed. Most of us don't have experiences like this (nor did most early Christians, so far as we can tell); but unless we allow sceptics to bully us we should be free to affirm that this sort of thing has indeed happened to some people (usually completely unexpectedly), and that such people usually regard it as hugely important and life-changing.

The three watchers and the others were of course terrified. Peter (we're getting to know him quite well now) blurts out the first thing that comes into his head, trying vaguely not only to prolong the moment but to hook it in to one of the Jewish festivals. That wasn't the point, but the sheer oddity of his bumbling suggestion is itself strong evidence of the story's basic truth. Nobody inventing a tale like this would make up such a comic moment, lowering the tone of the occasion in such a fashion.

But what are we to say? Can we look at the whole thing (as Jesus had previously urged Peter to look at things) not just from a human point of view, but from God's point of view? With caution and humility, we might try.

Take a step back. What has happened in the **gospel** so far? Jesus has, metaphorically speaking, led the **disciples** up the high mountain of a new view of God's **kingdom**. In extraordinary actions and puzzling but profound words he has unveiled for them what God is up to. Those 'outside' look and look, but never see; the disciples are having their eyes opened, so that they can see for the first time the inner reality of God's kingdom, and the central truth that – even though he doesn't look like what they might have expected! – Jesus really is the **Messiah**. Thus the story so far keeps telling us about eyes being opened, in several senses, and it all concentrates on Jesus himself and God's kingdom that is arriving with him.

Now Jesus takes the disciples literally up a high mountain, and something similar happens, though on another level. Western culture is increasingly realizing, what most other cultures have never forgotten, that the world we live in has many layers, many dimensions, and that sometimes these dimensions, normally hidden, may appear. Then, like the child with the microscope, we can look for a moment into a different reality, gasp with wonder, and ever afterwards see everything differently.

That's how it was on this mountain (which, by the way, was probably Mount Hermon, just north of Caesarea Philippi, though the rival candidate, Mount Tabor in central Galilee, is also possible). What was the inner reality of Jesus' work? He was continuing and completing the tasks of the great prophet Elijah, and, behind him, of the greatest prophet of old, Moses himself. Both of them, interestingly, had disappeared from view rather than died in the ordinary way, surrounded by their families and friends; legends grew up about their being somehow spared proper death. Now they reappear, with the veil of ordinariness drawn back for a moment, and Jesus is with them, shining with a brilliant light.

People are often fuzzy about what this means. It isn't a revelation of Jesus' divinity; if it were, that would make Elijah and Moses divine too, which Mark certainly doesn't want us to think. Once again, Mark believes in Jesus' divinity, but hasn't yet told us why. Rather, as the similar experiences of mystics in various ages and cultures would suggest, this is a sign of Jesus being entirely caught up with, bathed in, the love, power and kingdom of God, so that it transforms his whole being with light, in the way that music transforms words that are sung. This is the sign that Jesus is not just indulging in fantasies about God's kingdom, but that he is speaking and doing the truth. It's the sign that he is indeed the true prophet, the true Messiah.

That, too, is what the heavenly voice is saying. Jesus is God's special, beloved son. Elijah and Moses were vital in preparing the way; Jesus is finishing the job. Mark is happy for later Christian readers to hear, in the phrase 'son of God', fuller meanings than the disciples would have heard. For them, the primary meaning, as with the voice at the **baptism**, is that Jesus is Messiah. That's enough to be going on with.

Once again Jesus tells them not to reveal what they have seen. This time he gives them a cryptic time-frame: 'until the **son of man** has been raised from the dead'. Not surprisingly, this puzzles them. In Jewish thought of the time, 'the **resurrection**' would happen to all the righteous at the end of time, not to one person ahead of all the others. What could Jesus mean by implying that 'the son of man' would rise from the dead, while they would be still living the sort of normal life in which people would tell one another what they had seen months or years before? Mark's readers would already know about Jesus' resurrection, but the characters in his story certainly didn't, and weren't expecting it. Like much that Jesus said, it remained cryptic and puzzling until after the event.

The final exchange is even more teasing. The disciples are trying to work it out; scripture, they know, tells them that Elijah will prepare the way for the Messiah. (Mark has already quoted the relevant passage, right at the start of his **gospel**.) Jesus has other scriptures to hand as well, though, which speak to him of his own vocation; this time, he seems to be blending Daniel 7 with Isaiah 53, a powerful combination we'll look at later on. But the fateful identification, the one that matters, is his cryptic comment about Elijah having already come. **John the Baptist** has done that job. Now there is nothing left but the final messianic task, the task which Jesus has already declared will involve his own suffering and death.

All this could remain puzzling to us, too. We don't generally experience things as dramatic as this story. We don't often try to interpret the details of our lives and our times according to a detailed scriptural plot. But each of us is called to do what the heavenly voice said: Listen to Jesus, because he is God's beloved son. And as we learn to listen, even if sometimes we get scared and say all the wrong things, we may find that glory creeps up on us unawares, strengthening us, as it did the disciples, for the road ahead.

MARK 9.14–29

The Demon-Possessed Boy

[14]The four of them made their way back to the other disciples. There they saw a large crowd surrounding them, and legal experts arguing with them. [15]As soon as the crowd saw Jesus they were astounded, and they all ran up to greet him.

[16]'What's all the fuss about?' he asked.

[17]'Teacher,' said someone from the crowd, 'I brought my son to you. He's got a spirit that stops him speaking. [18]Whenever it takes hold of him it throws him on the ground; he foams at the mouth, and grinds his teeth, and goes rigid. I spoke to your disciples about casting it out, but they couldn't.'

[19]'You unbelieving generation!' replied Jesus. 'How much longer must I be with you? How much longer must I put up with you? Bring the boy to me.'

[20]They brought him to him. When the spirit saw Jesus, it immediately threw the boy into a convulsion, and he fell on the ground and rolled about, foaming at the mouth.

[21]'How long has it been like this with him?' asked Jesus.

'Since childhood,' replied the man. [22]'Often it even throws him into the fire or water to kill him. But if you can do anything . . . please, please help us! Have pity on us!'

[23]'What d'you mean, "If you can"?' said Jesus. 'Everything is possible to someone who believes.'

[24]At this the father gave a great shout. 'I do believe!' he roared. 'Help me in my unbelief!'

[25]Jesus saw that the crowd was getting bigger by the minute. He scolded the unclean spirit: 'Speechless and deaf spirit,' he said, 'I command you – come out of him, and never go back again!'

²⁶The spirit yelled, gave the boy a huge convulsion, and came out. The boy seemed to be dead; in fact, several people did say 'He's dead!' ²⁷But Jesus took him by the hand and helped him to his feet, and he stood up.

²⁸'Why couldn't we cast it out?' asked his disciples, once they were back in the house by themselves.

²⁹'This sort', replied Jesus, 'can only be cast out by prayer.'

Our mountain walk started quite easily. We strolled along the first mile or two, following the red flashes of paint on nearby rocks, which marked the route. Only a gentle incline; we didn't even break into a sweat. We began to notice, little by little, that we were going uphill; we were even tempted, once or twice, to stop for a short rest. There was a steep drop away to our right, and a wall of rock to our left, but it didn't seem too dangerous.

But then, suddenly, we turned a corner; and there before us, with a red flash teasing us at the top, was a terrifying 100-foot wall of sheer rock. An old wire rope ran up it, beside a very rudimentary wooden ladder. If we wanted to go any further on this walk, it was time for summoning up new courage and energy. We took a deep breath.

That's the mood Mark wants us to catch as Jesus comes back after the transfiguration. At Caesarea Philippi he had told his followers that it was time to take up the cross. His vocation, and the **disciples'** awareness of it, has been confirmed by the heavenly voice. The road now leads to Jerusalem. Up until now it has been comparatively easy to follow Jesus; from here on it's going to be harder and harder.

It begins with a problem for the disciples. They had previously been able to cast out **demons** in Jesus' name, but this one had them beaten. They were as puzzled as we, the readers, are likely to be; we didn't realize that there were, so to speak, different degrees of demons, some being harder to deal with than others. All Jesus will say, by way of explanation, is that this kind takes prayer (presumably prayer was always part of the operation; this must mean special prayer, a particularly focused spiritual effort). We are, perhaps, meant to assume that Jesus' time on the mountain was, for him, a time of particularly intense prayer, giving him on his return particularly heightened power.

But the main impression we get is of the disciples' inability to deal with the problem, and the crowd's consequent impatience with them. They have turned a corner in their pilgrimage; now it's getting harder. People today often suppose that the early years of a person's Christian pilgrimage are the difficult ones, and that as you go on in the Christian life it gets more straightforward. The opposite is frequently the case. Precisely when you learn to walk beside Jesus, you are given harder tasks, which will demand more courage, more spiritual energy. Did we suppose following Jesus was like a summer holiday?

The incident seems to have made Jesus, too, reflect on just how bad things now are. His response to the problem (echoing 8.12) is to comment sorrowfully on 'this faithless generation', and to wonder aloud how much longer he will be with them. Something in the father's statement of the problem, in the crowd's prurient but faithless interest, and in the disciples' inability to deal with it all, says to him that whatever is going on it isn't **faith**. That sad reflection confirms him in his belief, announced already at Caesarea Philippi, that he must now himself go the way of sorrow, the way of the cross, the path of his redeeming vocation.

Our eye is then led to the man at the centre of the fuss. As in several other stories, this is a parent desperate with anxiety over his child. (Are we supposed, perhaps, to see in these stories a reflection of the grieving love of the Father for his Child, Israel? For his image-bearing daughters and sons throughout the world? For his unique son, Jesus himself, as he goes obediently, mute before his captors, to a certain death?)

In this part of the scene, too, the mood is tense; a corner has been turned, and everything seems more demanding. In the first half of the **gospel**, many people come to Jesus with what appears comparatively easy faith. They touch him and are healed; it seems as simple as that. But for this man, in this situation, faith is hard. Not for nothing are his words regularly quoted as an ideal prayer for someone caught in the middle between faith and doubt, living in the shadowy world of half-belief where one is never sure whether one can see properly or not.

After the disciples' failure to heal his son, the man isn't sure whether Jesus himself will manage it. His request is made with almost a shrug of the shoulders: 'If there's anything you can do'. Jesus teasingly rebukes him, and bounces the question right back: 'What's this "If you can" nonsense? Just believe and it will happen!' This puts the man on the spot. It's now his turn to stare at the wall of rock ahead of him. He desperately puts his foot on the first rung of the ladder, and gropes round for help: 'I do believe! Help me in my unbelief!' His words, shouted out in the mixture of despair and trust that so often seems to characterize our prayers when things are tough, bring yet more people running to see what's going on. Jesus, the beloved son on his way to his own death and **resurrection**, rebukes the spirit; it leaves the boy apparently dead, but Jesus (in Mark's words) 'raises him up, and he arises' (both words are regular resurrection words in the New Testament).

In the story overall, Mark has told us that things are now going to be much harder, but that Jesus, and with him God's whole saving project, is going to get there in the end. It will take all his resources of spiritual and physical endurance, but he will indeed climb the rock and complete the walk, right to the summit. He will take up his own cross, be faithful to the end, and bring in the **kingdom**. The question, though, for us must be: are we going with him? Are we left muddled, unable to do even what we used to be able to? Are we facing a new turn in our pilgrimage, needing fresh reserves of spiritual strength, needing to spend more time, and more intensity, in our prayers?

And when faced with crises ourselves, do we know how to pray with whatever faith we may have? 'I believe; help me in my unbelief!' When we find ourselves at that point, the only thing to do is to put the first foot on the ladder, ask for help and start to climb.

MARK 9.30–37

True Greatness

> [30]They went away from there and were travelling through Galilee. Jesus didn't want anyone to know, [31]because he was teaching his disciples.
>
> 'The "son of man"', he was saying, 'is to be given over into human hands. They will kill him; and, when he's been killed, after three days he will rise again.'
>
> [32]They didn't understand the saying, and were afraid to ask him.
>
> [33]They came to Capernaum. When they got into the house he asked them, 'What were you arguing about on the road?'
>
> [34]They said nothing, because on the road they had been arguing about which of them was the greatest.
>
> [35]Jesus sat down and called the Twelve. 'If you want to be first,' he said, 'you must be last of all, and servant of all.' [36]He took a small child, and stood it in the middle of them. Then he hugged the child, and said to them, [37]'If anyone welcomes one child like this in my name, they welcome me. And if anyone welcomes me, it isn't me they welcome, but the one who sent me.'

I don't know whether Mark wants us to feel sorry for the **disciples** at this point, but quite frankly I do.

Earlier in the **gospel** Jesus said things to them in code, and they didn't get it. The **parables** were secret, hidden messages which they gradually learnt – away from the crowds, in the house – how to understand. When Jesus warned them about the leaven of the **Pharisees** and Herod (8.15) they thought he was making a comment about them forgetting to bring bread. They have struggled to get their minds round the fact that he often says things that have a clear meaning at the surface level, but what he wants is for them to look under the surface and find a hidden meaning somewhere else.

And now he tells them something which we, the readers, realize he means quite literally; and they, not surprisingly, are puzzled because they are looking for a hidden meaning and can't find it. This isn't public teaching; it's part of the hidden, inner meaning of his whole career, the bit that the crowds won't see until it actually happens. Jesus doesn't, at this stage, even attempt to tell parables about his approaching fate. Nearer the time he will do strange things, and say even stranger things, about it; but at this stage he is simply trying to tell them what he can see is going to happen. He will be handed over; he will be killed; he will rise again.

Why couldn't they understand? Basically, because no such fate could possibly have been part of their game plan, their understanding of what a **Messiah** might do. You might as well expect a footballer, planning the biggest game of the season, to explain to his friends that he was going to play with his legs tied together. Probably not all Jews of the time believed that God would send a Messiah; but nobody at all believed that, if and when God did send one, that Messiah would have to suffer, still less have to die.

However – and this must have increased their confusion – the language Jesus used for saying this contained two phrases which could have been used as code for something else. My guess is that the disciples were trying to decode things which Jesus meant in a quite straightforward sense.

The first is our old friend 'the **son of man**'. Clearly Mark intends us to understand that on this occasion Jesus simply meant 'I'. Of course, Mark knows that the phrase carries echoes of the great dream-picture in Daniel 7, where 'one like a son of man', duly interpreted, refers to 'the people of the saints of the most high'. But the phrase could also be used as an indirect way of saying 'I'. That, of course, is how it was meant, and quickly understood, in 8.31; but after the sharp exchange at that point between Jesus and Peter the message still doesn't seem to have sunk in.

The second phrase which they might have taken as code was 'after three days he will rise'. As we saw earlier (9.10), though most Jews believed that God would raise the dead bodily at the end of the **present age**, they were not expecting that one person would rise from the dead while the present age continued on its way. They must have wondered what on earth – literally, what *on earth* – he was talking about.

At this stage we can not only sympathize with the disciples; we must ask ourselves whether we do the same thing. When God is trying to say something to us, how good are we at listening? Is there something in scripture, or something we've heard in church, or something we sense going on around us, through which God is speaking to us – and if so, are we open to it? Are we prepared to have our earlier ways of understanding things taken apart so that a new way of understanding can open up instead?

A sign that the answer may still be 'no' is if, like the disciples in the next paragraph, we are still concerned about our own status, about what's in it for us. If we are thinking that by following Jesus we will enhance our own prestige, our sense of self-worth (so highly prized today, but so easily leading to a narcissistic sense that the gospel exists to make us feel good about ourselves), or even our bank balance, then we're very unlikely to be able to hear what God is actually saying. Certainly Jesus must have been frustrated and disappointed that the disciples could only worry about their own relative status. That's the trouble with understanding half the message – the half they wanted to understand: if Jesus is Messiah, then we are royal courtiers-in-waiting! They will spend the next several chapters with the same idea in their heads, until the shocking truth dawns.

To try to jolt them out of their upside-down thinking, Jesus, not for the last time, uses a child as a teaching aid. Aside from normal family affection children were not rated highly in the ancient world; they had no status or prestige. The point Jesus is making here is that the disciples won't gain particular favour or social standing because they are his followers; anyone who receives even a child in Jesus' name will receive Jesus himself, and thereby will receive also 'the one who sent me' – a way of referring to God which may remind us more of John's gospel. In other words, anyone at all associated with Jesus can become the means of access to royalty, and even to divinity; the disciples aren't special in that sense at all.

This lesson resonates out into the centuries of church history in which so many have thought that being close to Jesus, even working full-time for him, made them somehow special. Those who have really understood his message know that things aren't like that. As Jesus goes to the cross, turning upside down everything his disciples had imagined, he is also turning upside down the way people, including Christians, still think. If we feel sorry for the disciples in their confusion, we should ask ourselves just how confused we ourselves still are.

MARK 9.38–50

Warnings about Sin

[38]'Teacher,' said John, 'we saw someone casting out demons in your name. We stopped him, because he wasn't following us.'

[39]'Don't stop him,' said Jesus. 'No one who does powerful things by my name will be able to say bad things about me soon afterwards. [40]Anyone who's not against us is on our side. [41]Anyone who even gives

you a cup of water in my name, because you belong to the Messiah –
I'm telling you the truth, that person won't go unrewarded.

⁴²'Think about these little ones who believe in me,' he went on. 'If
anyone causes one of them to slip up, it would be much better for that
person to have a huge millstone put around their neck, and be thrown
into the sea.

⁴³'And if your hand causes you to slip up, cut it off. It's better for you
to go into life maimed than to have two hands and go into Gehenna,
into the fire that never goes out.

⁴⁵'And if your foot causes you to slip up, cut it off. It's better for you
to go into life lame than to have two feet and be thrown into Gehenna.

⁴⁷'And if your eye causes you to slip up, throw it away. It's better for
you to go into the kingdom of God with one eye than to have two eyes
and to be thrown into Gehenna, ⁴⁸where

their worm lives on for ever
and the fire can never be quenched.

⁴⁹'You see, everyone will be salted with fire. ⁵⁰Salt is great stuff; but if
salt becomes unsalty, how can you make it salty again? You need salt
among yourselves. Live at peace with each other.'

During the Second World War, while London was being heavily
bombed, one of the canons of Westminster Abbey watched as his house,
and everything in it, went up in flames after a direct hit. The clothes he
stood up in were all he had left. In the morning, he went to Oxford to
visit a friend and, while there, went to a shop to buy some new clothes.
The shop assistant was surprised by all the things he was asking for.
'Don't you know there's a war on?' she asked.

Of course he did, and that's the point of the story. But what Jesus now
says to the **disciples** implies that they don't know. There is a serious business afoot, which will have serious consequences; and unless they realize
this they will be in real danger. Battle has been joined; martial law is now
appropriate. If the disciples are to be Jesus' associates in the final and
vital stage of his plan they must sort their ideas out and see things from
his strategic point of view. Don't they know there's a war on?

Looking at these short sayings like this helps to make sense of them
as a sequence, though actually this is the one part of Mark's **gospel**
where it seems to me very likely that Mark has collected together, and
edited, sayings from completely different contexts. Even if that is the
case, we should assume that he has something in mind as an overall
theme, and the idea of a battle now being joined, with serious consequences, fits the bill.

To begin with, Jesus assumes that Israel as a whole is, by implication, taking sides as to whether his mission is or is not from God. John

wants to restrict working in Jesus' name to the official group of disciples, but Jesus has no such qualms; if someone is casting out **demons** by mentioning Jesus' name, such a person is honouring Jesus, and is hardly likely to be found speaking evil of Jesus and his movement. The difference in attitude isn't just about being exclusive (John) or inclusive (Jesus); it's about the difference between seeing Jesus' work as a private and privileged operation and seeing it as an event that is moving swiftly towards a showdown.

John's attitude (which of course fits with the approach in the previous paragraph, in which the disciples were arguing about who would be the greatest) is a symptom of a disease that afflicts the church to this day. How easy it is for any of us, especially professional clergy and theologians, to assume that the church belongs to us. How easy, too, for people who have always worshipped and prayed within one particular tradition or style to feel that this is the 'proper' way. That isn't to say, of course, that some styles may not be richer, or more satisfying, than others. But out there in the world, beyond even rudimentary theological education and training, there are millions of Christians whom Jesus may be referring to as 'little ones who believe'. If those who have training and education do anything that excludes such people, they are in deep trouble.

This probably gives us the right focus for the sayings about cutting off hands and feet, and plucking out eyes. Virtually all readers agree that these commands are not to be taken literally. They refer to precious parts of one's personality – to aspects of one's full humanness – which may from time to time cause one to stumble, which may, that is, bring about one's ruin as a follower of Jesus. The immediate meaning seems to be that John and the others had better watch out in case their desire for honour when Jesus becomes king (if only they knew!) prevents them in fact from being his disciples at all. Anything that gets in the way must go.

Such sayings, though, demand that we apply them in various ways to wider issues. The first thing to note is that discipleship is difficult, and demands sacrifices. Many today write and speak as if the only purpose in following Jesus were to find complete personal fulfilment and satisfaction, to follow a way or path of personal spirituality which will meet our felt needs. That is hardly the point. There's a war on. God is at work in our world; so are the forces of evil; and there really is no time or space for self-indulgent spiritualities that shirk the slightest personal cost, or even resist it on the grounds that all the desires and hopes one finds within one's heart must be God-given and so must be realized.

The second thing, within that, is that what we are asked to give up is not something that is sinful in and of itself. Of course we should reject sin; there's nothing special in that (difficult though it may be), but that's just the beginning. We should also be prepared to reject something which is good and God-given – as hands, feet and eyes are! – but which, at the moment at least, is leading us down the wrong path. This is not (as is sometimes suggested) to be morbid or dualistic, to regard as evil that which God created as good. It is to recognize, once more, that there's a war on.

This passage, for the first time in Mark, introduces us to the stern warning that those who drift down the wrong road are heading for the rubbish heap. 'Gehenna' is the valley that runs past the south-west corner of the old city of Jerusalem; a week ago, ironically, I sat there and watched a fireworks display. In ancient times it was used as Jerusalem's rubbish tip, smouldering perpetually; by Jesus' day it had already become a metaphor for the fate, after death, of those who reject God's way. Jesus seems to combine the two meanings. As we shall see later (and as emerges more fully in the other gospels), he was continually warning his contemporaries that unless they followed his way of the **kingdom**, his way of peace, they, together with the nation and its capital city, were heading for literal physical destruction, in a great cataclysm that would reduce Jerusalem to a large-scale and horrifying extension of its own smouldering rubbish tip. Here he draws on this larger theme to make the personal warning: don't think you can drift along doing whatever you feel like. There's a war on; the kingdom is breaking in; sacrifices are required; to think otherwise is to risk total ruin.

The end of the chapter brings us back to the squabbling disciples (suggesting that, for Mark at least, the rest of the passage is about them as well). Salt purifies; so does fire. They are called, as Jesus' people, to be the salt of the earth (Matthew 5.13), but, as with the rest of the nation, they must beware of losing their particular flavour and so becoming worthless. If they are to be followers of the prince of peace they must learn to live at peace within themselves.

The next chapter will show that they still had some way to go in learning this basic lesson. But this only makes the question for us more immediate and direct. Have we learnt the lesson? Do we know there's a war on? Are we taking appropriate action?

MARK 10.1-16

Teachings on Divorce

¹Jesus left the region, and went to the districts of Judaea across the Jordan. A large crowd gathered around him, and once more, as his custom was, he taught them.

²Some Pharisees approached him with a question. 'Is it permitted,' they asked, 'for a man to divorce his wife?' They said this to trap him.

³'Well,' answered Jesus, 'what did Moses command you?'

⁴'Moses permitted us,' they replied 'to write a notice of separation and so to complete the divorce.'

⁵'He gave you that command,' said Jesus 'because you are hard-hearted. ⁶But from the beginning of creation

male and female he made them; ⁷and that's why the man must leave his father and his mother and cleave unto his wife; ⁸so that the two become one flesh.

'There you are, then: they are no longer two, but one flesh. ⁹What God has joined, humans must not split up.'

¹⁰When they were back indoors, the disciples asked him about this.

¹¹'Anyone who divorces his wife,' said Jesus, 'and marries someone else commits adultery against her. ¹²And if she divorces her husband and marries someone else she commits adultery.'

¹³People brought children to Jesus for him to touch them. The disciples reprimanded them. ¹⁴But Jesus was angry when he saw it, and said to them, 'Let the children come to me! Don't stop them! The kingdom of God belongs to people like that. ¹⁵I'm telling you the truth: anyone who doesn't receive the kingdom of God like a child will never get into it.'

¹⁶And he hugged them, laid his hands on them, and blessed them.

In Britain during the early 1990s, from time to time a journalist would telephone a bishop or theologian to ask about divorce. It happened to me once. It's a question every church, every member of the clergy, has to think about at some time today, especially in the Western world. A newspaper article on divorce will be widely read. Everybody knows someone who is going through, or has just gone through, the break-up of a marriage.

But of course the journalists weren't wanting to write a piece about the church's attitude to divorce in general. They were wanting to write about Prince Charles and Princess Diana. Once it became clear that their marriage was in real trouble the journalists never left it alone for a minute. Anyone trying to pronounce on the broader question of divorce would at once be seized on: 'Are you then saying that Prince Charles . . .'

Something very similar was happening when the **Pharisees** asked Jesus about divorce. Why does Mark say they put the question as a trap? Why does Jesus only give the detailed answer when he's back safely in the house with the **disciples** (just like he did with the **parable** of the sower, and with the saying about purity in chapter 7)? Well, look and see where this incident is taking place. It's down by the Jordan, in the Judaean wilderness. Who used to work there? **John the Baptist**. Why did John get put in prison, and finally lose his head? For criticizing Herod Antipas for marrying his brother's wife. It all makes sense.

This doesn't mean that what Jesus has to say about divorce in the passage is irrelevant to the broader question; far from it. But it brings the story into three-dimensional reality. Herod's irregular marital arrangements (his wife, Herodias, had had to divorce Philip so that it could happen) were among the reasons why it was clear, to John the Baptist and plenty of others, that he could never be the true king that God intended to give to Israel. The criticism of Herod went with the announcement that the **Messiah**'s coming was expected at any time. Now, as Jesus goes to Jerusalem following the disciples' recognition of him as Messiah, we shouldn't be surprised that the Pharisees try to trap him. Will he allow himself to say something about divorce which can then be presented as treasonable?

Jesus, of course, can spot the trap a mile off; but he loses no integrity in how he deals with it. In public, a debate about the meaning of different scriptural texts; in private, a sharp and direct comment to the disciples (including what amounts to a specific reference to Herodias, since in Jewish law a woman could not normally divorce her husband). Though in Matthew's version of the incident, and in Paul's discussion in 1 Corinthians 7, we find permission for divorce under certain circumstances, the present passage is not designed to give detailed case law, or discuss exceptions to the rule, but to state the rule itself as clearly as can be done.

Jesus' public discussion is extraordinarily interesting on several levels. The Pharisees quote Moses, who doesn't command or encourage divorce, but allows it and places strict controls on it (one has to go through the proper written procedures – a measure designed to protect the vulnerable woman from exploitation). But this wasn't answering Jesus' actual question, which was 'What did Moses *command*?' Jesus doesn't say Moses was wrong with the 'permission' in Deuteronomy; but he insists that one should go back to Genesis, to the account of creation itself, to discover the creator's will. (Jesus and the Pharisees both assume, of course, that Moses wrote Genesis.)

Genesis is where you find the command in question. It's quite clear: the bond of husband and wife creates not merely a partnership or a working agreement but a new entity, a new human being. And as far as Jesus is concerned, what Genesis says about marriage, God says.

Jesus' comment on the Mosaic permission is important as a clue to what he thought was going on in his own ministry. Moses 'gave you that command because you are hardhearted'; in other words, Israel in Moses' day was not able to fulfill the creator's intention, and needed laws that would reflect that second-best reality. Hardheartedness, the inability (to use our version of the same metaphor) to have one's heart in tune with God's best intention and plan, thwarted God's longing that Israel should be his prototype of renewed humanity. The problem was not with the ideal, nor with the law, but with the people: Israel was, when it all came down to it, just like everybody else. Hardhearted. Eager to take the precious gift of genuine humanness and exploit or abuse it.

But this means that, for Jesus' comment to make sense, *he must be offering a cure for hardheartedness.* If he is now articulating a rigorous return to the standard of Genesis, to God's original intention, he is either being hopelessly idealistic or he believes that the coming of the **kingdom** will bring about a way for hearts to be softened. The fact that debates about divorce have concerned the church ever since indicates that this cure doesn't work automatically or easily. Equally, though, the fact that millions of Christians have prayed for grace to remain faithful to their marriage vows, often under great stress, and have found the way not only to survive but to celebrate as 'one flesh', indicates that the implicit promise is true.

In today's church, particularly in the West, anyone who even reads verses 10–12 out loud is likely to be called cruel, unfeeling, unforgiving, exclusive and a host of other names. So many people are bruised by the whole experience of marriage breakdown that to raise the topic, let alone to take a strong line on it, seems (as they might say) 'unChristian'. But the next paragraph in Mark reminds us of another dimension. Who, today, is liable to earn Jesus' anger at preventing little children feeling the warmth of God's love and welcome? Hardly the churches, where (though there is always plenty of room for improvement) youth work often flourishes today. Rather, the people who suppose that children and their feelings don't matter, and that adults can make whatever arrangements suit them. Marriage break-up can devastate children, even grown-up children, with long-lasting ill effects. Which is kinder, more Christian: to say that these things don't matter, or to take a strong line, like Jesus, on behalf of the truly weak and vulnerable?

MARK 10.17–31

The Rich Young Ruler

[17]As he was setting out on the road, a man ran up and knelt down in front of him.

'Good teacher,' he asked, 'what should I do to inherit the life of the Age to Come?'

¹⁸'Why call me "good"?' replied Jesus. 'No one is good except God alone. ¹⁹You know the commandments:

Don't kill.
Don't commit adultery.
Don't steal.
Don't swear falsely.
Don't defraud.
Honour your father and your mother.'

²⁰'Teacher,' he said, 'I've kept all of them since I was little.'

²¹Jesus looked hard at him, and loved him.

'One more thing,' he said. 'Go away, and whatever you possess – sell it, and give it to the poor. You will have treasure in heaven! Then: come and follow me.'

²²At that, his face fell, and he went off sadly. He was very wealthy.

²³Jesus looked slowly around. Then he said to his disciples, 'How difficult it is for the wealthy to enter the kingdom of God!'

²⁴The disciples were astonished at what he was saying. So Jesus repeated once more, 'Children, it's very hard to enter the kingdom of God! ²⁵It would be easier for a camel to go through the eye of a needle than for a rich man to enter God's kingdom.'

²⁶They were totally amazed, and said to each other, 'So who then can be saved?'

²⁷'It's impossible for mortals,' Jesus said, looking hard at them, 'but it's not impossible for God. All things are possible for God.'

²⁸'Look here,' Peter started up, 'we've left everything and followed you.'

²⁹'I'll tell you the truth,' replied Jesus. 'No one who has left a house, or brothers or sisters, or mother or father, or children, or lands, because of me and the gospel, ³⁰will fail to receive back a hundred times more in the Present Age: houses, brothers, sisters, mothers, children, and lands – with persecutions! – and finally the life of the Age to Come. ³¹But plenty of people at the front will end up at the back, and the back at the front.'

When I was a boy, grown-ups used to divide their history into two periods: Before the War, and After the War (or Since the War). The Second World War had torn a hole in their world. Everything was different now: a different government and society, different hopes and needs, different possibilities and dangers.

Many first-century Jews divided their immediate future in the same way. Something would happen, they believed, which would make everything different. A great event would occur which would bring justice and peace, freedom for Israel, punishment for evildoers (whether

Jews or Gentiles), a time of prosperity when all the prophecies would be fulfilled, all the righteous dead would be raised to new life, all the world would burst out into a new and endless spring.

Their way of talking about all this was to distinguish between the **present age** and the **age to come**. The present age, their own time, was full of sin and injustice, lying and oppression. Good people suffered; wicked people got away with it. But in the age to come that would all be different. And the question pressing on any Jew who believed this was: can I be sure that I will be one of those who will inherit the age to come, and, if so, how? The phrase '**kingdom** of God', as we have seen, is another way of talking about the same thing: the age to come is the period of time in which God is at last ruling the world as he always wanted to.

That is the question the rich man (Matthew tells us he was young; Luke, that he was a ruler; hence the composite phrase, 'the rich young ruler') asks Jesus. A long Christian tradition, of course, has assumed that he wanted to know how he could be sure of going to **heaven** when he died, but that wasn't how he would have put it. God was going to make the whole world a new place; when that happened, you wouldn't want to be away in a dis-embodied heaven, but here on earth to enjoy the great blessing.

A further word of explanation is needed here. When Jesus says 'You will have treasure in heaven', he doesn't mean that the young man must go to heaven to get it; he means that God will keep it stored up for him until the time when, in the age to come, all is revealed. The reason you have money in the bank is not so that you can spend it in the bank but so that you can take it out and spend it somewhere else. The reason you have treasure in heaven, God's storehouse, is so that you can enjoy it in the age to come when God brings heaven and earth together at last. And 'eternal life', as most translations put it, doesn't mean 'life in a timeless, otherworldly dimension', but 'the life of the age to come' (the word 'eternal' translates a word which means 'belonging to the Age').

If you'd asked any **Pharisee**, or any member of one of the other sects of the time (such as the **Essenes**), what you should do to inherit the age to come, they would almost certainly have given two sorts of reply. First, they would have given you their own detailed interpretation of the Jewish law. The law itself defined Israel as God's people; but granted that Israel as a whole was (as the prophets had said) full of sinners, it was necessary to follow a more precise understanding of the com-mandments. Rabbinic law, and the **Dead Sea Scrolls**, have plenty of material like that. But, second, they would probably have urged you to join their own group: to become a Pharisee, an Essene, or whatever.

Then you would be able to enjoy, even in the present age, the security of knowing that you would inherit the age to come.

The question was, then: what was Jesus' attitude to the basic Jewish law? And what sort of a movement might he be leading? Jesus' reply must have puzzled the young man greatly. All he did was to restate the basic commandments which every Jew knew well. Or at least, some of them; notice which ones he misses out. He starts the list with numbers 6 to 9 (murder, adultery, theft, perjury), adds an extra one ('don't defraud'), and then goes back to number 5 (honouring parents). He omits numbers 1 to 4 (putting God first, no idols, not taking God's name in vain, and the **sabbath**) and number 10 (covetousness).

Now watch how the rest of the conversation comes round the back with a fresh twist on all of these (excepting only the sabbath). Jesus' basic demand is not for some logic-chopping extra observance, some tightening of definition here, some sharpening of exact meaning there. It is for idols and covetousness to be thrown to the winds: sell up and give to the poor! And it is for a radical rethink on what putting God first, and not taking his name in vain, might mean: Why do you call me good? No one is good but God; come and follow me. Jesus' new movement is indeed a radical revision of what it meant to be God's people, to follow the law of Moses. Because he, Jesus, is here, a whole new world opens up: the age to come is not now simply in the future (though it is that too); it is bursting through into the present, like a chicken so keen to be born that it's already sticking its beak through the shell ahead of the right time.

The discussion that follows the rich man's sad departure reflects the **disciples**' shock at being told that wealth won't buy you a place in the age to come. Their surprise only makes sense if we assume that they regarded wealth as a sign of God's pleasure – a common view in both Judaism and paganism, though there was already much in the Old Testament which challenged that attitude.

Jesus slices through their amazement. Riches can no more go into the age to come than a camel can go through a needle – a typical and deliberate overstatement, like saying 'you'll get your riches into God's kingdom when you can put the entire ocean into a bottle'. Everything will be upside down and inside out; all things are possible to God; the first will be last and the last first. In particular, though, those who have left family and possessions to follow Jesus will receive things back even in the present age – a new and ever-enlarging family of their fellow-disciples, with homes open to them wherever they go (and persecutions waiting for them too, a theme Mark wants to rub in); and, of course, in the age to come, the God-given life of that new age.

All the early Christians came to believe that with Jesus' death and **resurrection** the age to come had indeed broken in to the present age.

That's one of the hardest points for us to grasp today about their way of looking at the world, and at God. But if we even begin to take it seriously, we'll see that there is nowhere to hide from Jesus' uncompromising – though cheerful and celebratory – demand for discipleship. The call 'Come on! Follow me!' echoes down through history, and everyone is judged by the answer they give.

MARK 10.32–45

The Request of James and John

³²They were on the road, going up to Jerusalem. Jesus was walking ahead of them; they were amazed, and the people following were afraid.

Again he took the Twelve aside and began to tell them what was going to happen to him. ³³'Look,' he said, 'we're going up to Jerusalem. The son of man will be handed over to the chief priests and the legal experts, and they will condemn him to death, and hand him over to the pagans. ³⁴They will taunt him and spit at him and flog him and kill him – and after three days he will rise again.'

³⁵James and John, Zebedee's sons, came up to him.

'Teacher,' they said, 'we want you to grant us whatever we ask.'

³⁶'What do you want me to do for you?' asked Jesus.

³⁷'Grant us,' they said, 'that when you're there in all your glory, one of us will sit at your right, and the other at your left.'

³⁸'You don't know what you're asking for!' Jesus replied. 'Can you drink the cup I'm going to drink? Can you receive the baptism I'm going to receive?'

³⁹'Yes,' they said, 'we can.'

'Well,' said Jesus, 'you will drink the cup I drink; you will receive the baptism I receive. ⁴⁰But sitting at my right hand or my left – that's not up to me. It's been assigned already.'

⁴¹When the other ten disciples heard, they were angry with James and John. ⁴²Jesus called them to him.

'You know how it is in the pagan nations', he said. 'Think how their so-called rulers act. They lord it over their subjects. The high and mighty ones boss the rest around. ⁴³But that's not how it's going to be with you. Anyone who wants to be great among you must become your servant. ⁴⁴Anyone who wants to be first must be everyone's slave. ⁴⁵Don't you see? The son of man didn't come to be waited on. He came to be the servant, to give his life "as a ransom for many".'

What comes to mind first when you think of the crucifixion of Jesus?

Perhaps you think of going to church and singing well-known hymns: 'There is a green hill far away', or 'When I survey the wondrous cross'.

Perhaps you think of a picture, or a statue, of the cross: a crucifix, reminding you of the sorrow and suffering of Jesus, and somehow bringing consolation and hope into your own sorrow and suffering.

Perhaps you think of the brutality that could have dreamed up that way of killing people – and of the similar brutalities that still deface God's world today.

Perhaps you have an image in your mind of the crowds at the foot of the cross, some mocking Jesus, some in tears. Perhaps, in your picture, you are there with them, watching him die.

Mark is going to tell us the story of how Jesus was crucified. And he wants us to hold in our minds several pictures which will give us the full meaning of the scene, for Jesus, for Israel, for the world and for ourselves. In this passage he wants, as it were, to sow the seeds of these different pictures. These seeds will germinate during the next few chapters, and come to flower as Jesus celebrates his final meal with his followers, prays in Gethsemane, stands before the authorities and finally meets his death. It will help us at this stage of the **gospel** if we look at these seeds one by one.

This is the third time Jesus has solemnly warned the **disciples** about what's going to happen to him. It isn't taking him by surprise. It's part of the vocation which has gripped him since, at least, the voice at his **baptism**, which echoed Isaiah's prophecy about the servant, to which in this passage he returns explicitly. The great central section of Isaiah (chapters 40—55) has as its main character, after Israel's God himself, an anointed, messianic figure who suffers and dies for the sins of Israel and the world. This is 'YHWH's servant', and at the end of the passage Jesus refers back to Isaiah 53, the fourth 'servant song', which speaks in awe and gratitude of the servant's redeeming death.

Many thinkers in our own day have found it incredible that Jesus would have thought about his own death in this deliberate, focused way. Well, his followers at the time found it incredible too; that's the second 'seed' Mark is sowing here. Jesus' disciples couldn't believe the way he was leading them to Jerusalem with such determination. People who were following found it scary. So did many thinkers in the next few centuries, who struggled to find ways of telling the story of Jesus without having the cross at the middle of it. So do many in our own day. But from Jesus' own pronouncements onwards the claim that he not only died by crucifixion but did so as the climax of a thought-out vocation has always been at the centre of authentic Christianity.

People have said, again and again, that this 'authentic Christianity' is actually a way of compromise with political power. (This is presumably because the cross has sometimes been used to encourage a private piety which leaves the larger problems of the world untouched.) This is, though, the exact opposite of the truth. This is the third 'seed' Mark is sowing here.

James and John want to turn Jesus' messianic journey to Jerusalem into a march to glory – a glory in which they will sit on either side of him when he reigns as king. They have clearly heard all the language about suffering, death and rising again simply as a set of pictures, perhaps meaning 'It's going to be tough, but we're going to come out on top.' But the cross is not, for Jesus or for Mark, a difficult episode to be got through on the way to a happy ending. It is precisely God's way of standing worldly power and authority on its head. When, at the end of this passage, Jesus quotes the servant song ('. . . to give his life as a ransom for many'), he is making the point, with which Isaiah would have emphatically agreed, that the **kingdom** of God turns the world's ideas of power and glory upside down and inside out.

This full and major Markan statement about the meaning of the cross, in context, is first and foremost a *political* interpretation. The cross isn't just about God forgiving our sins because of Jesus' death (though of course this is central to it). Because it is God's way of putting the world, and ourselves, to rights, it challenges and subverts all the human systems which claim to put the world to rights but in fact only succeed in bringing a different set of humans out on top. The reason James and John misunderstand Jesus is exactly the same as the reason why many subsequent thinkers, down to our own day, are desperate to find a way of having Jesus without having the cross as well: the cross calls into question all human pride and glory. This is bound to carry political meanings, and dangerous ones at that.

Jesus' conversation with the ambitious brothers gives us the fourth 'seed' that Mark is planting. 'Can you drink the cup I'm going to drink? Can you receive the baptism I'm going to receive?' These are dense and difficult words. The 'cup' seems to be the cup of God's wrath, spoken of by the prophet Jeremiah. Jesus, here and in Gethsemane (14.36), faces the fact that the wickedness of the whole earth, and of Israel in particular, is pulling down upon its own head the just judgment of God. This takes specific and concrete form: as in the Old Testament, God's wrath is what happens when foreign armies come and destroy God's people, God's city. Jesus' task is to go ahead and take the full force of that 'wrath' on himself.

The 'baptism' looks back to the beginning of the story. Just as Jesus' own baptism by John committed him to his vocation of suffering messiahship, at the head of God's new **covenant** people, so his forthcoming death is itself to be understood as a kind of baptism – going down beneath the waters of death, so that sins might be forgiven. This is how some very early Christians understood their own baptism in relation to that of Jesus (Romans 6.3–11; Colossians 2.11–15). If we want to see Jesus' death the way Mark sees it we must let these seeds in particular germinate and grow to full flower.

The final 'seed' is provided by Jesus' wry comment about those who will sit at his right and his left. James and John don't know what they're asking for, but Mark's reader, after a few chapters of waiting in suspense, will discover. When Jesus 'sits in his glory', with one at his right and another at his left, it will be on the cross. Mark has given us a stark picture both of what true kingly glory looks like and of what Jesus' death will mean. We must now let him water these seeds and watch them start to grow.

As we do so, we must remember again that one of Mark's underlying themes throughout these chapters is that of following Jesus. When we look at the picture he's drawing, we too may be amazed, horrified and afraid. But Jesus is going up to Jerusalem, turning the world's values and power-systems on their heads, setting off to give his life as a ransom for many. If we want to receive what he has to offer, we have no choice but to follow.

MARK 10.46–52

Jesus Heals a Blind Beggar

[46]They came to Jericho. As Jesus, his disciples and a substantial crowd were leaving the town, a blind beggar named Bartimaeus, the son of Timaeus, was sitting by the road. [47]When he heard it was Jesus of Nazareth, he began to shout out: 'Son of David! Jesus! Take pity on me!'

[48]Lots of people told him crossly to be quiet. But he shouted out all the louder, 'Son of David – take pity on me!'

[49]Jesus came to a stop. 'Call him,' he said.

So they called the blind man.

'Cheer up,' they said, 'and get up. He's calling you.'

[50]He flung his cloak aside, jumped up, and came to Jesus.

Jesus saw him coming. [51]'What do you want me to do for you?' he asked.

'Teacher,' the blind man said, 'let me see again.'

[52]'Off you go,' said Jesus. 'Your faith has saved you.' And immediately he saw again, and he followed him on the way.

It took some weeks of persuasion before they came to see me. The grown-up son was desperate to get his ailing and depressed mother into some kind of a home where she would be properly cared for. As long as she lived with him he couldn't do his own work or have any private life. She swamped him with demands for help and attention. We looked at several options. There were small communities, large communities, nursing homes, sheltered housing. Any of them would have been real possibilities. The mother, though, saw some flaw in each of them which became, to her, fatal. None of them would do. After an hour she turned to the son with triumph gleaming in her eyes. 'There you are!' she said. 'He can't do anything for us.'

But the truth was that she didn't *want* anybody to do anything for her. She wanted to go on being a victim, putting moral pressure on her son (and everybody else in sight) to feel sorry for her.

Jesus' question to Bartimaeus addresses exactly that possibility. 'What do you want me to do for you?' Do you, Bartimaeus, want to give up begging? Do you want to have to live differently, to work for a living, to have no reason to sit by the roadside all day whining at pass-ers-by? It's quite a challenge, and Bartimaeus rises to it splendidly. He wants the new life; not only sight, but the chance to follow Jesus. Fancy seeing for the first time for many years, and imagine that the first thing you saw was Jesus on his way up to Jerusalem.

Mark is quite clear: Bartimaeus is a model to imitate. Unlike the **disciples**, who hadn't really understood what Jesus was about, he is already a man of **faith**, courage and true discipleship. He recognizes who Jesus is ('**son of David**'); he clearly believes Jesus can help him ('your faith has saved you'); he leaves his begging (the cloak would be spread on the ground to receive money; Jericho is seldom cold enough for anyone to wear a cloak during the day), and he follows Jesus on the way ('the way' was the early Christian's word for what we call 'Christianity').

He makes a stark contrast with the disciples. Remember how, when Jesus said to James and John, 'What do you want me to do for you?', all he got was a request for power, prestige and glory. As with the blind man in chapter 8, the healing of Bartimaeus is a sign that Jesus is trying to open his followers' eyes, this time to see him not just as **Messiah** but as the one who would give his life to bring salvation to all.

When Jesus says 'Your faith has saved you', the word 'saved' refers once again to physical healing (compare 5.34). For any early Christian, though, it would carry a wider and deeper meaning as well. The different dimensions of salvation were not sharply distinguished either by Jesus or by the **gospel** writers. God's rescue of people from what we think of as physical ailments on the one hand and spiritual peril on the other were thought of as different aspects of the same event. But again not for the first time, we see that the key to salvation, of whatever kind, is faith. That's why anyone, even those normally excluded from pure or polite society, can be saved. Faith is open to all; and often it's the unexpected people who seem to have it most strongly. And faith consists not least in recognizing who Jesus is and trusting that he has the power to rescue.

This is the kind of story that lends itself particularly well to slow, patient meditation. Take some time and imagine yourself in the crowd that day in Jericho. It's hot, dry and dusty (it almost always is there). You're excited; you're with Jesus; you're going up to Jerusalem. And here is someone shouting from the roadside. It's a nuisance. It's possibly even dangerous (if enough people call him 'son of David', someone in authority is going to get alarmed). Examine your own feelings. Try to remember other times when you've felt like that. Then watch as Jesus, never put out by what annoys his followers (remember the children, earlier in the chapter) turns to speak to the blind man. How do you feel about that? Do you want this beggar in the party? How about when Jesus speaks warm and welcoming words to him? Has he ever spoken to you like that? How do you feel as you set off together up the hill to Jerusalem?

Now imagine yourself as the blind man. We all have something, by no means necessarily a physical ailment, that we know is getting in the way of our being the people we believe God wants us to be and made us to be. Sit by the roadside and listen to the crowd. Examine your own feelings when you discover it's Jesus coming by. Call out to him, and when he summons you, put everything aside and go to him. And when he asks you what you want him to do, go for it. Don't look back at the small, selfish comforts of victimhood. Ask for freedom, for salvation. And when you get it, be prepared to follow Jesus wherever he goes next.

Now for the real challenge. Do you have the courage to think through the story from Jesus' point of view?

MARK 11.1–11

The Triumphal Entry

¹So they approached Jerusalem. They got as far as Bethphage and Bethany, on the Mount of Olives, when Jesus sent two of his disciples on ahead with a specific task.

²'Go to the village over there,' he said to them, 'and as soon as you enter it you will find a colt tied up – one that nobody has ever ridden before. Untie it and bring it here. ³And if anyone says to you, "Why are you doing that?" then say, "The master needs it, and he will return it at once."'

⁴They went off and found the colt tied up beside a door, out in the street; and they untied it.

⁵Some of the bystanders said to them, 'Why are you untying the colt?' ⁶They gave the answer Jesus had told them, and they let them carry on. ⁷So they brought the colt to Jesus and laid their cloaks on it, and he mounted it. ⁸Several people spread out their cloaks in the road. Others did the same with foliage that they had cut in the fields. ⁹Those in front, and those coming behind, shouted out, 'Hosanna! Welcome in the Lord's Name! ¹⁰Here comes the kingdom of our father David! Hosanna in the highest!'

¹¹Jesus entered Jerusalem, went into the Temple, and looked all round. It was already getting late, and he returned to Bethany with the Twelve.

If you've ever been to the Holy Land, you will know that to go from Jericho to Jerusalem involves a long, hard climb. Jericho is the lowest city on earth, over 800 feet below sea level. Jerusalem, which is only a dozen or so miles away, is nearly 3,000 feet *above* sea level. The road goes through hot, dry desert all the way to the top of the Mount of Olives, at which point, quite suddenly, you have at the same time the first real vegetation and the first, glorious sight of Jerusalem itself. Even if you were climbing that road every week on business, there would still be a sense of exhilaration, of delight and relief, when you got to the top.

Now add to that sense of excitement the feeling that Jewish pilgrims, coming south from Galilee, would have every time they went up to Jerusalem for a festival (as they did several times a year). They were coming to the place where the living God had chosen to place his name and his presence; the place where, through the regular daily sacrifices, he assured Israel of forgiveness, of fellowship with himself, of hope for their future. They were coming there to celebrate the great Jewish stories of the past, which were mostly stories of freedom and hope. They would meet with relatives and old friends. There would be singing, prayer, dancing, feasting. All that was implied by a pilgrim convoy coming up the hill from Jericho to Jerusalem.

Now add to that anticipation and gladness the mood of Jesus' followers as they came up the hill. It was Passover time – freedom time! But it was also, as far as they were concerned, **kingdom** time: the time when Passover dreams, the great hope of freedom, of God's sovereign and saving presence being revealed in a quite new way, would at last come true. The long climb up through the Judaean wilderness was the climb to the kingdom.

Everything Mark tells us in this brief account of how they arrived at Jerusalem is designed to emphasize this, with the focus on Jesus himself as the King. He decides to ride into the city, and commandeers a colt for the purpose. (Matthew tells us it was a donkey; if all we had was Mark and Luke we wouldn't have known, since the word 'colt' could equally mean a young horse. Mark makes nothing of the theme of humility which Matthew inserts at this point.) Whether Jesus had arranged this ahead of time with friends in Bethany, or whether it was an on-the-spot decision, doesn't matter here; what matters is the sovereign freedom with which he acts.

Then comes the climax. You don't spread cloaks on the road – especially in the dusty, stony Middle East! – for a friend, or even a respected senior member of your family. You do it for royalty. And you don't cut branches off trees, or foliage from the fields, to wave in the streets just because you feel somewhat elated; you do it because you are welcoming a king. Two hundred years before, Judas Maccabaeus defeated the Syrian king Antiochus Epiphanes, entered Jerusalem and cleansed and rebuilt the **Temple** – and the people waved ivy and palm branches as they sang hymns of praise. Judas started a royal dynasty that lasted a hundred years. (The story is told in 2 Maccabees 10.1–9; compare 1 Maccabees 13.51.) Actually, just as Mark doesn't make it clear that Jesus rode on a donkey, so he doesn't say the people waved palm branches; the word for what they cut from the fields could just as easily mean corn or straw, or leafy branches cut from trees. The point Mark wants to make, however, is clear. From chapter 8 onwards the **disciples** have believed that Jesus is the true and rightful King of the Jews, on his way to the capital city to be hailed as such. This is the moment for his royal reception.

The shout of the crowd brings this out exactly. 'Hosanna' is a Hebrew word which mixes exuberant praise to God with the prayer that God will save his people, and do so right away. The beginning and end of their cheerful chant is taken from Psalm 118.25–26, which is itself all about going up to Jerusalem and the Temple. The sentence that follows means, literally, 'Blessed is the one who comes'; but in Hebrew and Aramaic that's the way you say 'welcome'. In the middle of the chant they have inserted the dangerous prayer: Welcome to the kingdom of our father David! This is what the scene is all about – as Mark's readers have known for some while, and as we saw in the shout of blind Bartimaeus in 10.47–48.

The scene ends, dramatically, with nothing happening – or not just yet. Jesus goes into the Temple, looks around, and comes out again, back to Bethany where he is to lodge with the **Twelve** during the few days leading up to Passover. (Jerusalem was extremely crowded during major festivals; many pilgrims would choose to stay in the outlying villages rather than within the city walls.) Mark leaves us, for the moment, in suspense as to what will happen when this King makes his presence felt in his own city.

Over the next few chapters, in fact, Mark will show us what Jesus meant when, in chapter 10, he radically redefined kingship. This is not to be the sort of royalty that either Israel or the rest of the world were used to. But the passage already raises questions for us in our own following of Jesus and loyalty to him. Are we ready to put our property at his disposal, to obey his orders even when they puzzle us? Are we ready to go out of our way to honour him, finding in our own lives the equivalents of cloaks to spread on the road before him, and branches to wave to make his coming into a real festival? Or have we so domesticated and trivialized our Christian commitment, our devotion to Jesus himself, that we look on him simply as someone to help us through the various things we want to do anyway, someone to provide us with comforting religious experiences? In our world where most countries don't have kings and queens, and where those monarchies that remain are mostly constitutional offices with the real power lying elsewhere, have we forgotten what, in biblical terms, a true king might be like?

MARK 11.12–25
Jesus Cleanses the Temple

¹²The next day, as they were leaving Bethany, Jesus was hungry. ¹³From some distance away he saw a fig tree covered with leaves, and hoped to find some fruit on it; but when he came up to it he found nothing but leaves. (It wasn't yet the season for figs.)

¹⁴He addressed the tree directly. 'May no one ever eat fruit from you again', he said. And his disciples heard.

¹⁵They came into Jerusalem. Jesus went into the Temple and began to drive out the traders, those who bought and sold in the Temple, and overturned the tables of the money-changers and the seats of the dove-sellers. ¹⁶He permitted no one to carry any vessel through the Temple. ¹⁷He began to teach: 'Isn't this what's written', he said,

'My house shall be called a house of prayer
for all the world to share?

But you've made it a brigand's den!'
¹⁸The chief priests and the legal experts heard, and looked for a way to get rid of him. But they were afraid of him, because the whole crowd was astonished at his teaching.

¹⁹When evening came, they went back out of the city.

²⁰As they were returning, early in the morning, they saw the fig tree withered from its roots.

²¹'Look, Teacher!' said Peter to Jesus, remembering what had happened before. 'The fig tree you cursed has withered.'

²²'Have faith in God', replied Jesus. ²³'I'm telling you the truth: if anyone says to this mountain, "Be off with you – get yourself thrown into the sea", if they have no doubt in their heart, but believe that what they say will happen, it will be done for them. ²⁴That's why I'm telling you, everything that you request in prayer, everything you ask God for, believe that you receive it, and it will happen for you.

²⁵'And when you are standing there praying, if you have something against someone else, forgive them – so that your father in heaven may forgive you your trespasses.'

What is the largest, most important building in your country? The one with the most historic meanings and associations? The one where famous people come, either to work or to visit? The one that stands for, and symbolizes, the very centre and meaning of your country, its life, its rulers and its people?

Now supposing you were convinced that this building was shortly to be devastated, say in an earthquake, or by enemy action. And supposing you believed that this was God's judgment upon it, because the rulers of your country were wicked beyond repair. And supposing you felt obliged to tell people – to warn them solemnly, to give them a sign of what was to come, to urge them to change their ways while there was still time.

How would you do it?

(You may say that's a lot of supposing; most of us never have thoughts like that from one year's end to the next. But unless we imagine ourselves in something like the situation Jesus faced we will never understand this passage; and since this passage is central to the rest of the **gospel** we'll never understand that either.)

Mark has given us the story, once again, in 'sandwich' form. The outer part concerns the fig tree, the inner part concerns the **Temple**. Each story helps us understand the other.

By itself, the fig tree incident looks most peculiar. It wasn't yet time for figs; surely Jesus was being petty and petulant, cursing the tree for doing what fig trees always do, putting out leaves in the spring but not yet bearing fruit? By the way he's told the story, though, Mark makes it clear that the fig tree is a dramatic acted **parable**, indicating the meaning of what Jesus was going to do in the Temple.

By itself, the Temple incident is ambiguous. Many people have thought that Jesus was simply protesting against commercialization. On this view, he only intended to clean up the Temple – to stop all this non-religious activity, and leave it as a place for pure prayer and worship. (That's a suspiciously modern attitude; keeping religion and economic life strictly separate has had fairly devastating consequences, not least in the Two-Thirds World.) But Mark makes it clear, by the placing of the Temple incident within the two halves of the fig tree story, that he sees Jesus' actions as, again, a dramatic acted parable of judgment. This was Jesus' way of announcing God's condemnation of the Temple itself and all that it had become in the national life of Israel.

The key comes in the biblical quotations that sum up Jesus' charge against the Temple. Harking back to the old prophetic books of Isaiah and Jeremiah, Jesus is reminding his hearers that the Temple had always been an ambiguous thing. Right from the time it was built and dedicated by Solomon, it was clear that it could never in fact be the full and final dwelling-place of the true God (1 Kings 8.27). Although God had promised to bless Israel through the Temple, if Israel began to take it for granted, to use the Temple and the promises attached to it as an excuse for immoral and unjust behaviour, then the Temple itself could and would be judged. That's what the early chapters of Jeremiah are all about, including the quotation that comes here: God's house has become a brigand's cave.

In what sense was it a brigand's cave? Not in the sense that people were using it to make money on the side. The word 'brigand', in Jesus' day, wasn't a word for 'thief' or 'robber' in the ordinary sense, but for the revolutionaries, those we today would call the ultra-orthodox, plotting and ready to use violence to bring about their nationalist dreams.

Part of Jesus' charge against his fellow-Jews was that Israel as a whole had used its vocation, to be the light of the world, as an excuse for a hard, narrow, nationalist piety and politics in which the rest of the world was to be, not enlightened, but condemned. We can see something of this attitude both in the **Dead Sea Scrolls** and in the tendency to violent revolution throughout the period in which Jesus lived. The Temple had been intended to symbolize God's dwelling with Israel for the sake of the world; the way Jesus' contemporaries had organized things, it had come to symbolize not God's welcome to the nations but God's exclusion of them. The holy brigands who were bent on violent rebellion against Rome – which in Jesus' view was exactly the wrong way to bring about the kingdom of God – looked to the Temple as the central focus of their ideology. And the guardians of the Temple itself were notorious for their rich and oppressive lifestyle. Violence towards outsiders; injustice towards Israel itself; that was what the Temple had come to mean. As with the fig tree, Jesus' only word for the place was one of judgment.

How did his actions in the Temple mean that? The purpose of the Temple was to be the place of **sacrifice**. Hour by hour worshippers came to the Temple, changed money into the official coinage, bought animals that were guaranteed perfect for sacrifice (if you brought an animal from some distance, there was a good chance it might be attacked on the way and so no longer be a perfect specimen, able to be sacrificed), and brought them to the **priests** who completed the killing and offering. The sacrificial system, and with it the reason for the Temple's existence, depended on money-changing and animal purchase. By stopping the entire process, even just for a short but deeply symbolic moment, Jesus was saying, more powerfully than any words could express: the Temple is under God's judgment. Its reason for existing is being taken away.

In addition, as we shall see, the **kingdom**-message of judgment went hand in hand with Jesus' kingdom-agenda of defeating evil in a way far deeper and more complete than either the holy brigandry of revolution or the symbolic world of animal sacrifice. 'The **son of man** . . .', he said in the previous chapter, 'came to give his life as a ransom for many.' Jesus used sacrificial language, here and in the Upper Room (chapter 14), to describe the death he would die, the death through which God's sovereign and saving presence, that is, God's kingdom, would come to its full effect. The sacrificial system was therefore doubly redundant. It was part of the Temple system which had come to stand for the wrong things; it was part of the signpost system set up by God to draw the eye to the climactic achievement of Jesus himself on the cross.

We should think twice, therefore, before we 'apply' this passage, as is sometimes done, to occasions when we feel that people are trying to commercialize religion, to mix God and mammon. Yes, that's a danger, and the church must always watch out for it. But Jesus' protest was far deeper, and if we applied it today it wouldn't just be the churches that ought to tremble, but the lawcourts and legislative assemblies, the royal palaces and banking centres, the places where power is so often wielded to the benefit of the already powerful and the downtreading of the already powerless, the places where people with power or wealth turn in on themselves instead of outwards in generosity towards the world. That's where Jesus wants to stride today, to turn over tables and drive out traders.

But beware. This kind of symbolic gesture doesn't come cheap. Jesus engaged in it only as the climax of a whole career of healing, teaching, feeding and simply loving people into God's new life. And his action led directly to his violent death.

One more thing. In encouraging his followers to pray with confident boldness for the present order to be replaced by God's new order ('this mountain', in context, almost certainly refers to the Temple mountain), Jesus is quite clear that there can be no personal malice or aggression involved in such work. Even at the very moment where Jesus is denouncing the system that had so deeply corrupted God's intention for Israel, his final word is the stern command to forgive. Perhaps only those who have learnt what that means will be in a position to act with Jesus' authority against the injustice and wickedness of our own day.

MARK 11.27–33

The Authority of Jesus Is Questioned

²⁷Once more they went into Jerusalem. As Jesus was walking in the Temple he was approached by the chief priests, the legal experts and the elders.

²⁸'By what right do you do these things?' they asked. 'Who gave you the right to do them?'

²⁹'I have one question for you, too,' replied Jesus, 'and if you tell me the answer I shall tell you by what right I do these things. ³⁰Was the baptism of John from heaven, or was it a human invention? What's your answer?'

³¹'Well now,' they muttered to each other, 'if we say it was from heaven, he will say, "Then why didn't you believe him?" ³²But if we say it was a human invention . . .' They were afraid of the crowd, because everyone regarded John as a prophet.

³³'We don't know,' they said to Jesus.

'Nor will I tell you,' replied Jesus, 'by what right I do these things.'

It is a busy Friday afternoon, in the middle of the city rush-hour. The traffic has built up for some time, and now there is gridlock. Nobody can move. Horns are blaring, taxi-drivers swearing. Hot and tired commuters are eager to get home for the weekend. Nobody knows what to do.

All at once, out of the shadows, steps a young man. He walks into the middle of the road, dressed in casual clothes, and begins to direct the traffic. Drivers are surprised, but they do what he indicates. The blockage unblocks itself. Traffic starts to flow again.

The young man is about to melt back into the crowd when (too late, of course) the police arrive. They have been upstaged. What they want to know from the young man is, who do you think you are? Who gave you the right to behave like this?

That's the mood of this passage. The **Temple** has been going about its business for centuries, run by the chief **priests** and their subordinate officials. Suddenly a young man has come in and taken charge. Everybody seems to be hanging on his words. Who does he think he is? What gives him the idea that he has the right to behave like this?

Mark's readers know, of course, what the answer is: Jesus is the true king, anointed (at his baptism) but not yet enthroned. It is the king who has ultimate authority over the Temple. (This was a sore point with the priests at the time; Herod the Great had exercised authority over them, and now the Romans were claiming certain rights over appointments and so on.) David planned the Temple, his son Solomon built it, and it had been intimately connected with Israel's royalty ever since. Prior to the rise of Herod, the Hasmonean royal family had acted as both kings and priests. Now Jesus has come into the city as its rightful, if unexpected, king. That's the true answer to the question.

But Jesus won't say that in so many words, or not yet. He begins, instead, a series of riddles which Mark's readers should be able to decode but which kept the authorities guessing. As so often in this **gospel**, the most important and powerful things are not spoken in straightforward language; they appear as teasing questions, to which Jesus' hearers, and now Mark's readers, have to work out the right answer.

In this case, it's not difficult. Jesus' counter-question about John's baptism isn't simply a difficult question thrown down as a challenge to shut them up. It is a coded way of answering their own question. As Mark's readers know, Jesus was anointed with the **spirit** and power at the time of John's baptism; John had pointed to him as the Coming One, the one who would act with power, and the voice at the baptism had declared to Jesus himself, in words echoing the royal psalms and prophecies, that he was the true King, God's own beloved son. He was the one for whom Israel had waited a thousand years. If the chief priests knew what was really going on at John's baptism, their question would have answered itself. What Jesus did in the Temple was simply the long-range outworking of what had happened at his baptism. In terms of the story I began with, the young man who has apparently come from nowhere to direct the traffic turns out to be the man secretly appointed to head the city's police force – though the police themselves don't know this yet.

And of course the chief priests find themselves wrong-footed. They can neither say that God sent John (Why then had they not repented? Why then had they not sought out, and followed, the one to whom John pointed?), nor that John was just a wild man following his own crazy ideas (that would have gone down like a lead balloon with the crowds thronging the Temple courtyards). They have to admit they do not know – although Mark has made it clear that their interest was not in knowing the actual truth, but in discovering an answer which would save their political face.

The question of Jesus' authority has thus come full circle. In the early chapters of the gospel this was the thing that most impressed people in

Galilee (1.22, 27; 2.10; 3.15). Now the authority with which he taught and healed was turned into explicit authority over the highest institution within Judaism. Who did he think he was? From here there is a straight line to the questions before the chief priest after Jesus' arrest (14.55–64). The incident in the Temple is the key to the unfolding drama.

If we take the New Testament seriously, it appears that those who follow Jesus, who are equipped with his spirit, are themselves given authority, under his direction, to act in his name in the world. Have we even begun to consider what this might mean? Where, to use picture language, are the traffic jams in our world waiting for people to step quietly forward and take charge? Where are the Temples that need to be challenged and warned? Where are the people who will know how to give wise answers to the question, Who do you think you are?

MARK 12.1-12

The Parable of the Tenants

[1]Jesus began to speak to them with parables.

'Once upon a time,' he began, 'there was a man who planted a vineyard. He built a fence around it, dug out a wine-press, built a watchtower, and then let it out to tenant farmers. He himself went abroad. [2]When the time came he sent a slave to the farmers to collect from them his portion of the vineyard's produce. [3]They seized him, beat him and sent him away empty-handed.

[4] 'So again he sent another slave to them. This one they beat about the head, and treated shamefully. [5]He sent another, and they killed him. He sent several more; they beat some and killed others.

[6]'He had one more to send: his beloved son. He sent him to them last of all, thinking "They will respect my son".

[7]'But the tenant farmers said to themselves, "This is the heir! Come on – let's kill him, and we'll get the inheritance!" [8]So they seized him and killed him, and threw him out of the vineyard.

[9]'So what will the vineyard owner do? He will come and destroy those tenants, and give the vineyard to others. [10]Or haven't you read the scripture which says,

There is the stone the builders refused;
now it's in place at the top of the corner.
[11]This was the way the Lord planned it;
we were astonished to see it.'

[12]They tried to find a way of arresting him, because they realized he had directed the parable against them. But they were afraid of the crowd. They left him and went away.

Shakespeare's play *The Merchant of Venice* is normally listed as a comedy. The main characters all end up with their problems resolved. But the last two or three times I have seen the play I have come away feeling that it is after all a tragedy.

Shylock, the rich Jew, is portrayed to begin with as a villain, the others sneering at him in the typical way of an older European anti-Semitism. Gradually, however, we discover his real feelings, the depth of his personal sorrows. Though Shakespeare keeps us in two minds, we find ourselves increasingly sympathizing with him, rather than with the shallow and trivial 'heroes'. By the end, Shylock has been defeated, forcibly converted to Christianity – though the main characters show little evidence of authentic Christian character – and the happy party continues as though he didn't matter. I think it is, after all, a tragedy in disguise.

The first main **parable** Jesus told in Mark's **gospel**, back in chapter 4, was a longish story about different seeds falling into different soils. It had an equally long explanation: this seed refers to this sort of people, that to that sort, and so on. It was a story which went through various stages of failure and finally arrived at success. One lot of seed failed, and another, and another, but at last there was a harvest. It was, essentially, a comedy.

Now we have a parable where we might think the same thing is going to happen, but it doesn't. One slave is sent, then another, then another, without result; but when the final messenger is sent, instead of him coming home in triumph with the fruit, he is ignominiously killed. We thought this play, too, might be a comedy, but it turned out to be a tragedy. Here is the true Jew, come to claim his father's rightful property; and the rebellious tenants, like the flippant and sneering characters in Shakespeare, kill him and throw him out.

This parable didn't need an explanation. No going back into the house to tell the **disciples** what it was all about; everybody could tell right away. This was partly because Jesus was reusing a well-known theme from the prophet Isaiah. In his fifth chapter, Isaiah writes a poem – a love-song, he calls it – about God planting Israel like a vineyard, watching over it, hoping for good grapes, and finally discovering wild grapes. Israel had gone to the bad, despite all his care. All that is left is judgment; the vineyard will be broken down, and wild animals will come and take over. It's a terrifying picture of what happens if the people of God persistently reject the purpose for which God has called them.

Jesus has taken the story and told it somewhat differently. God is still the vineyard-owner, Israel still the vineyard. But Jesus weaves into the story the idea, which many Jews of his day would have believed, that God was waiting at a distance, addressing his people through prophets, longing for the time when Israel would at last obey his call to be the people he wanted them to be. The prophets, as was well known, had mostly been rejected by the people; Israel had persisted in going its own way. Now, at last, God was sending one who was doing the job of a prophet, but who was himself more than a prophet. He was the beloved son. Mark's readers know what this means: Jesus is the **Messiah**, the **son of God**, marked out as such in his **baptism**, confirmed as such at the transfiguration. And now, as Jesus knew would happen, Israel – in the person of its highest authorities, the chief **priests** – is going to reject him too, and kill him. There is no happy ending to this story. As it stands, it is pure tragedy. The vineyard tenants overreach themselves; they realize it's either him or them. Either the son will inherit, or they will.

This parable is designed to add a further powerful layer of explanation to the developing story of what's going on now that Jesus has reached Jerusalem. His action in the **Temple**, like the actions of Jeremiah and other great prophets, was meant as a stark warning to Israel, but the warning would not be heeded. Instead, faced with someone behaving with an authority which has the word 'royal' stamped all over it, the authorities must either submit or do away with him.

Instead of an explanation, or a 'happy ending', Jesus adds a scriptural quotation, from the same psalm (118) that the excited worshippers were using when singing their hosannas a few days before (11.9). This psalm, well known from many Jewish celebrations, is about going up to Jerusalem to worship in the Temple, in the presence of the Lord. It mentions the fact that part of the glory of the Temple architecture is the stone which wouldn't fit any other part of the building but which is just what's needed for the capstone, the stone at the very summit of a corner or an arch.

That's the image Jesus needs for his point: what he has come to do, and to be, can't be fitted into a different sort of building, and indeed will be rejected by 'builders' who have their own interests in mind (in this case, the chief priests, determined to hang on to power and prestige). No wonder they were now actively attempting to do away with him. Mark uses this story as a further way of leading us on from Jesus' action in the Temple to his arrest, trial and death.

Those who follow Jesus often have to speak and act in ways which the surrounding culture won't understand and won't like. The church has a prophetic mission to the wider world, because the God who planted Israel as a vineyard is the creator God, by whom in fact the whole world was designed as a fruitful garden. Often those who have exercised a prophetic vocation have suffered and died for their pains. Those in whom the **spirit** of the Beloved Son has come to live can, after all, expect no less. Living as a Christian is not guaranteed to be like being a character in a comedy; often it feels more like a tragedy. But God's promise remains: when builders reject a stone, sometimes that is because it's designed to be the capstone.

MARK 12.13–17

On Paying Taxes to Caesar

¹³They sent some Pharisees to Jesus, and some Herodians, to try to trick him into saying the wrong thing.

¹⁴'Teacher,' they said, 'we know you are a man of integrity; you don't regard anybody as special. You don't bother about the outward show people put up; you teach God's way truly.

'Well then: is it lawful to give tribute to Caesar or not? Should we pay it, or shouldn't we?'

¹⁵He knew the game they were playing. 'Why are you trying to trap me?' he said. 'Bring me a tribute-coin; let me look at it.'

¹⁶They brought one to him.

'This image,' he asked, 'whose is it? And whose is this super-scription?'

'Caesar's,' they replied.

¹⁷'Well then,' said Jesus, 'give Caesar back what belongs to Caesar – and give God back what belongs to God!'

They were astonished at him.

I have on my desk one of the tribute-pennies from the reign of Tiberius Caesar. It is almost certainly the type that features in this story. It's about the size of my thumbnail, but you can make out the writing quite clearly – and the imperial head of Tiberius. You don't have to look at it for too long to see that this conversation wasn't simply about taxation policy.

That was itself bad enough, though. Paying taxes to Rome was a running sore to devout Jews. It wasn't only the cost, though for many that would be serious (they would also pay local taxes, **Temple** taxes and, for those in Galilee, taxes to Herod as well). It was what the tax represented. The Jews celebrated the fact that they were God's free people, but they agonized over the fact that it wasn't true. Ever since the Babylonian invasion half a millennium before, they had been ruled by others. Under the Hasmoneans, in the period roughly 163 BC to 63 BC, they were semi-independent; but since then Rome had taken over. And where Rome ruled, Rome taxed, and Rome was hated for it.

But the coin itself went further. Jews were forbidden to make carved images. They debated whether this included images of plants and flowers, but images of human beings were out of the question; and here is

Tiberius, staring coldly out at the world from every small Roman coin. And the writing! Around the head the words say, in Latin: 'Augustus Tiberius, son of the divine Augustus'. On the other side, it says: 'High Priest' (the Emperors were routinely high priests of the main Roman cult). 'Son of a god'; 'high priest' – if the Romans had gone out of their way to be offensive to the Jews, they could hardly have done it better. And when Jesus, who Mark's readers now know to be the true king, the son of God, is standing there in the Temple ruled by the Jewish chief **priest**, the irony could hardly be sharper.

So it was (what we would call) a religious question, not simply a political or social one, that faced Jesus. Some devout Jews were so shocked by this type of coin that they would try never to touch or use one (they could use Jewish coins instead), or even perhaps to look at one. Jesus, by asking his questioners to produce a coin, isn't exactly saying that he wouldn't normally touch the stuff himself, but he is at least embarrassing them by making them find one for him to look at.

Here, as in 3.6, the **Pharisees** and **Herodians** are acting together. Their trap is clear. They are trying to force Jesus either to support the paying of taxes to Rome, thus alienating the crowds, or to denounce the tax, in which case they could tell the governor, Pontius Pilate, that Jesus was guilty of a straightforward capital charge, namely inciting revolt. But they reckoned without Jesus' brilliant response.

To understand what he meant, a word about the background. Two hundred years earlier, one of the slogans of the Maccabean revolt against the Syrians had been 'pay back the **Gentiles** what they deserve – and obey the commands of the law!' (1 Maccabees 2.68). This put into a crisp double command the Jewish duty to the Gentiles and to God. What the first half meant was: give as good as you get. In other words, vengeance: repayment in kind for the violence the Gentiles have used.

Now a very different revolt is under way. Jesus had opposed violent revolution, and his **kingdom**-movement was attacking a deeper and more far-reaching evil than simply pagan domination. He is not going to be drawn into the sterile should-we/shouldn't-we debate. Nor is he giving a timeless ethical ruling which settles once for all the relationship between church and state – though some have mistakenly tried to build such a theory on this very narrow foundation. He is hitting the ball back over the net at twice the speed it came. We need to separate out three different things he's doing, each of which took them completely by surprise.

First, 'give Caesar what belongs to Caesar' can be taken, of course, as a way of saying 'yes, pay the tax', but without the sting of 'yes, submit to the Romans as your masters'. The fact that Jesus has drawn attention to the blasphemous image and writing gives his command the flavour of 'send this filthy stuff back where it came from!' It is contemptuous, without opening Jesus to the charge of sedition.

Second, though, it nicely echoes the Maccabean slogan. 'Give the pagans what they deserve'; or, if you like, 'pay the Gentiles back in their own coin'. It could be taken as a coded revolutionary slogan; after all, the kingdom of God is all about the one true God becoming king of the world, demoting the petty princelings who style themselves sons of God, high priests, or whatever. Yet again, in context, it doesn't leave Jesus open to a direct charge. His words are, after all, literally saying, 'yes, pay the tax'.

Third, the command to give God what belongs to God opens all kinds of further questions. Did he also mean that, because humans bear God's image, all humans owe themselves, their very lives, to God, and should give those lives back, as one might give a coin back to Caesar? Did he mean, standing there in the Temple courtyards, that the sacrifical system, which was supposed to be the way of giving God his due, needed to be superceded by a more complete worship? Did he mean – against the normal revolutionaries – that if you really gave your whole self to God you would discover that using violence to fight violence, using evil to fight evil, simply wouldn't do? I think he probably meant to hint at all of that, and perhaps even more.

What he didn't mean – despite many attempts to squash his words into this shape – was that you could divide human life, and the world, into two segments (the 'religious' part and the 'political' or 'social' part). That's a much later idea, which gained ground only in the eighteenth century. It has had a huge influence on the modern world, but is increasingly being seen today as at best inadequate and at worst dangerous. It would prevent, for instance, any Christian critique of public policy, including economic policy, which is sometimes sorely needed in our world. Jewish thought, and Christian thought as it emerged within Judaism, have always seen the entire world and everything in it as created by the one God. All aspects of it fall under his sovereign and saving rule.

To repeat, then: this passage isn't designed as a full-scale statement of Christian truth on 'religion and society' or 'church and state'. It was a quick and sharp-edged quip for a particular occasion. But what Jesus said will bear a lot of thinking through and working out. The kingdom of God goes beyond the sterile either/or questions which crafty people (often with flattery, as here) like to pose. God grant us wisdom to see to the heart of things, and to give ourselves wholly to our true God and King.

MARK 12.18-27

Marriage and the Resurrection

[18]Some Sadducees approached Jesus (Sadducees, by the way, deny the resurrection).

[19]'Teacher,' they said, 'Moses wrote for us that "If a man's brother dies, and leaves a wife but no child, the brother should take the wife and raise up descendants for his brother." [20]Well now: there were once seven brothers. The first married a wife, and died without children. [21]The second married the widow, and died without children. The third did so as well, [22]and so did all seven, still without leaving children. Finally the woman died too. [23]So: when they rise again in the resurrection, whose wife will she be? All seven had her, after all.'

[24]'Where you're going wrong,' replied Jesus, 'is that you don't know the scriptures, or God's power. [25]When people rise from the dead, they don't marry, nor do people give them in marriage. They are like angels in heaven.

[26]'However, to show that the dead are indeed to be raised, surely you've read in the book of Moses, in the passage about the bush, what God says to Moses? "I am Abraham's God, Isaac's God and Jacob's God"? [27]He isn't the God of the dead, but of the living. You are completely mistaken.'

After the death of Princess Diana in 1997, 'books of remembrance' were placed in public buildings throughout Britain, and indeed in many other parts of the world, particularly in churches and cathedrals, so that people could sign their names as a tangible mark of their sorrow. Hundreds of thousands did so.

I read some of the contributions in the books in Lichfield Cathedral, where I worked at the time. I was struck by the remarkable range of beliefs about what happens after death. Several people spoke of Diana having become a star in the sky. Some wrote about God wanting her company and so taking her from us sooner than we'd expected. Again and again people wrote that she'd been an angel in disguise, and had now gone back to being a regular angel again – or that, having showed she was clearly angelic material, she had now graduated to being a proper one.

There is no warrant for any of this in the Bible, so one must assume it's the sort of thing that occurs to people naturally, in a kind of folk-religion, when they try to come to terms with the sense of loss that millions felt when Diana died. But the present passage, Jesus' discussion with the **Sadducees**, is as close as you get to the suggestion of humans becoming angels.

It doesn't actually mean that. This is a complex and difficult question, and we have to take it step by step if we're to see both what was at stake for Jesus and his opponents and what we can learn for ourselves.

The Sadducees, the Jewish priestly aristocracy, didn't believe in the **resurrection**. This wasn't because (as people sometimes imagine) they held 'liberal' beliefs. Far from it. They were the conservatives, politically and theologically. They regarded resurrection as a dangerous new idea. They denied that it was taught in the earliest parts of the Bible, the 'five books of Moses' (from Genesis to Deuteronomy, known as the Pentateuch), the part they regarded as truly authoritative. As far as they could see, it depended on very late, and (to them) dubious, books like Daniel – and on the speculations of groups like the **Pharisees**. (The Pharisees were influential among ordinary Jews, so it's likely that most Jews believed in resurrection as well.)

In particular, the Sadducees saw belief in resurrection as politically risky. It had become popular particularly during the revolutionary movements of the second century BC, as a way of affirming that the martyrs had a glorious future awaiting them, not immediately after death, but in the eventual resurrection when they would be given new bodies. This belief was based on the fundamental idea of God as the maker, and therefore the remaker, of the world. People who believe that God is going to recreate the whole world, including Israel, and even including their own dead bodies, are much more likely to do daring and risky things. Wealthy ruling classes prefer people not to think thoughts like that.

And now here was Jesus, doing and saying things which made it look as if he was mounting a one-man revolutionary movement, albeit with a difference. The Sadducees wanted to see whether he was on the same side as the dangerous, revolutionary Pharisees.

And the answer was: certainly, but again with an important difference. The Sadducees tell Jesus a (presumably hypothetical) story which depends on an ancient Jewish law (Deuteronomy 25.5–10 with Genesis 38.8). If a man dies married but childless, his younger brother is commanded to marry his widow, and count the children as his brother's, thus keeping up the family line and inheritance. In the story, this happens seven times to one woman. The Sadducees hold this up as evidence that resurrection is ridiculous; if all come back to life, whose wife will the woman be?

Jesus boldly rebukes them: clearly, he says, they don't know their Bibles, nor yet how powerful God is! He then offers a double argument against their objection.

His first answer is that resurrection does not mean mere resuscitation, coming back into exactly the same sort of physical life as before, but *transformation*, with a different sort of bodily life.

People are easily confused here. I frequently hear 'resurrection' used to mean simply 'life after death'; and since many imagine life after death taking place in a disembodied state called '**heaven**', where (among other things) angels may be found, they understand a passage like this to be saying: after death you will go to heaven, and be a disembodied spirit like an angel – and that will be 'resurrection'.

That is precisely what this passage, and the New Testament teaching about resurrection in general, does *not* mean. The whole point of the Jewish doctrine of resurrection was that it meant a new embodied life, a life that would be given at some future date, *after* whatever sort of 'life after death' God's people were enjoying at the present. Saying that the resurrected dead will be 'like angels in heaven' does *not* mean that they will be like them in all respects, including disembodiment. They are like the angels in this respect only: that they will not marry. They are beyond death; they will not need to propagate the species or continue the family (which was the point of the law about the brother marrying the widow); they will have gone into a new mode of bodily life in which such things are irrelevant. (This raises questions about the kind of relationships that will be enjoyed in the resurrection world, but this would take us off track at the moment.)

That is Jesus' first point: resurrection, which he affirms, will not simply reproduce every aspect of our present humanity. It will be a recognizable and re-embodied human existence; but a great change will have taken place as well, whose precise nature we can at present only guess at.

Second, Jesus finds a passage at the heart of the Pentateuch, acknowledged by Sadducees as authoritative, which, he claims, demonstrates that the dead will indeed be raised. When God meets Moses at the burning bush, he introduces himself as Abraham's God, Isaac's God and Jacob's God. If this is how God chooses to reveal himself, argues Jesus, it cannot be the case that the patriarchs are dead and gone for ever.

This again can be misunderstood. Jesus is not simply saying that Abraham, Isaac and Jacob are still alive in the presence of God, and that their present afterlife is what is meant by 'resurrection'. Everybody knew that Abraham, Isaac and Jacob had *not* yet been raised from the dead. The point is precisely that they are 'dead' at present, but that since God desires to be known as their God he must be intending to raise them from death in the future.

'Resurrection', in other words, is not another, somewhat nicer, description of 'being dead'. It is the reversal of death, the gift of a new body to enjoy life in God's new world. We should beware of regarding death itself, the dissolution and decay of the physical body, as anything other than an enemy. That's the first step to denying the goodness of

God's creation. Believing in the resurrection doesn't just offer the best hope of all for our ultimate future; it gives to the present created world its full value. What God has made, he will remake.

MARK 12.28–34

The Most Important Commandment

[28]One of the legal experts came up, and overheard the discussion. Realizing that Jesus had given a splendid answer, he put a question of his own.

'Which commandment', he asked, 'is the first one of all?'

[29]'The first one', replied Jesus, 'is this: "Listen, Israel: the Lord your God, the Lord is one; [30]and you shall love the Lord your God with all your heart, and with all your soul, and with all your understanding, and with all your strength." [31]And this is the second one: "You shall love your neighbour as yourself." No other commandment is greater than these ones.'

[32]'Well said, Teacher', answered the lawyer. 'You are right in saying that "he is one and that there is no other beside him", [33]and that "to love him with all the heart, and with all the intelligence, and with all the strength" and "to love one's neighbour as oneself" is worth far more than all burnt offerings and sacrifices.'

[34]Jesus saw that his answer came out of deep understanding.

'You are not far from God's kingdom', he said to him.

After that, nobody dared put any more questions to him.

If the house is on fire, what will you grab as you escape?

Your children, of course, if they can't walk themselves.

Your wallet. Your computer. Your passport and personal documents.

A precious photograph. The wristwatch your grandfather gave you. A stack of letters from someone you love dearly.

You look on from a safe distance as everything else is burnt to ashes. You realize the significance of what you've just done. You have made some important choices. These things are more valuable to you than tables and chairs, china and glass, clothes, books, hi-fi equipment, and all the thousand other things that find a place in a home. You have discovered where your priorities really lie.

The question the lawyer asked Jesus was like that. Faced with the whole volume of Jewish law, which commandment really matters? Which one will you grasp on to in a moment of crisis? And what is the significance of that choice? What are you saying about the others?

This is about far more than 'how to construct a code of personal ethics', but let's take that aspect of it first. The Jewish law begins with worship, with the love of God, because if it's true that we're made in God's image we will find our fullest meaning, our true selves, the more we learn to love and worship the one we are designed to reflect. No half measures: heart, soul, mind and strength – that is, every aspect of human life – is to be poured out gladly in worship of the one true God. Whatever we do, we are to do for him. If we truly lived like that for a single day, God's **kingdom** would have come on earth as it is in **heaven**. And – this is the point – Jesus seems to think that through his kingdom-work this commandment is now within our reach.

Nor does Jesus stop there. The lawyer hasn't asked him about his second choice, but it's so important to his whole mission that he adds it anyway. 'Love your neighbour as yourself'; this doesn't mean loving others *instead of* ourselves, but showing to all people the same respect and care that we show to ourselves. Elsewhere in the **gospel** stories (e.g. Luke 10) this is developed and applied in more detail. Again, if people lived by this rule, most of the world's greatest problems would be solved overnight. Once more, Jesus implies that his kingdom-work will bring this commandment within reach. He really expects his followers to live it out, because he believes that God is now fulfilling his ancient promise to renew people's hearts. That's where writers like Paul take up the story.

Jesus' answer to the **scribe's** question carries another important implication. His 'first commandment' is a version of the central Jewish prayer, the *Shema* ('Shema' means 'listen', as in 'Listen, Israel . . .'). Devout Jews, from Jesus' day to our own, pray this prayer regularly every day. Jesus is claiming nothing less than this: that through his work, his teaching, and the things he has come to Jerusalem to achieve, the central prayer and hope of Judaism is being fulfilled. This isn't designed as a 'new religion', a way of life somehow different from what pious Jews sought after. This is the fulfilment of the law and the prophets.

But this in turn leads to the clear implication, which is hugely important for what Mark is telling us about Jesus in Jerusalem. The lawyer, musing on Jesus' answer, draws out a meaning which Jesus hadn't said out loud but which was certainly there. If these commandments are the primary ones; if this is what worshipping, loving and serving God is all about, then all that the **Temple** stands for, the daily, weekly and annual round of **sacrifices** and offerings, is virtually unnecessary. When a crisis comes, loving God and one's neighbour still matters; sacrifices don't.

The lawyer has grasped, and agreed with, Jesus' underlying meaning. This is partly why Jesus did what he did in the Temple. He was offering a fulfilment of Judaism which would make the Temple itself out of date. No wonder Jesus commends him with the breathtaking words: 'You are not far from God's kingdom.'

At one level, then, this passage enables us to understand more fully what Jesus thought his work was all about, and how his overall mission was bound to challenge the centrality of the Temple – a highly controversial, not to say dangerous, thing to suggest. Jesus really did believe that through his kingdom-mission Israel's God would enable people to worship and love him, and to love one another, in a new way, the way promised in the prophets, the way that stemmed from renewed hearts and lives.

At another level, this comes as a considerable challenge to all contemporary Christians. Would anyone looking at us – our churches, our lives, the societies that claim in some sense to be 'Christian' – ever have guessed that the man we claim to follow saw his followers as being people like this? Or to put it another way: when the crisis comes, what remains solid in your life and the life of your community? Wholehearted love of God and neighbour? Or the mad scramble of everyone trying to save their own skins?

MARK 12.35–44

David's Son and the Widow's Mite

[35]By way of response to it all, Jesus began to teach in the Temple.

'Why do the experts say', he asked, 'that the Messiah is the son of David? [36]David himself, inspired by the holy spirit, said:

> The Lord said to my Lord:
> sit at my right hand,
> until I place your enemies
> right underneath your feet.

[37]'David himself calls him "Lord"; how then can he be his son?'

The whole crowd listened to him with delight.

[38]During his teaching, he said, 'Beware of the lawyers! They like to walk about in long robes, and to be greeted in the marketplaces. [39]They take the chief seats in the synagogue, and the best places at dinner parties. [40]They devour the property of widows, and make long prayers without meaning them. They will receive all the more condemnation.'

[41]As he sat opposite the Temple treasury, he watched the crowd putting money into the alms boxes. Lots of rich people put in substantial amounts. [42]Then there came a single poor widow, who put in two tiny coins, together worth a single penny.

[43]Jesus called his disciples.

'I'm telling you the truth', he said. 'This poor widow just put more into the treasury than everybody else. [44]You see, all the others were

126

contributing out of their wealth; but she put in everything she had, out of her poverty. It was her whole livelihood.'

The final scene in the Temple courtyards takes us to a dense and difficult riddle which Jesus himself puts to his hearers (and which they cannot answer), and to a small but striking incident by the Temple treasury. The riddle and the incident are, at one level, completely different, but as we shall see, at a deeper level, they belong together powerfully.

We take the riddle first – the question about David's Lord and **David's son**. The question of **messiahship** in general, and Jesus' messiahship in particular, has been swirling around Mark's **gospel** most of the time, and particularly since chapter 8. Now Jesus himself addresses it head on.

Who exactly will the Messiah be? What can we say about him? The question belongs here in Mark not least because, as we have seen, what Jesus had done in the Temple had raised the question, 'Who did he think he was?' and the implied answer was 'The Messiah, the one who has authority over the Temple'. Several of the subsequent discussions – the question about **John the Baptist**, the **parable** about the wicked tenant farmers, and the question about tribute to Caesar – all relate to this in various ways, as we have seen.

Jesus appears to challenge the normal Jewish assumption, based on long scriptural tradition including Psalm 2, Psalm 89, and particularly 2 Samuel 7, that the great coming king would be born from the family of David. It's impossible, though, to think that either Jesus or Mark was denying that the Messiah would be a descendent of David. The whole early church was clear that he was indeed from that family (e.g. Romans 1.3; Matthew 1.17; Luke 2.27, 32). What we find, instead, is a challenge to the idea that the Messiah will be *simply* a king from David's line. He will be David's Lord *as well as* David's son.

To make this point, Jesus uses Psalm 110, which became very important in the early church as a way of talking about Jesus' ascension and lordship over the world. He assumes that it's written by David himself, and discovers that it refers to someone David calls 'my Lord' – someone, in other words, who is apparently senior to David, not junior as a descendent would be. Who can this be? We should be used by now to Jesus saying things which point beyond themselves, telling riddles which he doesn't totally explain, pointing towards a larger truth which he is eager to communicate but which cannot be spoken, or not at the time, in straightforward language.

What he appears to be saying is that when you understand messiahship in terms of this psalm, you find that the Messiah – who will, of course, be a descendent of David – will also be one whom David will rightly call Lord. He is raising the corner of the curtain that hides the biggest secret of all. Not only is he the Messiah, coming with royal authority to Jerusalem and the Temple. Not only is he going to die to bring about the true **kingdom** (though the **disciples** haven't understood this yet). He is doing all of this not simply as David's son but as David's Lord.

Mark has not given us, yet, other ways of saying this; but it didn't take the early church long to find that some of the ways of talking about the Messiah – 'son of God', for instance – could be filled with new meaning, capable of expressing the astonishing and revolutionary belief that Jesus was not just speaking about Israel's God acting decisively to establish the kingdom. He believed he was *embodying* Israel's God doing all this. Messiahship was, so to speak, a suit of clothes designed for God's own use. And Jesus saw this as foreshadowed in the Psalms themselves.

The psalm continues, beyond the verse that Jesus has quoted, to speak of this coming King or Lord as a **priest** – and a priest for ever. This passage is therefore pointing towards something which again has been bubbling up under the surface ever since Jesus arrived in Jerusalem, and will come to its head when Jesus confronts Caiaphas in chapter 14. Jesus is claiming authority over the Temple – claiming, indeed, the right to declare God's judgment on it – not simply as a prophet, but as the King; not simply as the King, but as the true priest; not simply as the priest-King, but as the living embodiment of Israel's God. This is complex, and perhaps difficult for us to grasp all at once. But these are the themes that make sense of the whole of Mark's gospel, and in a measure of Jesus himself.

The chapter ends with a brief warning against the pomp and pretension of some of the **legal experts**. They give themselves airs, and have a great reputation for piety, but are only interested in lining their pockets. The world has not changed, it seems. Not only lawyers, but also politicians and other leaders in the civic world, are again and again discovered to be putting on a show to gain favour while underneath they are after money. What a contrast: when David's Lord became David's son, he did not use this as a means of gaining popularity or wealth, but gave up his life.

Giving up one's life, indeed, is the theme of the final short scene, where Jesus contrasts the rich people who can afford to give plenty to the Temple treasury, and make sure others see that they're doing it, with the poor widow who has given, literally, 'her whole life', the two copper coins which were all she had to live on that day. Her **sacrifice**, though small, was total. Once again, when we read this story in the light of Jesus' riddle about David's Lord and David's son we discover a strange affinity. One might have thought she was 'merely' putting in two copper coins, but in fact she was putting in everything she had. One might have thought the Messiah was 'merely' David's son – a human king among other human kings. But in fact, in the Messiah, Israel's God has given himself totally, given all that he had and was.

At the end of this chapter, we are left on tiptoe with expectation. Jesus has declared God's judgment on the Temple, and has claimed the highest possible authority for doing so. At the same time, he must know that what he has done is bound to lead, not just to interrogation and arguments in the Temple courtyards, but to arrest, trial and death. What will happen to the Temple? What will happen to Jesus? And how are these two related? It is these themes which the following chapters will now explore.

MARK 13.1–13

Signs of the End

[1]As they were going out of the Temple, one of Jesus' disciples said to him, 'Teacher! Look at these huge stones, and these huge buildings!'

[2]'You see these enormous buildings?' said Jesus. 'There will not be one single stone left on top of another. They will all be torn down.'

[3]Peter, James, John and Andrew approached him privately as he was sitting on the Mount of Olives opposite the Temple.

[4]'Tell us', they asked. 'When will these things happen? What will be the sign that these things are about to be completed?'

[5]'Take care that nobody deceives you', Jesus began to say to them. [6]'Plenty of people will come in my name, saying "I'm the one!", and they will lead plenty astray. [7]But whenever you hear about wars, and rumours of wars, don't be disturbed. These things have to happen, but it doesn't mean the end is here. [8]One nation will rise up against another; one kingdom will rise up against another. There will be earthquakes in various places, and famines too. These are the first pains of childbirth.

[9]'But watch out for yourselves. They will hand you over to courts, they will beat you in synagogues; you will stand before rulers and kings because of me, as a witness against them. [10]And the message of the kingdom must first be announced to all the nations. [11]And when they put you on trial and hand you over, don't work out beforehand what you are going to say, but say whatever is given you at that moment. It won't be you speaking, you see, but the holy spirit.

[12]'One brother will hand over another to death. Fathers will hand over children. Children will rebel against parents and have them put to death. [13]And you will be hated by everyone because of my name. But the one who is patient through to the end – that one will be saved.'

The place to start to understand this passage is in the middle, at verse 8: 'These are the first pains of childbirth.'

Jesus' **disciples** would have known more about birth pangs than most modern men. I watched three of my four children being born, but that's the limit of my first-hand experience of such matters. In the ordinary world of the ancient Middle East, and many other places to this day, a good deal of intimate family life goes on in a semi-public world. Everyone knows everyone else's business; children grow up knowing from direct observation what today's children learn from television; and the way babies are born – and the agonies it takes for a woman to give birth – are part of the common knowledge of everyday life.

The picture of birth pangs had been used for centuries by Jews as they reflected on the way in which, as they believed, their God was intending to bring to birth his new world, his new creation, the **age to come** in which justice and peace, mercy and truth would at last flourish. From the great prophets onwards they spoke of the world going through the labour-pains that would herald the birth of the new day. Many writers from Jesus' time whose works have come down to us spoke of the Jewish hope in this fashion. Since, as we have already seen, Jesus believed that his **kingdom**-mission, his **message**, was the divinely appointed means of bringing this new world to birth, we shouldn't be surprised that he sometimes spoke of it in this way as well.

The whole chapter is introduced by a double question about the **Temple**. Herod's Temple, still incomplete in Jesus' day, had the reputation of being the most beautiful building in the whole world, and was certainly the largest and most imposing structure for hundreds of miles in any direction. Jesus solemnly predicts that the whole thing will be demolished – putting into words the message he had acted out when he stopped the sacrificial system from functioning earlier in the week. The **disciples** are astonished. They, after all, have just said how impressed they are at the sight of the place. And they ask, not unnaturally, when these things are going to take place.

It's important to remind ourselves of that question, because many people have read Mark 13 (and its parallels in Matthew and Luke) as a chapter mainly about 'the end of the world', which it certainly isn't. As we shall see in the next two sections, there are passages where Jesus draws on the cosmic language of scripture to talk about the future, giving rise to the belief that the whole chapter is about the large-scale future of the cosmos. But as the present section indicates, the main apparent subject is nothing so grandiose, certainly not on the surface. The main subject remains the fate of the Temple in Jerusalem – and of Jesus' followers in the time leading up to the Temple's demise.

Verses 3–13, in fact, are a preparation for the answer to the question about the Temple. They assume for the moment that there is going to be a great catastrophe which will cause the Temple to be destroyed, and that in the run-up to this catastrophe Jesus' followers will be at grave risk. In line with his warnings about his own death, Jesus clearly envisages a time when he will no longer be there in person to lead them and encourage them. They will face what he has faced and what he will shortly face – trials, beatings, the threat of death – and all because of their allegiance to him. He sees them as a group continuing, after he has gone, to be defined as his followers. And he sees that they will suffer for it.

However, they are not to assume that as soon as they hear a rumour of a great war starting up somewhere (we need to remind ourselves that without electronic media people often wouldn't hear about a war until months or even years after it had happened, and reports would often be highly garbled) that means that Jerusalem is about to fall. Nor will an earthquake in one place necessarily mean that another one is about to strike the holy city. One of the arts that Jesus' followers must learn after his departure is patience. False teachers, frightening rumours and natural disasters will all tempt them to panic. They must resist the temptation. 'These are the first pains of childbirth.'

But they are at least the beginnings. The world is going to be plunged into convulsions, Jesus says; and his followers, called like him to live at the place where the purposes of God and the pain of the world cross paths with each other, will find themselves caught up in those convulsions. Special help will be given them, not least when they are on trial (the command not to consider ahead of time what to say was not meant to apply to preachers (!), but to those on trial for treason because of belonging to Jesus). The warning that they would be 'hated by all people' was dramatically fulfilled a generation later when, in Rome itself, the Christians were viciously persecuted by Nero, being regarded (as one Roman historian put it) as 'notoriously depraved', and as holding to a 'deadly superstition'. The history of the early church, in fact, shows that all these warnings were needed.

The particular final crisis came and went in AD 70, as we shall see in the next section. But Jesus' warnings to his followers are to be taken very seriously by all who are called to work for the kingdom today. Many Christians today face persecution every bit as severe as that which the early church suffered; and those Christians who don't face persecution often face the opposite temptation, to stagnate, to become cynical, to suppose that nothing much is happening, that the kingdom of God is just a pious dream.

Jesus told us we would need patience to hold on and see the thing through. We should not be surprised if we are called, through whatever circumstances, to practise that virtue – however unfashionable it may be in our hurried and anxious world.

MARK 13.14–27

Further Signs of the End

[14]'However,' Jesus continued, 'when you see "the desolating abomination" set up where it ought not to be' (let the reader understand) 'then those who are in Judaea should run away to the mountains. [15]If you're on the house-top, don't go down, and don't go in to get anything from the house. [16]If you're out in the countryside, don't turn back again to pick up your cloak.

[17]'It will be a terrible time for pregnant and nursing mothers. [18]Pray that it won't happen in winter. [19]Yes, those days will bring trouble like nothing that's ever happened from the beginning of creation, which God created, until now, or ever will again. [20]In fact, if the Lord had not shortened the days, no one would be rescued. But for the sake of his chosen ones, those whom he appointed, he shortened the days.

[21]'So at that time, if someone says to you, "Look – here is the Messiah!" or, "Look – there he is!", don't believe them; [22]because false messiahs and false prophets will arise, and will perform signs and portents to lead astray even God's chosen ones, if that were possible. [23]But you must be on your guard. I've told you everything ahead of time.

[24]'But in those days, after that suffering,

The sun will be dark as night
and the moon will not give its light;
[25]the stars will fall from heaven
and the powers in heaven will shake.

[26]'Then they will see "the son of man coming on clouds with great power and glory". [27]And then he will dispatch his messengers, and will gather in his chosen ones from the four winds, from the ends of earth to the ends of heaven.'

When Albert Schweitzer, the great medical missionary, theologian and musician of the early twentieth century, was a young man, he studied the organ in Paris under Charles Marie Widor. One day in 1899 Widor confessed to Schweitzer that he couldn't understand Bach's chorale preludes. The mood of the music kept shifting unpredictably.

'Naturally,' replied the young Schweitzer, 'many things in the chorales must seem obscure to you, because they can only be explained by the texts that go with them.'

Schweitzer was right. Widor hadn't known that the chorale preludes were designed to go with particular Lutheran hymns. Once you understood the texts behind the music, the music itself became clear. We meet the same problem in the middle of Mark 13. Mark begins with something so obscure that he adds a note – 'let the reader understand!' – which shows that he realized that not all readers *would* understand. Throughout, you can only make sense of what's going on if you know, as it were, the texts behind the music – in other words, the scriptural echoes and allusions that make up a good deal of the passage.

Before we begin to unravel these texts and echoes, we must remind ourselves that the chapter began with questions about the fall of the **Temple**. So far, in verses 5–13, Jesus has warned his followers not to panic at the various things that will happen in the coming days. Even when put on trial for their lives, they are not to assume this means that the Temple is at last to face its doom. The end is not yet.

But now in verse 14 the mood changes. Up until this point they are to stand firm; now, at a given signal, they are to take to their heels. Something will happen that will tell them it's time to run – to run without looking back, without picking up belongings, to flee so quickly that those with young children will have difficulty keeping up. That's the moment when a disaster is coming upon Jerusalem that will make all the previous woes of the world, and all that will ever be, look tame by comparison.

What is Jesus talking about? And what is the sign?

He is talking about the moment when foreign armies will take over the Temple. We, with historical hindsight, know that this happened in AD 70. We can read, in the historian Josephus, the terrible tale of the siege of Jerusalem; how people starved, ate their own babies to stay alive, fought each other both for scraps of dirty food and for small-scale political gains in the factional fighting, more Jews being killed by other Jews than by the invading Romans. Jesus clearly wanted his followers to get out and run. There was no place for misguided national loyalty, for staying to the bitter end of that appalling time.

The sign is 'the desolating abomination': an appalling object or person whose presence signifies imminent destruction. The text behind this is Daniel 11.31 and 12.11, which speaks of pagan armies invading Jerusalem, stopping the regular **sacrifices** in the Temple, and setting up instead 'a desolating abomination'. Jesus doesn't seem to know what precisely this might be, but it sounds like a pagan idol, an image to another god in place of the one true God, set up in the middle of the Temple. This will be the sign that it's time, not to stay and be patient, but to get out and run.

It will also be a time when deceivers will run riot and lead many astray. Again, Josephus tells us of many would-be messiahs, many prophets, during the Roman–Jewish war of AD 66–70. They were offering rescue, trying to gain a following, promising signs and wonders. They all came to nothing.

But the climax of it all – the destruction of the Temple itself – can only be spoken of through prophetic words, summoning up the image of cosmic catastrophe. Consider what was happening. In the year AD 69 one Roman emperor succeeded another – four in all, Nero, Otho, Vitellius, Vespasian – each time with violence, murder and civil war. And as Vespasian made his way to Rome to receive the crown, his adopted son Titus entered Jerusalem, burnt the Temple, destroyed the city and crucified thousands of Jews.

What language could one use to describe such a year? It won't do simply to list the events, ghastly though they are. The only way of doing justice to such a time is in prophetic language, used originally (in Isaiah 13.10 and 34.4) to describe the fall of Babylon and Edom: the language of a dark sun and a quenched moon, of stars falling from the sky.

This is not a prediction of 'the end of the world', though many in Jerusalem at the time must have wished it was. Had it been the end of the world, what would have been the point of running away so frantically? No; but it was the end of *their* world, the close of the way of life that had failed, by the combination of injustice towards those inside and revolutionary violence towards those outside, to obey God's call to be the light of the world.

By the same token, the fall of the Temple would be the sure sign that God had vindicated Jesus as the true representative of his people. As a prophet, Jesus had predicted its destruction. As **Messiah**, he had solemnly enacted it. He had hinted at an even stronger reason: the Messiah was identified with David's Lord, who would sit at God's right hand until those who had opposed him were defeated. Now he brings in the final devastating biblical text: Daniel 7.13. 'They will see "the **son of man** coming on clouds with great power and glory".'

In Daniel 7 itself, this is not about the *return* of 'the son of man', but about his 'coming' *to* God after suffering. It is about triumph and vindication, and about simultaneous judgment falling on the system that has opposed God's call and God's **gospel**; and about Israel's representative sitting down, as David's Lord does in Psalm 110, at God's right hand. From Jesus' point of view, in other words, it concerns that vindication of his entire programme and mission which God will bring to pass, after his own death, with the destruction of the Temple that has come to symbolize all that his gospel opposes. From Mark's point of view, it is about the complete vindication of Jesus: his **resurrection**, his ascension, and the outworking of his prophecies against the Temple as sealing the whole process.

What else must happen during those times? The establishment of a mission that, unlike Jesus' own, will now reach out to the **Gentile** world with the news that the creator God, Israel's God, has made a way of salvation for all – has done through Jesus what the Temple should have stood for but had instead opposed. Jesus' messengers will go out to the whole world, where God's chosen ones (a typically Jewish way of describing those who would come to believe the gospel) await the good news.

It is vital to read this passage as containing Jesus' prophecies, fulfilled 40 years later, against the Temple. That is what Mark, at least, believes this whole chapter is about. But we should not suppose that there are therefore no messages for our own day, nearly 2,000 years later. Where human societies and institutions set themselves up against the gospel and its standards, producing arrogant and dehumanizing structures, deep injustices and radical oppression, there may once more be a place for prophets to denounce and to warn, and for God's people to get out and run. If we do not find ourselves in that position, we should be grateful; but we should remember to pray for those, even today, who do.

MARK 13.28–37

Watching for the Son of Man

²⁸'Learn this lesson from the fig tree. When its branch becomes soft and sprouts leaves, you know that summer is near. ²⁹In the same way, when you see these things happen, you should know that it is near, right at the gates. ³⁰I'm telling you the truth: this generation won't disappear until all of this has happened. ³¹Heaven and earth will disappear, but my words won't disappear.

³²'No one knows, though, the day or the hour. The angels in heaven don't know it; nor does the son; only the father.

³³'Keep watch, stay awake. You don't know when the moment will arrive. ³⁴It's like a man who goes away from home: he leaves his house, giving each of his slaves authority for their own tasks; and he commands the doorkeeper to keep watch. ³⁵Keep watch, then, because you don't know when the master of the house is going to come. It might be at evening, or at midnight, or at cockcrow, or in the morning! ³⁶You don't want him to come suddenly and find you asleep. ³⁷What I am telling you, I am telling everyone: keep watch!'

Most modern Western houses don't have a doorkeeper. It's up to the owners to lock up, and perhaps set burglar alarms. But in some big cities, over the last few years, there has been quite a change. Many people now live in apartment buildings which employ a full-time guard by the main entrance. Where I live, there is a succession of courtyards, and by the outer one there is a gate, with people on duty 24 hours a day. They see everyone who enters or leaves. This is how it would have been with a great house in Jesus' day.

The thing gatekeepers have to do above all, of course, is to stay awake. This is the warning Jesus issues so solemnly to his followers, as they face the troubled time that's coming upon them, upon Israel, upon Jerusalem, and indeed in a measure on the whole world.

The first level of meaning, clearly, is once more about the imminent destruction of the **Temple**; this is the subject of the entire chapter. Jesus' main concern is to warn his followers of the signs that will immediately herald the end – the end of the Temple, the end of the Jewish national way of life up to that point. (After AD 70, the Jews set about reconstructing their way of life around the law, rather than the Temple; but even the law contains detailed regulations for Temple worship as a standing reminder of how things had been.)

Unlike the fig tree two chapters earlier, which suffered from having leaves but no figs, Jesus now uses the image of a fig tree in leaf, signalling that summer is almost here, as an illustration of how his hearers are to react. They need to watch for the crucial events, especially the arrival of pagans taking over the holy city and the Temple itself. That will be the sign of the end. The terrifying sentences at the end of the **parable** of the wicked tenants is amplified here in chapter 13: the vineyard owner will take the vineyard away and give it to others (12.9). The 'others', as far as chapter 13 is concerned, are foreign, pagan armies, trampling the holy places. When that happens, the end is not far away.

And Jesus is quite clear that this will take place within a generation. That, of course, is only logical. If it's true that he is the last in the line of the prophets, the son who comes to the vineyard as the last possible messenger that the father can send, there can be no one else to come after him. Knowing that this generation would see it all was not a matter of special insight, so much as a straightforward deduction from his own strong sense of vocation. The generation that rejects his **message** – as it was doing – must be the generation upon whom the end will fall. This warning is backed up with one of Jesus' most solemn assurances: his words will stand, though all else may pass away.

Jesus, however, does not know the precise day or hour. He, the 'son', does not know it, because only the Father does. This statement is remarkable. It implies that normally son and Father work very closely together; speaking of Jesus and God in this way is very unusual in Mark (though common in, say, John). But it also presses a sharp distinction between the two. Jesus knows a great deal, but he does not know this. Like a good deal of Jewish thought on God's control of history, this implies that God has planned the right time for all these events to take place. But unlike a good deal of 'apocalyptic' writing, ancient and modern, which tried then, and tries now, to figure out precise timings for events, reducing biblical prophecy to the level of a horoscope, this passage insists on leaving the issue to God.

The resulting command, then, is not 'sit down and work out a prophetic timetable' – always a more exciting thing to do – but 'keep awake and watch'. The little church in the first generation cannot afford to settle down and assimilate itself either to the Jewish or the pagan world. It must constantly remind itself that great events are afoot, that terrifying times are just ahead. Paul's letters clearly reflect this same sense of a brooding, imminent crisis.

But what does this mean for us, who look back on the events of AD 70 as a distant tragedy? Partly, it is important for us simply to absorb the once-for-all significance of the moment in history when this great transition took place. Christians increasingly need to realize that unless we understand the first century we will not understand our own times, or what sort of people we ourselves are called to be.

But it is also important for us to remind ourselves of our own call to watch, to be alert. The judgment that fell on the Temple is a foretaste, according to other passages in the New Testament, of the judgment that will fall on the whole world. This time there are to be no signs (despite the regular attempts to speculate on such things), no advance warnings. Just the ongoing command to God's people in Christ to be faithful to him, not to compromise with the standards and fashions of the **present age**, but to keep awake, watching, as Paul again says, for the day to dawn, in whose light the dim flickering candles of the present age will be needed no more.

MARK 14.1-11

Jesus Is Anointed at Bethany

[1]Passover – the feast of unleavened bread – was due in two days. The chief priests and the lawyers were plotting how to seize Jesus by a trick, and kill him.

[2]'We can't do it at the feast', they said. 'The people might riot.'

[3]Jesus was in Bethany, at the house of Simon (known as 'the Leper'). While he was at table, a woman came up with an alabaster pot containing extremely valuable ointment made of pure spikenard. She broke the pot and poured the ointment on Jesus' head.

[4]Some of the people there grumbled to one another.

137

'What's the point of wasting the ointment?' they asked. [5]'That ointment could have been sold for three hundred dinars, and given to
the poor.'

And they were angry with her.

[6]'Leave her alone', said Jesus. 'Why make trouble for her? She
has done a wonderful thing for me. [7]You have the poor with you
always; you can help them whenever you want to. But you won't
always have me.

[8]'She has played her part. She has anointed my body for its burial,
ahead of time. [9]I'm telling you the truth: wherever the message is
announced in all the world, the story of what she has just done will be
told. That will be her memorial.'

[10]Judas Iscariot, one of the Twelve, went to the chief priests, to
arrange to hand Jesus over to them. [11]They were delighted with his
proposal, and made an agreement to pay him. And he began to look
for a good moment to hand him over.

If the storm clouds are gathering over Jerusalem in chapter 13, in chapter 14 they are coming together over the head of Jesus himself. The
parallel between the two is important: the fate Jesus has predicted for
the **Temple** (destruction at the hands of pagan enemies) is precisely
what will now happen to him. In their different ways, several of the
New Testament writers are aware of this parallel, and make it part of
their understanding of Jesus' death.

From this point on, Mark's story is entirely focused on the coming
crucifixion of the **Messiah**. This opening section of the chapter is like a
dramatic painting, a large canvas with three sections. The middle section, the main story about the woman with the pot of ointment, domi-
nates; but we understand its dark meaning not least when we look to
left and right, to the chief **priests** plotting and then to Judas going off
to strike a bargain with them. In Mark's telling, each scene contributes
to the sense that the end is near. Jesus knows it; Judas and the priests
plot it; the unnamed woman with the perfume intuitively does the
right thing, and anoints Jesus for it.

It was, of course, Passover time. Passover time was freedom time.
Every year, and still to the present day, the Jewish people tell the story
of the **Exodus** from Egypt, leaving the slavery of Pharaoh and coming
through the wilderness to the promised land. Passover was the setting
Jesus chose for the final showdown with the Temple and its hierarchy,
the final conflict (he believed) between the freedom movement he had
been spearheading and the new pharaohs, the forces both of pagan
rule and of Temple misrule. He had been acting, up until now, somewhat like Moses, doing striking things which functioned as signs of the
coming freedom. Now it was time to confront the Red Sea itself. The

Passover theme will be in the background, an important influence, in much of what follows.

As far as the Jewish authorities were concerned, Passover time, for all the same reasons, would not be a good time to arrest Jesus. They were, understandably, afraid of a riot. That's why they were looking for a way to make off with him by stealth. In a city whose every corner was crowded with pilgrims (and Jerusalem had, and still has, many turns and twists, small alleys and hidden doorways), the chief priests, or their officers, had no hope of finding Jesus away from the crowds unless someone led them to him. That is what Judas undertook to do.

His motives are notoriously hard to guess. Disappointment, we may imagine; why, after the great entry into the city, with the crowds cheering and branches waving, had Jesus contented himself with a token demonstration, and some dazzling verbal duelling with the local experts? This only goes part of the way, though, to an explanation. It is likely that other **disciples**, too, were feeling puzzled and perhaps anxious at this stage. None, it appears, had the slightest idea that Jesus had really meant what he had said, again and again, on the road.

Or that he meant the very strange things he said in defence of the woman with the pot of precious spikenard. It always happens, when people decide to worship Jesus without inhibition – to pour out their valuables, their stories, their dancing, their music, before him just the way they feel like doing – that others, looking on, find the spectacle embarrassing and distasteful. I, who have loved the formal church music of my tradition from boyhood, know only too well the temptation to look down on other, less inhibited, styles of music, which sometimes lack a certain polish but often add a certain integrity, a wholeness of spirit. Not everyone is called to pour out expensive ointment over Jesus' head; but if someone is, the rest should respect it.

The grumbles of the bystanders – which sound a lot like the embarrassed rationalizations of people who have their own emotions well covered up and don't like seeing other people's on display – call forth from Jesus a quite astonishing double comment. To their suggestion that the ointment might have been sold for a huge sum (literally, 'more than three hundred denarii'; if a denarius was roughly a day's wage, the sum implied is roughly a labourer's pay for a year), and given to the poor, Jesus, in spite of all his other teaching about the poor, nevertheless makes his own imminent death the prime consideration. He is trying to tell them something, though they still aren't listening. They won't have him with them much longer; and unless his whole vocation and public career has been totally misguided, having him with them is their whole reason for being who they are. We may compare 2.20, where Jesus speaks of 'the bridegroom being taken away'.

The second half of Jesus' comment places a startling interpretation on the woman's action. She has, he says, anointed his body for burial. She has done it ahead of time, presumably because, as Jesus knows, he will be killed in such a way that there may not be a chance for a proper anointing at the time. He is not implying that the woman has any actual knowledge of his coming fate. She has simply acted spontaneously, out of the fullness of her heart. She has, in fact, gone intuitively right to the heart of things, cutting through the male objections on the one hand, and contrasting with the male plots on the other. Not for nothing is this story sometimes held up as an example of a woman getting it right while all around her men are getting it wrong.

In particular, the contrast of reactions as Jesus goes to the cross invites Mark's readers to ponder their own position, feelings and attitudes. 'Were you there', asks the old song, 'when they crucified my Lord?' Yes, but the more important question is, What was going on inside you? Were you part of those who wanted to look the other way, because some people were so exuberant in their devotion? Were you, like Judas, hoping that, if Jesus was determined to die anyway, you at least might make something out of it? Were you glad to be rid of such a troublemaker? Or were you ready to give everything you had to honour this strange man, this unexpected Messiah, this paradoxical Passover-maker?

MARK 14.12–25

The Last Supper

¹²On the first day of unleavened bread, when the Passover lambs were sacrificed, Jesus' disciples said to him, 'Where would you like us to go and get things ready for you to eat the Passover?'

¹³He sent off two of his disciples, with these instructions.

'Go into the city, and you will be met by a man carrying a water-pot. Follow him. ¹⁴When he goes indoors, say to the master of the house, "The teacher says, where is the guest room for me, where I can eat the Passover with my disciples?" ¹⁵He will show you a large upstairs room, set out and ready. Make preparations for us there.'

¹⁶The disciples went out, entered the city, and found it exactly as he had said. They prepared the Passover.

¹⁷When it was evening, Jesus came with the Twelve. ¹⁸As they were reclining at table and eating, Jesus said, 'I'm telling you the truth: one of you is going to betray me – one of you that's eating with me.'

¹⁹They began to be very upset, and they said to him, one after another, 'It isn't me, is it?'

²⁰'It's one of the Twelve,' said Jesus, 'one who has dipped his bread in the dish with me. ²¹Yes: the son of man is completing his journey, as scripture said he would; but it's bad news for the man who betrays him! It would have been better for that man never to have been born.'

²²While they were eating, he took bread, blessed it, broke it, and gave it to them.

'Take it', he said. 'This is my body.'

²³Then he took the cup, gave thanks, and gave it to them, and they all drank from it.

²⁴'This is my blood of the covenant,' he said, 'which is poured out for many. ²⁵I'm telling you the truth: I won't ever drink from the fruit of the vine again, until that day – the day when I drink it new in the kingdom of God.'

On my fortieth birthday, my students gave me a surprise party. While I was taking a service in the college chapel, they carefully cleared the papers in my room, decorated it from floor to ceiling, and laid out a magnificent spread, with cakes and wine at the middle of it. I knew nothing about it until I walked through the door. It was a marvellous and memorable evening.

It's a deep human instinct – I believe a God-given one – that we mark significant moments with significant meals. Sharing a meal, especially a festive one, binds together a family, a group of friends, a collection of colleagues. Such meals say more than we could ever put into words about who we are, how we feel about one another, and the hopes and joys that we share together. The meal not only feeds our bodies; that seems in some ways the least significant part of it. It *says* something; and it *does* something, actually changing us so that, after it, part of who we actually are is 'the people who shared that meal together, with all that it meant'.

The great Jewish festivals all function in this way, most of them connected to the retelling of some part of the story of how God has rescued Israel from slavery in Egypt. Supreme among the festivals was Passover, when they not only told the story of how God had liberated them, but used to recline on couches at the table; in that world, free people didn't just sit, they reclined. Celebrating Passover was and is a deeply religious act, and also, for the many centuries in which Jews have suffered oppression, a deeply political act. It says, loud and clear, 'despite appearances, we are God's free people'. It sustains loyalty; it encourages **faith**, hope and love.

Take all that for granted, and now come into Jerusalem with the unsuspecting **disciples** as they follow one of Jesus' unnamed, secret friends in the city to an unidentified location. Jesus knows the end can't be far off, but he is determined that this Passover meal will be uninterrupted. This meal will say what he most wants to say to his followers, and because it's to be repeated, it will go on saying it. This meal will do what needs to be done, again and again, changing his followers, making them the people who depend on his death for their life, the people who discover that through his achievement God's **kingdom** is now coming on earth as in **heaven**. In that sense, the meal is a surprise party for the disciples, though it turns out to be a very sad one.

All the two know is that they're getting ready the special elements that make up the traditional Jewish Passover. What Jesus knows is that this will be a Passover with a difference. This is the time when he will go, as a greater Moses, ahead of the **Twelve**, ahead of Israel, ahead of the world, into the presence of a greater slave-master than Pharaoh, into a terror greater than walking through the sea, to lead the world to freedom. This Passover-meal-with-a-difference is going to *explain*, more deeply than words could ever do, what his action, and passion, the next day really meant; and, more than explaining it, it will enable Jesus' followers, from that day to this, to make it their own, to draw life and strength from it. If we want to understand, and be nourished by, what happened on Calvary, this meal is the place to start.

Jesus has, for some time now, been trying to teach the disciples about his forthcoming death; they have been, to put it mildly, slow to catch on. He has given a few words of explanation and interpretation, in terms of biblical background (the **son of man**, the servant), political meaning (turning worldly notions of rulership on their heads), and theological interpretation (giving his life a ransom for many). All of that lies behind this meal, but the meal itself goes far beyond theory.

To the annoyance of our rationalistic age, you can't put this meaning into words. You can only put it into action. Actions like this are so powerful that sometimes people in the churches have tried to contain or control them, to surround them with more and more words, like trying to cage in a tiger. But the actions – taking, blessing, breaking and giving the bread; taking, blessing and giving the cup – cannot be caged.

Of course, some words are necessary, otherwise the actions would degenerate into magic, perhaps unconnected with Jesus, with the historical moment of his death. The words Jesus himself used are crucial to the event. Jesus, we must assume, told the Passover story, as the head of the family always would; but this time, instead of saying words to link the bread and the wine back to the **Exodus** and forward to the final liberation of Israel, he said new words, which linked them directly to the death he would very shortly die, and to the coming of the kingdom of God that would be brought about by that death. This meal, with all its new-passover associations, was Jesus' primary means of enabling his followers not only to understand his death but to let it do its freedom-work in their lives and in the world. It drew to a head the kingdom-actions (not least the feastings) and kingdom-teaching of his whole public career. Jesus' death, seen and known in the light of this meal, makes sense of it all. This is how the kingdom will come.

All the more tragic, then, that on that night Jesus also spoke sorrowful words about someone who would betray him. They had come in secret to a secret destination; it would take treachery from within to put Jesus at the authorities' mercy. Jesus, with the scriptures in his head (not least passages in the Psalms which spoke of betrayal by an intimate friend), knew it was bound to happen, but grieved for the torment that would be suffered by the traitor.

Since this meal was and is so central, we shouldn't be surprised that its meaning, and the way it is enacted, has often been the subject of bitter disputes and divisions within the church. Sorrow hung over the Last Supper itself, and sorrow hangs over every re-enactment of it within a divided church. But the meal itself, whether kept simply or magnificently, whether the words are whispered or sung, towers above the disputes and failures of Jesus' followers then and now. Jesus intended it to be the central means whereby his kingdom-achieving death would be known, believed, appropriated and lived out. Each generation of Christians, and each subculture within Christianity, must find ways of enabling that to happen.

MARK 14.26–52

Jesus Is Arrested

²⁶They sang a hymn, and went out to the Mount of Olives.
²⁷'You're all going to desert me,' said Jesus, 'because it's written,

I shall attack the shepherd
and then the sheep will scatter.

²⁸'But after I am raised up, I will go ahead of you to Galilee.'
²⁹Peter spoke up.
'Everyone else may desert you,' he said, 'but I won't.'
³⁰'I'm telling you the truth,' Jesus replied. 'Today – this very night, before the cock has crowed twice – you will renounce me three times.'
³¹This made Peter all the more vehement. 'Even if I have to die with you,' he said, 'I will never renounce you.'
And all the rest said the same.
³²They came to a place called Gethsemane.
'Stay here,' said Jesus to the disciples, 'while I pray.'

³³He took Peter, James and John with him, and became quite overcome and deeply distressed.

³⁴'"My soul is disturbed within me", he said, 'right to the point of death. Stay here and keep watch.'

³⁵He went a little further, and fell on the ground and prayed that, if possible, the moment might pass from him.

³⁶'Abba, father,' he said, 'all things are possible for you! Take this cup away from me! But – not what I want, but what you want.'

³⁷He returned and found them sleeping. 'Are you asleep, Simon?' he said to Peter. 'Couldn't you keep watch for a single hour? ³⁸Watch and pray, so that you won't come into the time of trouble. The spirit is eager, but the body is weak.'

³⁹Once more he went off and prayed, saying the same words. ⁴⁰And again, when he returned, he found them asleep, because their eyes were very heavy. They had no words to answer him. ⁴¹But the third time he came, he said to them, 'All right – sleep as much as you like now. Have a good rest. The job is done, the time has come – and look! The son of man is betrayed into the clutches of sinners. ⁴²Get up, let's be on our way. Here comes the man who's going to betray me.'

⁴³At once, while he was still speaking, Judas, one of the Twelve, arrived, accompanied by a crowd, with swords and clubs, from the chief priests, the legal experts, and the elders. ⁴⁴The betrayer had given them a coded sign: 'The one I kiss – that's him! Seize him and take him away safely.'

⁴⁵He came up to Jesus at once. 'Rabbi!' he said, and kissed him.

⁴⁶The crowd laid hands on him and seized him. ⁴⁷One of the bystanders drew a sword and struck the high priest's servant, cutting off his ear. ⁴⁸Then Jesus spoke to them.

'Anyone would think,' he said, 'you'd come after a brigand! Fancy needing swords and clubs to arrest me! ⁴⁹Day after day I've been teaching in the Temple, under your noses, and you never laid a finger on me. But the scriptures must be fulfilled.'

⁵⁰Then they all abandoned him and ran away.

⁵¹A young man had followed him, wearing only a linen tunic over his otherwise naked body. ⁵²They seized him, and he left the tunic and ran away naked.

What do you do when the strong person in your life suddenly becomes weak?

Children face this when the parent on whom they have relied for everything is suddenly struck down with illness or grief. Colleagues working on a project are thrown into confusion if the team leader suddenly loses confidence. A church is dismayed if the pastor or preacher suddenly loses **faith**, or hope, or integrity.

We can only begin to imagine the effect on the **disciples** of the sudden change that came over Jesus in Gethsemane. Until that moment he had been in control: planning, directing, teaching, guiding. He had always been ready with a word or action. Now he is, as we say, falling apart, and warning them that they are going to collapse around him. As well they might.

The scene is so intimate and frightening that we feel almost embarrassed to be onlookers. Jesus' own horror, and the disciples' sleepy dismay, are raw human emotion, naked and unadorned. When the great Greek philosopher Socrates went to his death, he was calm and in control throughout the process. His followers, though distraught and in tears, remembered his steady teaching right up to the end, his coolly ironic last words. Not so with Jesus. This story is neither a Greek-style heroic tale nor a typical Jewish martyrdom. It is unique. Only if we enter into it – which we can hardly do without fear and trembling on our own part – will we understand the human depths, and hence the theological depths, of the story.

Once again we have a central scene flanked by two outer ones. In the middle is Jesus in the garden, overcome with horror, praying for another way, claiming the truth he had already taught the disciples (10.27), that all things are possible to God – and being told that there was no turning back. As ever, the Psalms give him words to express his torment, this time in a quotation from the refrain of Psalms 42 and 43 (42.5, 11; 43.5; 'Why so heavy, my soul? Why so disturbed within me?'). He comes through a time of great struggle, a three-times repeated prayer for rescue; eventually, it seems, he hears from the one he calls 'Abba, Father' the answer: No. ('Abba' is the Aramaic word for 'father'; not simply a children's word, but always carrying intimate affection and devotion.) If even Jesus received that answer to one of his most heartfelt prayers, we should not be surprised if sometimes it's that way for us too. He emerges, composed and in charge once more, though his last words to the disciples are full of ironic contradiction: 'Carry on sleeping – get up and let's go!'

To one side of this central scene is Jesus' frightening conversation with the disciples. They will all, he says, abandon him. Again he is conscious of scriptural warnings, all of which he senses rushing together into a dense fulfilment. He has shepherded his little flock, from the time he gathered them in Galilee until now; now he, the shepherd, will be struck down, and for a time at least the flock will run away to wherever they can hide. Even this, though it will reflect their cowardice and confusion, is part of the plan: Jesus must go alone into the 'time of trouble', the great dark moment that is coming upon him. The disciples have no place there. They must pray to be spared it.

145

And Peter, the Rock – impetuous as ever, opening his mouth first and thinking afterwards – Peter will be turned inside out by the whole process. The triple prayer of Jesus in the garden will find a ghastly parody in the triple renunciation that Peter will make. Three times Jesus will place himself in the hands, and the will, of his Abba. Three times Peter, Jesus' right-hand man, will deny that he even knows him.

To the other side of the central scene is Jesus' betrayal and arrest. Judas has found the perfect place: in the dark, outside the city, away from the crowds. The swords and clubs are unnecessary; they imply that Jesus is the kind of revolutionary leader that he has steadfastly refused to be, despite what many had hoped. Indeed, Judas himself may have wanted that kind of **Messiah**; the irony increases with every step.

One of the disciples gets carried away and tries to fight. John identifies him as Peter, but the others leave him anonymous, and Mark, aware of how out of keeping this behaviour was, won't even identify him as one of Jesus' followers, but just says 'one of the bystanders'. In the same way, though Mark has been talking in verses 48–49 about the crowd who have come to arrest Jesus, when in verse 50 he describes the disciples running away, he doesn't call them 'disciples'. He just says 'they all abandoned him and ran away'. They are not behaving as disciples, so he refuses them the title.

Finally, we have the young man who, like Joseph in Genesis 39.12, escapes by leaving his garment behind. It's often been suggested that this was Mark himself (the other **gospels** don't mention the incident); though it's impossible to prove it, it is a quite reasonable guess. Whether or not that is so, the imagery is striking, going back as far as Genesis 3. Like Adam and Eve, the disciples are metaphorically, and in this case literally, hiding their naked shame in the garden. Their disgrace is complete.

Gethsemane invites us to consider, above all, what it meant for Jesus to be, in a unique sense, God's son. The very moment of greatest intimacy – the desperate prayer to 'Abba, Father' – is also the moment where, hearing the answer 'No', he is set on the course for the moment of God-forsakenness on the cross (15.34). Until we have come to terms with this, we have not really begun to think what we mean when we say the Christian creeds.

The triple scene invites us to stop and ponder, once more, where we ourselves belong. Are we, like the disciples, full of bluster one minute, sleep the next, and confused shame the next? Are we ready to betray Jesus if it suits our other plans, or if he fails to live up to our expectations? Or are we prepared to keep watch with him in the garden, sharing his anguished prayer? We are not called to repeat his unique moment of suffering; he went through that alone on behalf of us all.

But as Christian writers from the very beginning (i.e. Paul) have seen, it is part of normal Christian experience that we, too, should be prepared to agonize in prayer as we await our own complete redemption and that of all creation. The church is called to live in the middle of this great scene: surrounded by confusion, false loyalty, direct attack and traitor's kisses, those who name the name of Christ must stay in the garden with him until the Father's will is done.

MARK 14.53–72

In the High Priest's House

⁵³They took Jesus away to the high priest. All the chief priests and the elders and legal experts were assembled. ⁵⁴Peter followed him at a distance, and came to the courtyard of the high priest's house, where he sat with the servants and warmed himself at the fire.

⁵⁵The chief priests, and all the Sanhedrin, looked for evidence for a capital charge against Jesus, but they didn't find any. ⁵⁶Several people invented fictitious charges against him, but their evidence didn't agree. ⁵⁷Then some stood up with this fabricated charge: ⁵⁸'We heard him say, "I will destroy this Temple, which human hands have made, and in three days I'll build another, made without human hands."'

⁵⁹But even so their evidence didn't agree.

⁶⁰Then the high priest got up in front of them all and interrogated Jesus.

'Haven't you got any answer about whatever it is these people are testifying against you?'

⁶¹Jesus remained silent, and didn't answer a word.

Once more the high priest questioned him. 'Are you the Messiah, the Son of the Blessed One?'

⁶²'I am,' replied Jesus, 'and you will see "the son of man sitting at the right hand of Power, and coming with the clouds of heaven".'

⁶³'Why do we need any more evidence?' shouted the high priest, tearing his clothes. ⁶⁴'You heard the blasphemy! What's your verdict?'

They all agreed on their judgment: he deserved to die.

⁶⁵Some of them began to spit at him. They blindfolded him and hit him, and said, 'Prophesy!' And the servants took charge of him and beat him.

⁶⁶Peter, meanwhile, was below in the courtyard. One of the high priest's servant-girls came up ⁶⁷and saw him warming himself. She looked closely at him, and said, 'You were with Jesus the Nazarene as well, weren't you?'

⁶⁸'I don't know what on earth you're talking about,' replied Peter.

He went outside into the forecourt, and the cock crowed.

⁶⁹The servant-girl saw him, and once more began to say to the bystanders, 'This man is one of them.' ⁷⁰But Peter again denied it.

> A little while later the bystanders said again to Peter, 'You really are one of them, aren't you? You're a Galilean!'
> [71]At that he began to curse and swear, 'I don't know this man you're talking about.' [72]And immediately the cock crowed for the second time. Then Peter remembered the words that Jesus had said to him: 'Before the cock crows twice, you will renounce me three times.' And he burst into tears.

Jesus retains his integrity at the cost of his life. Peter loses his integrity to save his skin. Mark has contrasted them vividly.

The double picture is put together in another of Mark's 'sandwiches'. Peter arrives in the high **priest**'s courtyard; but the reader already knows that Jesus has prophesied that he will renounce him three times. Jesus is then accused before the high priest of being, among other things, a false prophet. After the verdict, Jesus is taunted: he's such a hopeless prophet that when blindfold he can't tell who's hitting him. We then switch back to Peter: he does exactly what Jesus had said he would. That night, says Mark, Jesus was vindicated as a true prophet.

Within this framework, the detailed description of Peter's failure highlights the solitariness of Jesus. Betrayed by one associate, forsaken by ten more, and now publicly and bitterly renounced by his closest friend; he stands alone, defenceless, before the Jewish court, before the world. This too is important for the story Mark is telling: what Jesus has to do now, he has to do all by himself. No one else can give their life as a ransom for many. Nobody else can bring Israel's story of failure and redemption to its climax. If he is the **Messiah**, there comes a moment when he has to act solo. That moment has now arrived.

Of course, the human drama of Peter's blustering assertions and humiliating downfall (imagine, as a church leader, having your failure written into the foundation documents) deserves exploring from many angles. Like a scene in a Shakespeare play, it can be seen from many angles, bringing out the flavour of all our rebellions, all our false confidences, all our choosings of the safe, easy path over the hard way of truth. But Mark's telling of Peter's failure is designed to let Jesus' final statement of his vocation shine out the more brightly. What was at stake when Jesus stood before the high priest?

There are four stages, building in a crescendo, in Caiaphas' interrogation. We must take each in turn if we are to understand what Mark says was going on.

1. The bottom-line charge – and the one that is repeated in later Jewish sources – is that Jesus was a false prophet, leading Israel astray. There were scriptural warnings about such people, who would perform miraculous deeds and lure people away from following Israel's

God and Israel's law. Jesus' activity in Galilee, and the accusations there (e.g. 3.22), undoubtedly contributed to this charge. Jesus had undeniably done remarkable things; but this left open the question whether he was a true prophet or an imposter. They believed his threats against the **Temple** meant the latter. Hence the blindfold and the taunts at the end.

2. The more immediate issue, though, concerned Jesus' attitude to the Temple. The disputes of chapters 11 and 12 were generated by his dramatic demonstration in the Temple, and it had become clear that he was not only claiming some kind of authority over the Temple (i.e. at least challenging the authority of the high priest) but also warning that the Temple was under God's judgment and would be destroyed. The garbled version of these warnings which the false witnesses produce in verse 58 – which is quite close, actually, to John 2.19, but not to anything that Jesus says in Mark – shows that some word about his warnings had got out, even if it was muddled up with other sayings about a rather different three-day process. What Jesus had done in the Temple was the primary reason for his arrest and accusation.

3. The judges were aware, though, that what Jesus had done and said constituted a veiled claim to royal authority. He was making moves that could only be explained if he thought he was the true King, the Messiah. Now there was nothing wrong, let alone blasphemous, with thinking oneself to be Messiah. It might be dangerous, it might even be laughable (it must have seemed both that night), but it wasn't a capital offence under Jewish law. Nevertheless the court knew, and Jesus knew they knew, that if someone claimed to be a king, and the Roman governor heard about it, there could only be one result. Crucifixion, though practised widely in the Roman world for various offences, was the standard treatment for would-be rebel leaders. Hence the chief priest's key question, when Jesus remains silent about the Temple: Are you the Messiah?

Mark is aware of irony here. Caiaphas's question, in Greek, takes the form of a statement with a question mark at the end: 'You are the Messiah?' The words are identical to what Peter said in 8.29. Now Peter is outside, about to deny he even knows Jesus; and Caiaphas, inside, asks the question with contempt, knowing already what answer he would believe.

When he adds 'The son of the Blessed One', this doesn't mean he is thinking that the Messiah will be God's son in the later Christian sense. '**Son of God**', as we have seen, is an honorific title for the Messiah, and had been since the Psalms at least. But for Mark, and for Christian readers since, this phrase forms a transition to Jesus' shocking reply – as well as a link with the very beginning of the **gospel**, where the voice

149

from **heaven**, repeated at the transfiguration, assures Jesus, and then the **disciples**, that this is indeed who he really is.

4. Jesus incriminates himself at once on the political charge. Underneath his prophetic work, and his words against the Temple, he does indeed believe himself to be God's anointed. Everything he has done and said since his **baptism** has been based on that belief, and he isn't going to deny it now. But he goes much further. He draws together the two key biblical quotations he has already used to talk about the deeper meaning of messiahship: Psalm 110 (Mark 12.36) and Daniel 7.13 (Mark 13.26). The combination is explosive, and gives Caiaphas, in addition to the charge of being a rebel king, a charge he can present to his fellow-Jews as a sufficient reason for handing Jesus over: blasphemy.

It isn't that Jesus has, as it were, claimed simply to be divine (though some have seen the simple phrase 'I am' as an echo of the divine name). It is, rather, that these two biblical texts, taken together, answer all the questions simultaneously, and add to them the assertion that Jesus will be vindicated, exalted to a place at God's right hand. The answer says, in a tight-packed phrase: yes, I am a true prophet; yes, what I said about the Temple will come true; yes, I am the Messiah; *you will see me vindicated*; and my vindication will mean that I share the very throne of Israel's God. At last the masks are off, the secrets are out, the cryptic sayings and **parables** are left behind. The **son of man** stands before the official ruler of Israel, declaring that God will prove him in the right, and the court in the wrong.

Whether or not even this constituted a crime according to any official law-code we will never know. But the court was satisfied. Whatever precisely Jesus meant, they saw it as not only seditious but blasphemous. The insults and mockery that followed were the surface noise. What mattered was that Jesus could now be presented to Pilate as a rebel king, and to the Jewish people as a blaspheming false prophet, leading Israel astray. Mark's readers are left looking at Jesus and Peter in awe and dismay, realizing perhaps for the first time what Jesus had meant six chapters before when he spoke of saving one's life but losing it, or losing one's life but saving it.

MARK 15.1–15

Jesus before Pilate

[1]As soon as morning came, the chief priests held a council meeting with the elders, the legal experts, and the whole Sanhedrin. They bound Jesus, took him off to Pilate, and handed him over.

²'Are you the king of the Jews?' asked Pilate.

'You have said it', replied Jesus.

³The chief priests laid many accusations against him.

⁴Pilate again interrogated him: 'Aren't you going to make any reply? Look how many accusations they're making against you!'

⁵But Jesus gave no reply at all, which astonished Pilate.

⁶The custom was that at festival time he used to release for them a single prisoner, whoever they would ask for. ⁷There was a man in prison named Barabbas, one of the revolutionaries who had committed murder during the uprising. ⁸So the crowd came up and began to ask Pilate to do what he normally did.

⁹'Do you want me', answered Pilate, 'to release for you "the king of the Jews"?'

¹⁰He said this because he knew that the chief priests had handed him over out of envy. ¹¹The chief priests stirred up the crowd to ask for Barabbas instead to be released to them. So Pilate once again asked them, ¹²'What then do you want me to do with the one you call "the king of the Jews"?'

¹³'Crucify him!' they shouted again.

¹⁴'Why?' asked Pilate. 'What has he done wrong?'

'Crucify him!' they shouted all the louder.

¹⁵Pilate wanted to satisfy the crowd; so he released Barabbas for them. He had Jesus flogged, and handed him over to be crucified.

Today they sell crosses in fashionable jewellery shops. If you ask the shop assistants, you will find that many of them don't know where the symbol comes from, or what it means; and neither do many of their customers. It has become, ironically, a dead metaphor. Someone once remarked that if you want to wear a cross as an earring, it might be a good idea to wear an electric chair as its pair, to remind yourself what the cross was, and did, and meant.

The cross was a political symbol long before it became a religious symbol. Pilate knew, the crowds knew, the chief **priests** knew, and Jesus knew, what it meant. It was the ultimate symbol of Roman power. It said, 'We are in charge here, and this is what happens to people who get in our way.' They had crucified thousands of rebel Jews when Jesus was a boy in Galilee. They would crucify thousands more when they took Jerusalem in AD 70 – so many that they got bored, and experimented with hanging people up in different positions and attitudes, until they ran out of wood. And in between those two devastating repressions of revolts they crucified lots of people for a variety of reasons, often on small pretexts.

Polite Romans didn't even mention the word 'crucifixion' or 'cross'. The reality was so brutal, ugly and repellent. But crosses were the reality on which their empire was in fact constructed – the empire which boasted of bringing justice and peace to the whole world. Whether or not Mark was writing in Rome, as some have thought, his hearers certainly knew all this, and we need to remember it constantly if we are to understand him at this point.

Pilate feels under no obligation to hold anything approaching a fair trial. His main aim is to prevent riots, to get through the Passover season without major trouble, and if possible, while doing so, to assert his own authority over against the chief priests, who were always playing little power games against him. This wasn't a particularly bad day for Roman provincial justice; just business as usual.

Once again, then, the first level of meaning Mark's readers would find in this story would be *political*. Jesus was going to die the death they all knew about: the death of someone caught between the upper millstone of local trouble and the lower millstone of imperial Rome. Jesus had already spoken of his death as symbolizing the upending of the world's power structures; now he was about to act out his own words.

In particular, Jesus dies – Mark rubs our noses in this again and again in this chapter, six times in 32 verses – as 'the king of the Jews'. Pilate might have flogged an errant prophet if he was causing trouble. He would have dismissed a blasphemy case with a flick of his hand. But would-be kings spelt political trouble. This was the charge he had to take notice of, even though he knew Jesus wasn't leading the normal sort of messianic revolt (he didn't bother to round up any of his followers). Mark wants to be sure that we think of Jesus' death in terms of his messiahship, confronting the power of Rome, built as it was on the power of death.

But within this political meaning Mark wants us to discover the *theological* meaning. What was happening to God's **kingdom**, God's rescue operation, to the work Jesus had begun in Galilee? Mark will develop this in the rest of the chapter; but already two themes emerge in this passage which link it back to those days, and to the theological meaning of Jesus' work which emerged from the earlier chapters.

First, Jesus is silent. Mark has alerted us to a passage in Isaiah which, he says, Jesus himself took as his model: in Isaiah 53, the servant 'gives his life as a ransom for many'. This servant, the passage explains, is like a lamb led off to be slaughtered; he does not open his mouth. If Jesus is the **Messiah** in this passage, he is, for Mark, the Servant-King.

Second, Jesus is innocent. Even Pilate knows he's done nothing wrong; he hasn't been leading a revolt, he hasn't been stirring up dissension. Yet here he is, going off to meet the fate (destruction at the hands of Rome) that, in his own warnings, he had seen hanging over the **Temple**. Somehow he was going out ahead of Israel, to take its fate upon himself, to bring about God's kingdom of healing and forgiveness.

And therefore, within Mark's story, we find also the deeply *personal* meaning. The story of Barabbas invites us to see Jesus' crucifixion in terms of a stark personal exchange. Barabbas deserves to die; Jesus dies instead, and he goes free. Barabbas was the archetypal Jewish rebel: quite probably what we today would call a fanatical right-wing zealot, determined to stop at nothing to bring in a version of God's kingdom which consisted of defeating Roman power by Roman means – in other words, repaying pagan violence with holy violence. No doubt many Christians in Mark's community, and others who would read his book, had at one stage at least flirted with such revolutionary movements. Reading the story of the guilty man freed and the innocent man crucified, it would not be hard for them to identify with Barabbas, and to view the rest of the story with the awestruck gaze of people who think, 'There but for God's grace go I.'

Just so, Mark is saying. God's grace, God's sovereign and saving presence, is exactly what we are witnessing in this story. When we learn to read the story of Jesus and see it as the story of the love of God, doing for us what we could not do for ourselves – that insight produces, again and again, the sense of astonished gratitude which is very near the heart of authentic Christian experience.

MARK 15.16–32

The Crucifixion

¹⁶The soldiers took Jesus into the courtyard, that is, the Praetorium, and called together the whole squad. ¹⁷They dressed Jesus up in purple; then, weaving together a crown of thorns, they stuck it on him. ¹⁸They began to salute him: 'Greetings, King of the Jews!' ¹⁹And they hit him over the head with a staff, and spat at him, and knelt down to do him homage. ²⁰Then, when they had mocked him, they took the purple robe off him, and put his own clothes back on.

Then they led him off to crucify him. ²¹They compelled a man called Simon to carry Jesus' cross. He was from Cyrene, and was coming in from out of town. He was the father of Alexander and Rufus.

²²They took Jesus to the place called Golgotha, which in translation means 'Skull's Place'. ²³They gave him a mixture of wine and myrrh, but he didn't drink it.

²⁴So they crucified him; they 'parted his clothing between them, casting lots' to see who would get what. ²⁵It was about nine o'clock in the morning when they crucified him. ²⁶The inscription, giving the

charge, read: 'The King of the Jews'. [27]They also crucified two bandits alongside him, one on his right and one on his left.

[29]People who were passing by abused him. They shook their heads at him.

'Hah!' they said. 'You were going to destroy the Temple, were you? And build it again in three days? [30]Why don't you rescue yourself, and come down from the cross?'

[31]The chief priests and the lawyers were mocking him in the same way among themselves.

'He rescued others,' they said, 'but he can't rescue himself. [32]Messiah, is he? King of Israel, did he say? Well, let's see him come down from the cross! We'll believe him when we see that!'

The two who were crucified alongside him taunted him as well.

Peacekeeping forces, which have become a regular feature of our world, often have to contain themselves in the face of severe local provocation. They can easily build up a backlog of resentment and anger against the people who are causing them trouble, who are perhaps killing or wounding some of their comrades. Even where press cameras are on the lookout for trouble, and regulations are quite strict, one hears regular tales of soldiers who, frustrated beyond measure by niggling insurgents, seize the opportunity, when they have a prisoner all to themselves, to take revenge with brutal and sadistic torture.

It's a scene like that which opens Mark's account of Jesus' crucifixion. The Roman troops in Jerusalem wouldn't have been anxious about press reports, still less international courts of justice; they just got on with doing what they did well, which was keeping law and order through sheer brute force. Though some of their behaviour to Jesus is simply mockery (kings and senior nobles wore purple in the ancient world), the centre of it is deeply violent and offensive (the crown of thorns, the spitting, the beating with what was probably a centurion's staff). This is what they've always wanted to do to a King of the Jews, and they're not going to spoil the chance now they've got it. The result is humiliation and degradation.

This ugly scene is the first of several short snapshots. As with a photograph album, Mark builds up the story of Jesus' crucifixion through small pictures, one detail after another that together tell the story in a clipped sequence, moving swiftly from scene to scene. At no point does he stay for long on a particular theme, except for the main one, which emerges over and over: that Jesus is crucified as the King of the Jews. It is because he is bearing the fate and destiny of Israel, as its anointed representative, that his death means what it means to

Mark. Israel is where the world's violence and wickedness seems to have concentrated itself (if you were writing in AD 66–70 it would be easy to believe that); but the **Messiah**, the King, has already taken it upon himself, and so has made a way of rescue, of ransom, for any who will follow him.

The next snapshot is of a man named Simon, from Cyrene in North Africa – probably a Jew from the community there, in Jerusalem on pilgrimage. He is described as 'the father of Alexander and Rufus'. These names are not common in the New Testament; but Paul sends greetings to a Rufus in the Roman church (Romans 16.13), and it is possible that he lived there, and was a member of the church. First-century Christianity was quite a family affair. Memories of the dramatic events surrounding Jesus' death would have been told and retold within households, not least where one member had taken such a shocking part in the story.

Anyone who has been to Jerusalem and walked the Via Dolorosa, the likely route from the soldiers' barracks to Golgotha, will be able to envisage the procession. Prisoners often carried the cross-beam upon which they were to hang; the vertical pole would usually be on site already. Jesus was clearly too weak, after a sleepless night and repeated beatings, to carry his own cross-beam. Simon happened to be there in the crowd, and the soldiers used their legal privilege to compel him to carry it instead. It remained Jesus' cross, of course, not Simon's, but anyone who had read Jesus' words in Mark 8 about taking up one's cross and following him would be likely to make the connection.

Golgotha was then just outside the western wall. The city limits have extended since then, and the Church of the Holy Sepulchre, built over the probable site, is well within the current wall. The name 'Skull's Place' may refer to the shape of the hill, but the fact that Mark has bothered to translate the Aramaic name probably means that he understood it to mean a place of executions. He is heightening our sense of horror. Not only what is happening to Jesus, but the very place where it is happening, resonate with dismay and death.

Nor does Jesus, in Mark, mitigate his own suffering by drinking drugged wine. He chooses instead to drink to the dregs the 'cup' that his Father has given him (10.38; 14.36). His shame and humiliation are complete with the soldiers' stripping of his clothes; despite the modesty of virtually all carved and painted crucifixion scenes, people were in fact crucified naked. Mark was probably not the first to make the connection of the soldiers' gambling for his clothes with Psalm 22.19. Jesus quotes the opening line of the psalm as he dies (15.34), and the early church found many other points at which this psalm of the suffering but vindicated righteous man resonated with their memories of the events, and influenced the way they told the story to bring out its full meaning.

The custom in crucifixions was to fix a placard on the cross-beam indicating the crime of the condemned man. In Jesus' case, the 'crime' – in the eyes of Roman law – was that he had claimed to be King of the Jews. (When the Romans sacked Jerusalem in AD 70, they took Simon bar Giora, one of the messianic contenders of the time, back to Rome with them, and ceremonially executed him as 'King of the Jews' at the close of their triumphal procession, symbolizing the completeness of their victory.) Just to make the point sharper, Jesus was crucified between two bandits, or brigands: again, these were not small-time thieves or crooks, but revolutionaries. At the centre of Mark's picture, and of his thought, is the profound reflection: Jesus is dying the death that properly belonged to the violent kingdom-people, the nationalist guerillas. Luke draws this theme out much further, but it is there in embryo already in Mark. And – another heavily ironic reference to an earlier scene – we now at last discover who it is for whom 'it has been prepared' that they should find themselves at Jesus' right and left when he is enthroned as King (10.40).

The crucifixion scene closes, as it opened, with mockery. This time it comes from Jewish passers-by, including the leaders. The claims Jesus made, explicitly and implicitly, and his warnings against the **Temple**, are thrown back in his face. He can't even rescue himself, they say, let alone destroy and rebuild the Temple in three days. And – the sharpest cut of all – everyone knows that the Messiah should be defeating the Romans, not dying at their hands. If he really is the King, he should come down from the cross. That would give them reason to believe.

And Mark is saying, through it all: just because he is King of the Jews, he must stay on the cross. That is his royal task and reign. That is what he has come to do; it is the climax of his kingdom-vocation. The mocking and taunting, the shame and humiliation, come together with the dark extremes of pain and torture, as the inner core of what it all meant, the reason why the cross gives **faith** and hope to Mark's little community, and to all Christians as we meditate on these events. This, Mark is saying, is what happens when David's Lord becomes David's son. This is what it looks like when the son's vocation, given him by the Father, is acted out to the full. This is how the **kingdom** comes at last. We are perhaps meant to hear, with the ears of faith, the same voice that spoke at the **baptism** and transfiguration, saying with sorrow and pride the same words: 'This is my beloved son. I'm delighted with him'.

MARK 15.33–39

The Death of Jesus

[33]At midday there was darkness over all the land until three in the afternoon. [34]At three o'clock Jesus shouted out in a powerful voice, '*Eloi, Eloi, lema sabachthani?*' which means, 'My God, my God, why did you abandon me?'

[35]When the bystanders heard it, some of them said, 'He's calling for Elijah!'

[36]One of them ran and filled a sponge with sour wine, put it on a pole, and gave it him to drink.

'Well then,' he declared, 'let's see if Elijah will come and take him down.'

[37]But Jesus, with another loud shout, breathed his last.

[38]The Temple veil was torn in two, from top to bottom. [39]When the centurion who was standing facing him saw that he died in this way, he said, 'This fellow really was God's son.'

There are times when I envy musical composers, and this is one of them. If I were capable of setting this brief but shocking story to music, I know how I would start. Darkness at noon: low chords on the heavy brass, a brooding, twisting melody for the cellos and bassoons, a sense of growing foreboding, of apprehension and dread. From that start, and within that atmosphere, the varied themes of the rest of the passage could grow.

You can do that quite easily in music, but most of the words we try to use, as T. S. Eliot wryly observed, slip and slide and will not stay in place. We are too used to them, as indeed Christians are too used to the story of Jesus' death in general. We need, regularly, to find ways of making the story strange again, so that we can hear it once more as though it were new to us.

Because a strange story it is. If we were reading Mark for the first time, we might expect that, after the mocking of the crowds, all that would be left would be for Jesus to die. We might have imagined that this would take some time, since crucified people often hovered between life and death for days, and (as John informs us) only the imminent arrival of the Jewish **sabbath** would make the soldiers finish off the job more quickly. But nothing could have prepared us for the bizarre events that Mark relates in this short account of Jesus' last minutes.

Every step is more curious than the last. The darkness: it can't have been an eclipse, because Passover happened at full moon, so that the moon would be in the wrong part of the sky. Jesus' sudden and, to the bystanders, probably terrifying, yell of anguish. The bizarre misunderstanding, thinking he was calling Elijah. Then Jesus' death, much sooner than people would have expected. Then the **Temple** veil. Finally, the extraordinary remark of the centurion. The narrative bumps along from one to the next like an old car on a road full of potholes. What is Mark trying to tell us?

Let's begin at the end, because what the centurion said links up with the theme we have observed from the very start of the **gospel**. The opening line speaks of Jesus the **Messiah**, the **son of God**. The voice at the **baptism** hails Jesus as God's beloved son; the voice at the transfiguration says the same to Peter, James and John. The **parable** of the wicked tenants spoke of the beloved son, sent by the father but killed by the workers. Caiaphas asked Jesus if he was the Messiah, God's son. The crowds mocked him in the same words.

And now at last, not the high **priest**, not a leading rabbi, not even a loyal **disciple**, but a battle-hardened thug in Roman uniform, used to killing humans the way one might kill flies, stands before this dying young Jew and says something which, in Mark's mind, sends a signal to the whole world that the **kingdom** has indeed come, that a new age is being born, that God has done something the news of which will spread around the globe. The Roman centurion becomes the first sane human being in Mark's gospel to call Jesus God's son, and mean it. Yes, says Mark to his possibly Roman audience; and if him, why not more?

The earthshaking event which Mark thus describes goes with the darkness at noon and the tearing of the Temple veil. Out of the unexplained cosmic darkness comes God's new word of creation, as at the beginning. Matthew explains the tearing of the veil with an earthquake; Mark leaves it as a mystery, though he presumably means us to understand, in the light of the previous four chapters, that from now on the Temple is as good as finished. Its purpose has been taken over by the event which has just occurred. From now on, access into the presence of the living God is open to all through the death of his son.

And all happens because of the God-forsakenness of the son of God. The horror which overwhelmed Jesus in Gethsemane, and then seems to have retreated again for a few hours, came back in all its awfulness, a horror of drinking the cup of God's wrath, of sharing the depth of suffering, mental and emotional as well as physical, that characterized the world in general and Israel in particular. The dark cloud of evil, Israel's evil, the world's evil, Evil itself greater than the sum of its parts, cut him off from the one he called 'Abba' in a way he had never known before. And welling up from his lifetime of biblically based prayer there came, as though by a reflex, a cry not of rebellion, but of despair and sorrow, yet still a despair that, having lost contact with God, still asks God why this should be. The son, rejected by the tenants, looks in vain for his father and asks why. The question of Job – why do the innocent suffer? – mingles with the question not only of the psalmists but of millions in the ancient and the modern world, and becomes the question, to use later Christian language, that God himself uses when forsaken by God, that God the Son uses when forsaken, unthinkably, by God the Father. Unless we wrestle with this question we not only cut ourselves off from understanding the central Christian mystery and glory; we trivialize the gospel which meets the world at its point of deepest need.

The bystanders thought, from the sudden sound of *Eloi, Eloi*, that he was calling Elijah. They were wrong, but Mark uses it to remind us of an earlier theme which now returns to complete the picture. 'Elijah does come first,' Jesus had said, 'and restores all things; but how is it written of the **son of man** that he must suffer and be abused?' (9.12). The bystanders now, like the disciples then, thought that maybe Jesus (like many others) was still waiting for Elijah. But Jesus, who had begun his vocation through the work of the true Elijah, **John the Baptist**, had already passed this point. Elijah had come, had prepared the way, and had himself suffered for it. Now the son of man, through his own shame and suffering, had at last ushered in the kingdom of God.

His work was complete, and with another shout he died. Mark, perhaps, intends us to understand that he was conscious of this being his last breath.

MARK 15.40–47

The Burial of Jesus

[40]Some women were watching from a distance. They included Mary Magdalene, Mary the mother of the younger James and of Joses, and Salome. [41]They had followed Jesus in Galilee, and had attended to his needs. There were several other women, too, who had come up with him to Jerusalem.

[42]It was already getting towards evening, and it was the day of Preparation, that is, the day before the sabbath. [43]Joseph of Arimathea, a reputable member of the council who was himself eagerly awaiting God's kingdom, took his courage in both hands, went to Pilate, and requested the body of Jesus.

[44]Pilate was surprised that he was already dead. He summoned the centurion, and asked whether he had been dead for some time. [45]When he learned the facts from the centurion, he conceded the body to Joseph.

⁴⁶So Joseph bought a linen cloth, took the body down, wrapped it in the cloth, and laid it in a tomb cut out of the rock. He rolled a stone against the door of the tomb. ⁴⁷Mary Magdalene and Mary the mother of Joses saw where he was buried.

Yesterday a friend came to see me in great excitement. He had been in Jerusalem a few weeks earlier, and had happened to be present when an archaeologist stumbled upon a previously unknown first-century tomb, just outside the walls of the old city. It was preserved intact: bones, ossuaries (bone-boxes), everything, including one full skeleton still wrapped up, laid by itself in a niche in the cave. Presumably the family had not been able to return, as they would normally expect to, and collect the bones to put them in another ossuary.

There are, no doubt, still plenty of other archaeological excitements waiting to be discovered. But this one brings into focus for us what we might otherwise miss in a modern reading of the story: the manner of Jesus' burial, and the reasons why Mark is keen to tell us the story like this. We might suppose the burial narrative to be a sad and not particularly interesting appendix to the story of Jesus' death; for Mark, it trembles with the suppressed excitement of what he knows is going to happen next.

First, he wants to introduce us to the women who – as we now discover for the first time – have been accompanying Jesus and the **disciples** all along. Mark doesn't waste words; the reason he's telling us about them now is because they will be vital in the next chapter. They were, he says, present at the crucifixion and at the burial; they saw where the tomb was (implication: they knew, they weren't mistaken). He doesn't say they assisted Joseph in taking the body down and preparing it for the tomb, but it's perfectly reasonable to fill in the gaps in that way. Unfortunately for early Christian preachers, who would have preferred to have men as the first visitors to Jesus' tomb on the Sunday morning (women were regarded as worthless witnesses in the ancient world), but fortunately for us, because we know the early church would have been highly unlikely to make this story up, the two Marys and Salome will be the key players in the new drama that is about to unfold.

But for the moment another figure steps out of the shadows – making us wonder just how many others like him there were of whom there remains no record. The **sabbath** was coming closer. Something had to be done. If nobody took charge of Jesus' body, it would probably have been thrown into a common grave. Mark is careful to explain that Joseph was a member of the council, and well respected; presumably this means that people in Jerusalem might, even in Mark's day, know of him or his family, and could perhaps check the story. It also means, of course, that he had sat through the night session in the high **priest**'s house, and had heard the accusations and the condemnation. Luke explains at this point that he had not given his consent to the council's decision; Mark, as usual, leaves all that to our imagination.

It was a moment of great potential risk. To show any sympathy with someone who had just been crucified on a charge of sedition was bound to raise suspicions. Peter had been scared out of his wits by the mere suggestion that he was associated with Jesus. Joseph, Mark explains, had been eagerly longing for the **kingdom**; we must assume that this means he had been a keen, though secret, supporter of Jesus. He must have decided that if Jesus had died he had nothing more to lose by doing what he knew to be right.

It also meant, of course, that he would make himself ritually unclean, and unable to engage in some of the normal sabbath practices that evening and the next day. Joseph was treating Jesus as if he was a close member of the family, for whom it was his duty to see to burial before nightfal – as well as to fulfil the old biblical law not to let hanged corpses remain in place overnight. For this he was prepared to face uncleanness, suspicion and possible charges as an associate of Jesus.

Joseph's activities involve quite a lot of quick movement between three o'clock and the deadline of sundown, when the sabbath begins. He has to go from Golgotha to Pilate's headquarters, buy a shroud on the way back through the city, and finish the job in short order. He is kept waiting by Pilate, who summons the centurion from his post at Skull's Place to check that Jesus not only appears to have died but has in fact been dead for some time. This tells us why Mark has bothered with all this detail; one obvious retort to the early Christian claim about Easter was that Jesus had not really died, and that Joseph had cunningly taken him down half-dead in order to revive him later. There are, of course, other objections to this line of thought; but Mark is keen to squash it before it even begins.

The burial, like the burials found by my friend, was designed to be a two-stage one. The body, wrapped up and, ideally, covered with spices to offset the smell of decomposition, would be laid on a shelf or niche, usually at about waist height, within the cave. Other bodies would, in due course, be laid on other shelves in the same cave. Within a year or two the flesh would have decomposed, and the bones could then be gathered and placed in an ossuary, which would be stored for its final rest on another shelf, quite probably in the same tomb.

But in the case of Jesus the second stage was never reached. Mark finishes his account of the burial with a feeling of eager impatience. He has set everything in order for the next stage, but now it is the sabbath, and everything must rest, including the body of Jesus himself.

MARK 16.1–8

The Resurrection

¹When the sabbath was over, Mary Magdalene, Mary the mother of James, and Salome brought spices so that they could come and anoint Jesus. ²Then, very early on the first day of the week, they came to the tomb, just at sunrise. ³They were saying to one another, 'There's that stone at the door of the tomb – who's going to roll it away for us?'

⁴Then, when they looked up, they saw that it had been rolled away. (It was extremely large.)

⁵So they went into the tomb, and there they saw a young man sitting on the right-hand side. He was wearing white. They were totally astonished.

⁶'Don't be astonished', he said to them. 'You're looking for Jesus the Nazarene, who was crucified. He has been raised! He isn't here! Look – this is the place where they laid him.

⁷'But go and tell his disciples – including Peter – that he is going ahead of you to Galilee. You'll see him there, just like he told you.'

⁸They went out, and fled from the tomb. Trembling and panic had seized them. They said nothing to anyone, because they were afraid.

Mark's ending is missing. I am convinced of it. Two of our best manuscripts, both from the fourth century, end where this text breaks off. The alternative endings in several other manuscripts, which I shall deal with in an extra section after this one, seem clearly to be later writings, added by copyists who, agreeing with me that Mark couldn't have meant to stop there, were determined to fill in the gap.

Of course, there are many who think that Mark did after all intend to close the book with the women in fear and silence, but I disagree. I have become quite sure that there was more. I think a very, very early copy of Mark was mutilated. As with many other scrolls and books in the ancient world (and sometimes even in the modern), the last page, or the last column of the scroll, was torn off, presumably by accident.

But let's deal, first of all, with what is there, rather than with what isn't. The three women whom Mark listed as having watched the crucifixion, two of whom also saw where the tomb was (this variation in detail may well be a sign of historical memory), buy spices as soon as the **sabbath** is over, that is, on Saturday evening after sunset. They go to the tomb at first light on the Sunday (the first day of their working week), expecting to have difficulty with the massive stone, but hoping no doubt that someone stronger will be around to help.

We may note, already, what they are *not* saying to themselves (as they might be if this story were a later pious fiction). They were not going in order to witness Jesus' **resurrection**. They had no idea that

162

any such thing was even thinkable. They were going to complete the primary burial. This was a sad task, but a necessary one, both for reverence's sake, and to lessen the smell of decomposition as other bodies, in due course, would be buried in the same tomb over the coming year or so, prior to Jesus' bones being collected and put into an ossuary (the secondary burial).

They got the shock of their lives. The stone was already rolled away. A young man in white sat where Jesus' body had been, and calmly explained to them that Jesus had been raised from the dead and would see them again in Galilee. They were to go with a message to the **disciples**; the specific mention of Peter is presumably not to give him a place of primacy, but to ensure that, after his catastrophic denials, he was not regarded as beyond redemption. They, quite naturally, rushed off home, scared out of their wits. They must have passed several people on the way, but they didn't say a word. They were in shock.

Laborious attempts have been made in modern scholarship not just to suggest that Mark really did mean to stop there, but, as it were, to wallow in the dark uncertainty that results. Mark, we are told, is a book of mysteries. People in Mark are always being told to stay silent; now the women do just that. Instead of a cheap happy ending, they say, Mark has given us something far more powerful, a strange brooding puzzle which leaves every reader turning the matter over, wondering what on earth might have happened, and what it all might mean. These suggestions have an air of sophistication and literary imagination, but I am not convinced.

Mark has told us, over and over again, that Jesus tried to teach the disciples that he would suffer, be killed, and rise again from the dead. They didn't understand; presumably they thought he was talking in riddles. He wasn't, and Mark wants us to understand that he wasn't; he was speaking the truth. He told the disciples, after the transfiguration, that they were to tell no one about it 'until the **son of man** has been raised from the dead' (9.9). They were puzzled by this at the time, but Mark does not intend his readers to go on for ever being puzzled 'as to what this rising from the dead should mean' (9.10).

Mark has, in fact, presented Jesus throughout as a true prophet, and has now spent a good deal of time showing us how the first part of Jesus' prediction about his fate in Jerusalem came true. I find it incredible that he would break off just at the point where he was about to tell us how the second part came true as well.

It might just be possible to think that Mark did stop there – but that he intended anyone reading the book out loud, as they would, to call on one of the eyewitnesses present to tell the story of what they had seen, either that first Easter day or shortly afterwards. But I think it far more likely that he wrote a conclusion, in which the women spoke to the disciples, the disciples went to the tomb, and eventually (presumably in Galilee from what Mark has already said in 14.28 and 16.7), they met Jesus again. I suspect that the book concluded with Jesus not only confirming to them that he was indeed alive again in a new, though certainly bodily, way, but also commissioning them for the work that now awaited them (13.10; 14.9). The ending may not have been very long, but it will have been important as the intended conclusion to the book, drawing the themes to their proper destination.

But we can make a theological virtue out of necessity. Perhaps, in the strange providence of God, the way Mark's book now finishes encourages us all the more to explore not only the **faith** of the early church, that Jesus had indeed risen from the dead, but our own faith. There is a blank at the end of the story, and we are invited to fill it ourselves. Do we take Easter for granted, or have we found ourselves awestruck at the strange new work of God? What do we know of the risen Lord? Where is he now going ahead of us? What tasks has he for us to undertake today, to take 'the **gospel** of the **kingdom**' to the ends of the earth?

MARK 16.9–20

Two Extra Endings

[[They gave a brief account to the people around Peter of what they had been told. After this, Jesus himself sent out from East to West, through their work, the sacred and imperishable proclamation of eternal salvation. Amen.]]

⁹[When Jesus was raised, early on the first day of the week, he appeared first of all to Mary Magdalene, from whom he had cast out seven demons. ¹⁰She went and told the people who had been with him, who were mourning and weeping. ¹¹When they heard that he was alive, and that he had been seen by her, they didn't believe it.

¹²After this he appeared in a different guise to two of them as they were walking into the countryside. ¹³They came back and told the others, but they didn't believe them.

¹⁴Later Jesus appeared to the eleven themselves, as they were at table. He told them off for their unbelief and hardheartedness, for not believing those who had seen him after he had been raised.

¹⁵'Go into all the world,' he said to them, 'and announce the message to all creation. ¹⁶Anyone who believes and is baptized will be rescued, but people who don't believe will be condemned. ¹⁷And these signs will happen around those who believe: they will drive out demons in my name, they will speak with new tongues, ¹⁸they will pick up ser-

pents in their hands; and if they drink anything poisonous it won't harm them. They will lay their hands on the sick, and they will get better.'

¹⁹When the Lord Jesus had spoken with them, he was taken up into heaven, and sat down at God's right hand. ²⁰They went out and announced the message everywhere. The Lord worked with them, validating their message by the signs that accompanied them.]

These are the two 'extra' endings of Mark. They are not found in the best manuscripts, but are added in to several others in a bewildering variety of ways. The shorter, first one (in double square brackets) doesn't have a verse number. The longer second one is known as Mark 16.9–20. They represent at least two different ways – the second one may perhaps include more than one way – in which pious copyists, finding Mark short of a final column or page, decided to add what they thought a suitable conclusion.

The shorter ending is quite unlike Mark's style. It is grandiose and formal. It is a general statement of Christian **faith** in what happened after Easter, but it doesn't link in to the rest of Mark in any visible way, as we might have expected.

The longer ending looks very much like a compilation of bits and pieces from the **resurrection** narratives of Matthew and Luke, with some extra parts added. If, as most believe, Matthew and Luke were written later than Mark, this alone should arouse our suspicions. The passage starts, too, as though beginning the chapter again, introducing Mary Magdalene as though she hasn't already been mentioned several times in the preceding two paragraphs. We can't say for certain that nothing in this passage comes from the original Mark, but it doesn't seem to me likely.

That's not to say there's nothing we can learn here. The passage tells us, at least, how some fairly early Christians – nobody can say how early, but some time perhaps in the late second or early third century at the latest – saw the events of Easter and their significance. Great emphasis is laid, more than in other existing resurrection stories, on the initial unbelief of the **disciples**, despite the evidence of witnesses. Several details are then given about the way in which the **gospel** is to spread throughout the world, with particular reference to the miraculous signs that the disciples will now perform. Jesus is then taken up into **heaven**, and the disciples go about their world-changing task. Many elements of New Testament thinking are present here, but the overall effect is strangely flat. Quite unlike Mark, in fact, who can hardly be dull for a second.

The passage, though, can prompt us to think about our own discipleship, our own commission from the risen Jesus. Would he have to chide us for our unbelief and hardheartedness? Would we be found to be preaching the gospel with as much fervour as Jesus here commands? And how, in particular, would we apply today the very interesting instruction, in verse 15, to preach the gospel not just to every *creature* but to the entire *creation*?

GLOSSARY

the accuser, *see* the satan

age to come, *see* present age

apostle, disciple, the Twelve
'Apostle' means 'one who is sent'. It could be used of an ambassador or official delegate. In the New Testament it is sometimes used specifically of Jesus' inner circle of twelve; but Paul sees not only himself but several others outside the Twelve as 'apostles', the criterion being whether the person had personally seen the risen Jesus. Jesus' own choice of twelve close associates symbolized his plan to renew God's people, Israel (who traditionally thought of themselves as having twelve tribes); after the death of Judas Iscariot (Matthew 27.5; Acts 1.18), Matthias was chosen by lot to take his place, preserving the symbolic meaning. During Jesus' lifetime they, and many other followers, were seen as his 'disciples', which means 'pupils' or 'apprentices'.

baptism
Literally, 'plunging' people into water. From within a wider Jewish tradition of ritual washings and bathings, **John the Baptist** undertook a vocation of baptizing people in the Jordan, not as one ritual among others but as a unique moment of **repentance**, preparing them for the coming of the **kingdom of God**. Jesus himself was baptized by John, identifying himself with this renewal movement and developing it in his own way. His followers in turn baptized others. After his **resurrection**, and the sending of the **holy spirit**, baptism became the normal sign and means of entry into the community of Jesus' people. As early as Paul it was aligned both with the **Exodus** from Egypt (1 Corinthians 10.2) and with Jesus' death and resurrection (Romans 6.2–11).

Christ, *see* Messiah

circumcision, circumcised
The cutting off of the foreskin. Male circumcision was a major mark of identity for Jews, following its initial commandment to Abraham (Genesis 17), reinforced by Joshua (Joshua 5.2–9). Other peoples, e.g. the Egyptians, also circumcised male children. A line of thought from Deuteronomy (e.g. 30.6), through Jeremiah (e.g. 31.33), to the **Dead Sea Scrolls** and the New Testament (e.g. Romans 2.29) speaks of 'circumcision of the heart' as God's real desire,

167

by which one may become inwardly what the male Jew is outwardly, that is, marked out as part of God's people. At periods of Jewish assimilation into the surrounding culture, some Jews tried to remove the marks of circumcision (e.g. 1 Maccabees 1.11–15).

covenant

At the heart of Jewish belief is the conviction that the one God, YHWH, who had made the whole world, had called Abraham and his family to belong to him in a special way. The promises God made to Abraham and his family, and the requirements that were laid on them as a result, came to be seen in terms either of the agreement that a king would make with a subject people, or of the marriage bond between husband and wife. One regular way of describing this relationship was 'covenant', which can thus include both promise and law. The covenant was renewed at Mount Sinai with the giving of the **Torah**; in Deuter-onomy before the entry to the promised land; and, in a more focused way, with David (e.g. Psalm 89). Jeremiah 31 promised that after the punishment of **exile** God would make a 'new covenant' with his people, forgiving them and binding them to him more intimately. Jesus believed that this was coming true through his **kingdom** proclamation and his death and **resurrection**. The early Christians developed these ideas in various ways, believing that in Jesus the promises had at last been fulfilled.

David's son, *see* son of David

Dead Sea Scrolls

A collection of texts, some in remarkably good repair, some extremely fragmen-tary, found in the late 1940s around Qumran (near the north-east corner of the Dead Sea), and virtually all now edited, translated and in the public domain. They formed all or part of the library of a strict monastic group, most likely Essenes, founded in the mid-second century BC and lasting until the Jewish–Roman war of 66–70. The scrolls include the earliest existing manuscripts of the Hebrew and Aramaic scriptures, and several other important documents of community regulations, scriptural exegesis, hymns, wisdom writings, and other literature. They shed a flood of light on one small segment within the Judaism of Jesus' day, helping us to understand how some Jews at least were thinking, pray-ing and reading scripture. Despite attempts to prove the contrary, they make no reference to **John the Baptist**, Jesus, Paul, James or early Christianity in general.

demons, *see* the satan

disciple, *see* apostle

Essenes, *see* Dead Sea Scrolls

exile

Deuteronomy (29—30) warned that if Israel disobeyed YHWH, he would send his people into exile, but that if they then repented he would bring them back. When the Babylonians sacked Jerusalem and took the people into exile, prophets such as Jeremiah interpreted this as the fulfilment of this prophecy, and made further promises about how long exile would last (70 years, according to Jeremiah 25.12; 29.10). Sure enough, exiles began to return in the late sixth century BC (Ezra 1.1). However, the post-exilic period was largely a disappointment, since the people were still enslaved to foreigners (Nehemiah 9.36); and at the height of persecution by the Syrians Daniel 9.2, 24 spoke of the 'real' exile lasting not for 70 years but for 70 *weeks* of years, i.e. 490 years. Longing for the real 'return from exile', when the prophecies of Isaiah, Jeremiah, etc. would be fulfilled, and redemption from pagan oppression accomplished, continued to characterize many Jewish movements, and was a major theme in Jesus' proclamation and his summons to **repentance.**

Exodus

The Exodus from Egypt took place, according to the book of that name, under the leadership of Moses, after long years in which the Israelites had been enslaved there. (According to Genesis 15.13f., this was itself part of God's covenanted promise to Abraham.) It demonstrated, to them and to Pharaoh, King of Egypt, that Israel was God's special child (Exodus 4.22). They then wandered through the Sinai wilderness for 40 years, led by God in a pillar of cloud and fire; early on in this time they were given the **Torah** on Mount Sinai itself. Finally, after the death of Moses and under the leadership of Joshua, they crossed the Jordan and entered, and eventually conquered, the Promised Land of Canaan. This event, commemorated annually in Passover and other Jewish festivals, gave the Israelites not only a powerful memory of what had made them a people, but also a particular shape and content to their faith in YHWH as not only creator but also redeemer; and in subsequent enslavements, particularly the **exile**, they looked for a further redemption which would be, in effect, a new Exodus. Probably no other past event so dominated the imagination of first-century Jews; among them the early Christians, following the lead of Jesus himself, continually referred back to the Exodus to give meaning and shape to their own critical events, most particularly Jesus' death and **resurrection.**

faith

Faith in the New Testament covers a wide area of human trust and trustworthiness, merging into love at one end of the scale and loyalty at the other. Within Jewish and Christian thinking faith in God also includes *belief*, accepting certain things as true about God, and what he has done in the world (e.g. bringing Israel out of Egypt; raising Jesus from the dead). For Jesus, 'faith' often seems to mean 'recognizing that God is decisively at work to bring the **kingdom** through Jesus'. For Paul, 'faith' is both the specific belief that Jesus is Lord and that God raised him from the dead (Romans 10.9) and the response of grateful human love to sovereign divine love (Galatians 2.20). This faith is, for Paul, the solitary badge of membership in God's people in **Christ**, marking them out in a way that **Torah**, and the works it prescribes, can never do.

Gentiles

The Jews divided the world into Jews and non-Jews. The Hebrew word for non-Jews, *goyim*, carries overtones both of family identity (i.e. not of Jewish ancestry) and of worship (i.e. of idols, not of the one true God yhwh). Though many Jews established good relations with Gentiles, not least in the Jewish Diaspora (the dispersion of Jews away from Palestine), officially there were taboos against contact such as intermarriage. In the New Testament the Greek word *ethne*, 'nations', carries the same meanings as *goyim*. Part of Paul's overmastering agenda was to insist that Gentiles who believed in Jesus had full rights in the Christian community alongside believing Jews, without having to become **circumcised**.

Gehenna, hell

Gehenna is, literally, the valley of Hinnom, on the south-west slopes of Jerusalem. From ancient times it was used as a garbage dump, smouldering with a continual fire. Already by the time of Jesus some Jews used it as an image for the place of punishment after death. Jesus' own usage blends the two meanings in his warnings both to Jerusalem itself (unless it repents, the whole city will become a smouldering heap of garbage) and to people in general (to beware of God's final judgment).

good news, gospel, message, word

The idea of 'good news', for which an older English word is 'gospel', had two principal meanings for first-century Jews. First, with roots in Isaiah, it meant the news of yhwh's long-awaited victory over evil and rescue of his people. Second, it was used in the Roman world for the accession, or birthday, of the Emperor. Since for Jesus and Paul the announcement of God's inbreaking **kingdom** was both the fulfilment of prophecy and a challenge to the world's present rulers, 'gospel' became an important shorthand for both the message of Jesus himself and the apostolic message about him. Paul saw this message as itself the vehicle of God's saving power (Romans 1.16; 1 Thessalonians 2.13).

The four canonical 'gospels' tell the story of Jesus in such a way as to bring out both these aspects (unlike some other so-called 'gospels' circulated in the second and subsequent centuries, which tended both to cut off the scriptural and Jewish roots of Jesus' achievement and to inculcate a private spirituality rather than confrontation with the world's rulers). Since in Isaiah this creative, life-giving good news was seen as God's own powerful word (40.8; 55.11), the early Christians could use 'word' or 'message' as another shorthand for the basic Christian proclamation.

heaven

Heaven is God's dimension of the created order (Genesis 1.1; Psalm 115.16; Matthew 6.9), whereas 'earth' is the world of space, time and matter that we know. 'Heaven' thus sometimes stands, reverentially, for 'God' (as in Matthew's regular 'kingdom of heaven'). Normally hidden from human sight, heaven is occasionally revealed or unveiled so that people can see God's dimension of ordinary life (e.g. 2 Kings 6.17; Revelation 1, 4—5). Heaven in the New Testament is thus not usually seen as the place where God's people go after death; at the end, the New Jerusalem descends *from* heaven *to* earth, joining the two dimensions for ever. 'Entering the kingdom of heaven' does not mean 'going to heaven after death', but belonging in the present to the people who steer their earthly course by the standards and purposes of heaven (cf. the Lord's Prayer: 'on earth as in heaven', Matthew 6.10), and who are assured of membership in the **age to come**.

hell, *see* Gehenna

Herodians

Herod the Great ruled Judaea from 37 to 4 BC; after his death his territory was divided between his sons Archelaus, Herod Antipas (the Herod of the **gospels**), and Philip. The Herodians supported the claims of Antipas to be the true king of the Jews. Though the **Pharisees** would normally oppose such a claim, they could make common cause with the Herodians when facing a common threat (e.g. Jesus, Mark 3.6).

high priest, *see* priests

holy spirit

In Genesis 1.2, the spirit is God's presence and power *within* creation, without God being identified with creation. The same spirit entered people, notably the prophets, enabling them to speak and act for God. At his baptism by **John the Baptist**, Jesus was specially equipped with the spirit, resulting in his remarkable public career (Acts 10.38). After his **resurrection**, his followers were themselves filled (Acts 2) by the same spirit, now identified as Jesus' own spirit: the creator God was acting afresh, remaking the world and them too. The spirit enabled them to live out a holiness which the **Torah** could not, producing 'fruit' in their lives, giving them 'gifts' with which to serve God, the world and the church, and assuring them of future **resurrection** (Romans 8; Galatians 4—5; 1 Corinthians 12—14). From very early in Christianity (e.g. Galatians 4.1-7), the spirit became part of the new revolutionary definition of God himself: 'the one who sends the son and the spirit of the son'.

John (the Baptist)

Jesus' cousin on his mother's side, born a few months before Jesus; his father was a **priest**. He acted as a prophet, baptizing in the Jordan – dramatically re-enacting the Exodus from Egypt – to prepare people, by **repentance**, for God's coming judgment. He may have had some contact with the **Essenes**, though his eventual public message was different from theirs. Jesus' own vocation was decisively confirmed at his **baptism** by John. As part of John's message of the **kingdom**, he outspokenly criticized Herod Antipas for marrying his brother's wife. Herod had him imprisoned, and then beheaded him at his wife's request (Mark 6.14–29). Groups of John's disciples continued a separate existence, without merging into Christianity, for some time afterwards (e.g. Acts 19.1–7).

justification

God's declaration, from his position as judge of all the world, that someone is in the right, despite universal sin. This declaration will be made on the last day on the basis of an entire life (Romans 2.1–16), but is brought forward into the present on the basis of Jesus' achievement, because sin has been dealt with through his cross (Romans 3.21—4.25); the means of this present justification is simply **faith**. This means, particularly, that Jews and **Gentiles** alike are full members of the family promised by God to Abraham (Galatians 3; Romans 4).

kingdom of God, kingdom of heaven

Best understood as the king*ship*, or sovereign and saving rule, of Israel's God YHWH, as celebrated in several Psalms (e.g. 99.1) and prophecies (e.g. Daniel 6.26f.). Because YHWH was the creator God, when he finally became king in the way he intended this would involve setting the world to rights, and particularly rescuing Israel from its enemies. 'Kingdom of God' and various equivalents (e.g. 'No king but God!') became revolutionary slogans around the time of Jesus. Jesus' own announcement of God's kingdom redefined these expectations around his own very different plan and vocation. His invitation to people to 'enter' the kingdom was a way of summoning them to allegiance to himself and his programme, seen as the start of God's long-awaited saving reign. For Jesus, the kingdom was coming not in a single move, but in stages, of which his own public career was one, his death and resurrection another, and a still future consummation another. Note that 'kingdom of **heaven**' is Matthew's preferred form for the same phrase, following a regular Jewish practice of saying 'heaven' rather than 'God'. It does not refer to a place ('heaven'), but to the fact of God's becoming king in and through Jesus and his achievement. Paul speaks of Jesus, as **Messiah**, already in possession of his kingdom, waiting to hand it over finally to the Father (1 Corinthians 15.23–8; cf. Ephesians 5.5).

lawyers, legal experts, *see* Pharisees

leper, leprosy

In a world without modern medicine, tight medical controls were needed to prevent the spread of contagious diseases. Several such conditions, mostly severe skin problems, were referred to as 'leprosy', and two long biblical chapters (Leviticus 13—14) are devoted to diagnosis and prevention of it. Sufferers had to live away from towns and shout 'unclean' to warn others not to approach them (13.45). If they were healed, this had to be certified by a **priest** (14.2–32).

life, soul, spirit

Ancient people held many different views about what made human beings the special creatures they are. Some, including many Jews, believed that to be complete, humans needed bodies as well as inner selves. Others, including many influenced by the philosophy of Plato (fourth century BC), believed that the important part of a human was the 'soul' (Gk: *psyche*), which at death would be happily freed from its bodily prison. Confusingly for us, the same word *psyche* is often used in the New Testament within a Jewish framework where it clearly means 'life' or 'true self', without implying a body/soul dualism that devalues the body. Human inwardness of experience and understanding can also be referred to as 'spirit'. *See also* **holy spirit**; **resurrection**.

message, *see* good news

Messiah, messianic, Christ

The Hebrew word means literally 'anointed one', hence in theory either a prophet, **priest** or king. In Greek this translates as *Christos*; 'Christ' in early Christianity was a title, and only gradually became an alternative proper name for Jesus. In practice 'Messiah' is mostly restricted to the notion, which took various forms in ancient Judaism, of the coming king who would be David's true heir, through whom YHWH would bring judgment to the world, and in particular would rescue Israel from pagan enemies. There was no single template of expectations. Scriptural stories and promises contributed to different ideals and movements, often focused on (a) decisive military defeat of Israel's enemies and (b) rebuilding or cleansing the **Temple**. The **Dead Sea Scrolls** speak of two 'Messiahs', one a priest and the other a king. The universal early Christian belief that Jesus was Messiah is only explicable, granted his crucifixion by the Romans (which would have been seen as a clear sign that he was not the Messiah), by their belief that God had raised him from the dead, so vindicating the implicit messianic claims of his earlier ministry.

miracles

Like some of the old prophets, notably Elijah and Elisha, Jesus performed many deeds of remarkable power, particularly healings. The **gospels** refer to these as

173

'deeds of power', 'signs', 'marvels', or 'paradoxes'. Our word 'miracle' tends to imply that God, normally 'outside' the closed system of the world, sometimes 'intervenes'; miracles have then frequently been denied by sceptics as a matter of principle. However, in the Bible God is always present, however strangely, and 'deeds of power' are seen as *special* acts of a *present* God rather than as *intrusive* acts of an *absent* one. Jesus' own 'mighty works' are seen particularly, following prophecy, as evidence of his messiahship (e.g. Matthew 11.2–6).

Mishnah

The main codification of Jewish law (**Torah**) by the **rabbis**, produced in about AD 200, reducing to writing the 'oral Torah' which in Jesus' day ran parallel to the 'written Torah'. The Mishnah is itself the basis of the much larger collections of traditions in the two Talmuds (roughly AD 400).

parables

From the Old Testament onwards, prophets and other teachers used various story-telling devices as vehicles for their challenge to Israel (e.g. 2 Samuel 12.1–7). Sometimes these appeared as visions with interpretations (e.g. Daniel 7). Similar techniques were used by the **rabbis**. Jesus made his own creative adaptation of these traditions, in order to break open the world-view of his contemporaries and to invite them to share his vision of God's **kingdom** instead. His stories portrayed this as something that was *happening*, not just a timeless truth, and enabled his hearers to step inside the story and make it their own. As with some Old Testament visions, some of Jesus' parables have their own interpretations (e.g. the sower, Mark 4); others are thinly disguised retellings of the prophetic story of Israel (e.g. the wicked tenants, Mark 12).

parousia

Literally, it means 'presence', as opposed to 'absence', and sometimes used by Paul with this sense (e.g. Philippians 2.12). It was already used in the Roman world for the ceremonial arrival of, for example, the Emperor at a subject city or colony. Although the ascended Lord is not 'absent' from the church, when he 'appears' (Colossians 3.4; 1 John 3.2) in his 'second coming' this will be, in effect, an 'arrival' like that of the Emperor, and Paul uses it thus in 1 Corinthians 15.23; 1 Thessalonians 2.19; etc. In the **gospels** it is found only in Matthew 24 (verses 3, 27, 39).

Pharisees, lawyers, legal experts, rabbis

The Pharisees were an unofficial but powerful Jewish pressure group through most of the first centuries BC and AD. Largely lay-led, though including some priests, their aim was to purify Israel through intensified observance of the Jewish law (**Torah**), developing their own traditions about the precise meaning and application of scripture, their own patterns of prayer and other devotion, and their own calculations of the national hope. Though not all legal experts were Pharisees, most Pharisees were thus legal experts.

They effected a democratization of Israel's life, since for them the study and practice of Torah was equivalent to worshipping in the **Temple** – though they were adamant in pressing their own rules for the Temple liturgy on an unwilling (and often Sadducean) priesthood. This enabled them to survive AD 70 and, merging into the early rabbinic movement, to develop new ways forward. Politically they stood up for ancestral traditions, and were at the forefront of various movements of revolt against both pagan overlordship and compromised Jewish leaders. By Jesus' day there were two distinct schools, the stricter one of Shammai, more inclined towards armed revolt, and the more lenient one of Hillel, ready to live and let live.

Jesus' debates with the Pharisees are at least as much a matter of agenda and policy (Jesus strongly opposed their separatist nationalism) as about details of theology and piety. Saul of Tarsus was a fervent right-wing Pharisee, presumably a Shammaite, until his conversion.

After the disastrous war of AD 66–70, these schools of Hillel and Shammai continued bitter debate on appropriate policy. Following the further disaster of AD 135 (the failed Bar-Kochba revolt against Rome) their traditions were carried on by the rabbis who, though looking to the earlier Pharisees for inspiration, developed a Torah-piety in which personal holiness and purity took the place of political agendas.

present age, age to come, the life of God's coming age

By the time of Jesus many Jewish thinkers divided history into two periods: 'the present age' and 'the age to come' – the latter being the time when YHWH would at last act decisively to judge evil, to rescue Israel, and to create a new world of justice and peace. The early Christians believed that, though the full blessings of the coming age lay still in the future, it had already begun with Jesus, particularly with his death and **resurrection**, and that by **faith** and **baptism** they were able to enter it already. For this reason, the customary translation 'eternal life' is rendered here as 'the life of God's coming age'.

priests, high priest

Aaron, the older brother of Moses, was appointed Israel's first high priest (Exodus 28—29), and in theory his descendants were Israel's priests thereafter. Other members of his tribe (Levi) were 'Levites', performing other liturgical duties but not sacrificing. Priests lived among the people all around the country, having a local teaching role (Leviticus 10.11; Malachi 2.7), and going to Jerusalem by rotation to perform the **Temple** liturgy (e.g. Luke 2.8).

David appointed Zadok (whose Aaronic ancestry is sometimes questioned) as high priest, and his family remained thereafter the senior priests in Jerusalem, probably the ancestors of the **Sadducees**. One explanation of the origins of the **Qumran** Essenes is that they were a dissident group who believed themselves to be the rightful chief priests.

Qumran, *see* **Dead Sea Scrolls**

rabbis, *see* **Pharisees**

repentance

Literally, this means 'turning back'. It is widely used in Old Testament and subsequent Jewish literature to indicate both a personal turning away from sin and Israel's corporate turning away from idolatry and back to YHWH. Through both meanings, it is linked to the idea of 'return from **exile**'; if Israel is to 'return' in all senses, it must 'return' to YHWH. This is at the heart of the summons of both **John the Baptist** and Jesus. In Paul's writings it is mostly used for **Gentiles** turning away from idols to serve the true God; also for sinning Christians who need to return to Jesus.

resurrection

In most biblical thought, human bodies matter and are not merely disposable prisons for the **soul**. When ancient Israelites wrestled with the goodness and justice of YHWH, the creator, they ultimately came to insist that he must raise the dead (Isaiah 26.19; Daniel 12.2–3) – a suggestion firmly resisted by classical pagan thought. The longed-for return from exile was also spoken of in terms of YHWH raising dry bones to new life (Ezekiel 37.1–14). These ideas were developed in the second-**Temple** period, not least at times of martyrdom (e.g. 2 Maccabees 7). Resurrection was not just 'life after death', but a newly embodied life *after* 'life after death'; those at present dead were either 'asleep', or seen as 'souls', 'angels' or 'spirits', awaiting new embodiment.

The early Christian belief that Jesus had been raised from the dead was not that he had 'gone to **heaven**', or that he had been 'exalted', or was 'divine'; they believed all those as well, but each could have been expressed without mention of resurrection. Only the bodily resurrection of Jesus explains the rise of the early church, particularly its belief in Jesus' messiahship (which his crucifixion would have called into question). The early Christians believed that they themselves would be raised to a new, transformed bodily life at the time of the Lord's return or **parousia** (e.g. Philippians 3.20f.).

sabbath

The Jewish sabbath, the seventh day of the week, was a regular reminder both of creation (Genesis 2.3; Exodus 20.8–11) and of the **Exodus** (Deuteronomy 5.15). Along with **circumcision** and the food laws, it was one of the badges of Jewish identity within the pagan world of late antiquity, and a considerable body of Jewish law and custom grew up around its observance.

sacrifice

Like all ancient people, the Israelites offered animal and vegetable sacrifices to their God. Unlike others, they possessed a highly detailed written code (mostly in Leviticus) for what to offer and how to offer it; this in turn was developed in the **Mishnah** (*c.*AD 200). The Old Testament specifies that sacrifices can only be offered in the Jerusalem **Temple**; after this was destroyed in AD 70, sacrifices ceased, and Judaism developed further the idea, already present in some teachings, of prayer, fasting and almsgiving as alternative forms of sacrifice. The early Christians used the language of sacrifice in connection with such things as holiness, evangelism and the eucharist.

Sadducees

By Jesus' day, the Sadducees were the aristocracy of Judaism, possibly tracing their origins to the family of Zadok, David's **high priest**. Based in Jerusalem, and including most of the leading priestly families, they had their own traditions and attempted to resist the pressure of the **Pharisees** to conform to theirs. They claimed to rely only on the Pentateuch (the first five books of the Old Testament), and denied any doctrine of a future life, particularly of the **resurrection** and other ideas associated with it, presumably because of the encouragement such beliefs gave to revolutionary movements. No writings from the Sadducees have survived, unless the apocryphal book of Ben-Sirach (Ecclesiasticus) comes from them. The Sadducees themselves did not survive the destruction of Jerusalem and the **Temple** in AD 70.

the satan, 'the accuser', demons

The Bible is never very precise about the identity of the figure known as 'the satan'. The Hebrew word means 'the accuser', and at times the satan seems to be a member of YHWH's heavenly council, with special responsibility as director of prosecutions (1 Chronicles 21.1; Job 1—2; Zechariah 3.1f.). However, it becomes identified variously with the serpent of the garden of Eden (Genesis 3.1-15) and with the rebellious daystar cast out of **heaven** (Isaiah 14.12–15), and was seen by many Jews as the quasi-personal source of evil standing behind both human wickedness and large-scale injustice, and sometimes operating through semi-independent 'demons'. By Jesus' time various words were used to denote this figure, including Beelzebul/b (lit. 'Lord of the flies') and simply 'the evil one'; Jesus warned his followers against the deceits this figure could perpetrate. His opponents accused him of being in league with the satan, but the early Christians believed that Jesus in fact defeated it both in his own struggles with temptation (Matthew 4; Luke 4), his exorcisms of demons, and his death (1 Corinthians 2.8; Colossians 2.15). Final victory over this ultimate enemy is thus assured (Revelation 20), though the struggle can still be fierce for Christians (Ephesians 6.10–20).

scribes

In a world where many could not write, or not very well, a trained class of writers ('scribes') performed the important function of drawing up contracts for business, marriage, etc. Many scribes would thus be legal experts, and quite possibly **Pharisees**, though being a scribe was compatible with various political and religious standpoints. The work of Christian scribes was of vital importance in copying early Christian writings, particularly the stories about Jesus.

son of David, David's son

An alternative, and infrequently used, title for **Messiah**. The messianic promises of the Old Testament often focus specifically on David's son, for example 2 Samuel 7.12–16; Psalm 89.19–37. Joseph, Mary's husband, is called 'son of David' by the angel in Matthew 1.20.

son of God

Originally a title for Israel (Exodus 4.22) and the Davidic king (Psalm 2.7); also used of ancient angelic figures (Genesis 6.2). By the New Testament period it was already used as a **messianic** title, for example, in the **Dead Sea Scrolls**. There, and when used of Jesus in the **gospels** (e.g. Matthew 16.16), it means, or reinforces, 'Messiah', without the later significance of 'divine'. However, already in Paul the transition to the fuller meaning (one who was already equal with God and was sent by him to become human and to become Messiah) is apparent, without loss of the meaning 'Messiah' itself (e.g. Galatians 4.4).

son of man

In Hebrew or Aramaic, this simply means 'mortal', or 'human being'; in later Judaism, it is sometimes used to mean 'I' or 'someone like me'. In the New Testament the phrase is frequently linked to Daniel 7.13, where 'one like a son of man' is brought on the clouds of **heaven** to 'the Ancient of Days', being vindicated after a period of suffering, and is given kingly power. Though Daniel 7 itself interprets this as code for 'the people of the saints of the Most High', by the first century some Jews understood it as a **messianic** promise. Jesus developed this in his own way in certain key sayings which are best understood as promises that God would vindicate him, and judge those who had opposed him, after his own suffering (e.g. Mark 14.62). Jesus was thus able to use the phrase as a cryptic self-designation, hinting at his coming suffering, his vindication and his God-given authority.

soul, *see* life

spirit, *see* life, holy spirit

Temple

The Temple in Jerusalem was planned by David (*c*.1000 BC) and built by his son Solomon as the central sanctuary for all Israel. After reforms under Hezekiah and Josiah in the seventh century BC, it was destroyed by Babylon in 587 BC. Rebuilding by the returned **exiles** began in 538 BC, and was completed in 516, initiating the 'second Temple period'. Judas Maccabaeus cleansed it in 164 BC after its desecration by Antiochus Epiphanes (167). Herod the Great began to rebuild and beautify it in 19 BC; the work was completed in AD 63. The Temple was destroyed by the Romans in AD 70. Many Jews believed it should and would be rebuilt; some still do. The Temple was not only the place of **sacrifice**; it was believed to be the unique dwelling of **YHWH** on earth, the place where **heaven** and earth met.

Torah, Jewish law

'Torah', narrowly conceived, consists of the first five books of the Old Testament, the 'five books of Moses' or 'Pentateuch'. (These contain much law, but also much narrative.) It can also be used for the whole Old Testament scriptures, though strictly these are the 'Law, prophets and writings'. In a broader sense, it refers to the whole developing corpus of Jewish legal tradition, written and oral; the oral Torah was initially codified in the **Mishnah** around AD 200, with wider developments found in the two Talmuds, of Babylon and Jerusalem, codified around AD 400. Many Jews in the time of Jesus and Paul regarded the Torah as being so strongly God-given as to be almost itself, in some sense, divine; some (e.g. Ecclesiasticus 24) identified it with the figure of 'Wisdom'. Doing what Torah said was not seen as a means of earning God's favour, but rather of expressing gratitude, and as a key badge of Jewish identity.

the Twelve, *see* apostle

word, *see* good news

YHWH

The ancient Israelite name for God, from at least the time of the **Exodus** (Exodus 6.2f.). It may originally have been pronounced 'Yahweh', but by the time of Jesus it was considered too holy to speak out loud, except for the **high priest** once a year in the Holy of Holies in the **Temple**. Instead, when reading scripture, pious Jews would say *Adonai*, 'Lord', marking this usage by adding the vowels of *Adonai* to the consonants of YHWH, eventually producing the hybrid 'Jehovah'. The word YHWH is formed from the verb 'to be', combining 'I am who I am', 'I will be who I will be', and perhaps 'I am because I am', emphasizing YHWH's sovereign creative power.

STUDY GUIDE

Introducing the Study

Mark for Everyone is one of a series of commentaries written with the general reader in mind by noted New Testament scholar, N. T. Wright. Wright has written these commentaries to facilitate daily devotions, personal study or group discussion. They each include Wright's own translation of the biblical text divided into short segments followed by an accompanying section of background information and contextual explanation about each scripture segment.

In Wright's words: 'Many people think Mark's gospel was the first to be written, and certainly it has all the zip and punch of a quick, hasty story that's meant to grab you by the collar and make you face the truth about Jesus, about God and about yourself.' The 'zip and punch' of this gospel, on its own, may help encourage sufficient preparation (i.e., reading and reflecting) by members of the group and thereby facilitate thoughtful discussion.

To the Leader

'On the very first occasion when someone stood up in public to tell people about Jesus, he made it very clear: this message is for everyone' (page xiii).

N.T. Wright makes it clear that he intends his series of commentary guides – like the message of Jesus – to be for *everyone*; to that end, he has written these guides to make the texts of the Bible (in this case, Mark's gospel) accessible to any reader. Similarly, the task of the leader is to encourage and facilitate participation by *everyone*. Consider taking time at the start of the study to set the expectation that participants read in advance the selected sections from Wright's book (including the scripture passages) to be discussed in each session. Even minimal preparation will enhance the overall experience of the study. An easy way to do this is to send a weekly email to the group members with the selected pages from *Mark for Everyone* (see session guides) for them to read before each session.

181

Essentials for Participation

- Welcome the Bible as a dialogue partner and be open to the possibility of being challenged or changed by it.
- Welcome each other as dialogue partners who will bring unique insights to the group's experience, including different understandings of the Bible.

Essentials for Guiding Discussion

- Review questions provided in the session guides before using them. Make notes on your thoughts. This will enable you to see the extent to which the questions may need additional clarification to the group during their conversations with one another.
- Be open to silence during discussions; some people need more time than others to think before responding.
- Listen carefully to the group's conversation. Attentive listening is key to keeping the discussion moving along, encouraging individual contributions to the discussion, making connections among the various comments made and determining what follow-up questions might be needed.

The Session Readings

Session 1—Jesus Brings Good News: A Different Reality

Readings: Mark 1—3.6 (pages 1–23)

Mark 1.1–8	*The Preaching of John the Baptist*
Mark 1.9–13	Jesus' Baptism
Mark 1.14–20	The Calling of the Disciples
Mark 1.21–34	Exorcism and Healings
Mark 1.35–45	The Healing of a Man with a Skin Disease
Mark 2.1–12	*The Healing of the Paralytic*
Mark 2.13–17	The Calling of Levi
Mark 2.18–22	*Questions about Fasting*
Mark 2.23–28	Teachings on the Sabbath
Mark 3.1–6	Healing of the Man with the Withered Hand

Session 2—Jesus on the Move: Signposts Small and Spectacular

Readings: Mark 3.7—6.6 (pages 23–50)

Mark 3.7–19	The Twelve Are Appointed

Session 3—Jesus on a Mission: Picnics and Traditions

Readings: Mark 6.7—8.21 (pages 50–77)

Session 4—Jesus in Conversation: Invitations and Challenges

Readings: Mark 8.22—10.52 (pages 77–106)

Session 5—Jesus Gets Serious: Whips and Warnings

Readings: Mark 11.1—13.37 (pages 106–37)

Mark 11.1–11	The Triumphal Entry
Mark 11.12–25	*Jesus Cleanses the Temple*
Mark 11.27–33	The Authority of Jesus Is Questioned
Mark 12.1–12	The Parable of the Tenants
Mark 12.13–17	*On Paying Taxes to Caesar*
Mark 12.18–27	Marriage and the Resurrection
Mark 12.28–34	The Most Important Commandment
Mark 12.35–44	David's Son and the Widow's Mite
Mark 13.1–13	*Signs of the End*
Mark 13.14–27	Further Signs of the End
Mark 13.28–37	Watching for the Son of Man

Session 6—Jesus at the End: Passion and Puzzlement

Readings: Mark 14.1—16.20 (pages 137–66)

Mark 14.1–11	*Jesus Is Anointed at Bethany*
Mark 14.12–25	The Last Supper
Mark 14.26–52	Jesus Is Arrested
Mark 14.53–72	In the High Priest's House
Mark 15.1–15	Jesus before Pilate
Mark 15.16–32	*The Crucifixion*
Mark 15.33–39	*The Death of Jesus*
Mark 15.40–47	The Burial of Jesus
Mark 16.1–8	*The Resurrection*
Mark 16.9–20	Two Extra Endings

Leading the Sessions

The group sessions (60 minutes) will feature these movements:

- Gathering
- Attending to the Word in the Text
- Engaging the Word in Context
- Responding to the Word in the World
- Closing

Gathering

In addition to welcoming one another to the study, spend time at the start of each session centering in prayer and clearing the way for meaningful encounter with the Bible. Consider establishing a pattern of praying together, including both speech and silence. One suggestion: read aloud Mark 1.15 (the announcement of Jesus' message) each week from a different Bible translation. Follow that with a brief time of silent reflection, and then invite God's presence to undergird the group's study of God's Word.

Attending to the Word in the Text

Each session will highlight two or three scripture passages for the group to hear read aloud. Discussion of the scripture text will be guided by some basic questions of interpretation: What was the biblical writer's intent or purpose? What does the passage reveal about Jesus, Jesus' message or Jesus' mission?

Engaging the Word in the Context

Wright's brief commentary sections provide the basis for this part of the session. For the most part, the questions will explore Wright's comments about the two or three highlighted scripture passages the group just discussed. When appropriate, the group may discuss other of Wright's commentary sections. Keep in mind that, in this case, the idea of 'context' refers both to Wright's insights and to the group's thoughts about the biblical texts under discussion – both have value. So the questions here will invite engagement with Wright's and participants' comments.

Responding to the Word in the World

Encountering God's Word in scripture ideally should lead to engaging in God's work and purpose in the world. The questions in this section focus on making connections between the gospel expressed in the Bible and the gospel expressed in persons' faith and life. This is a place where attentive listening is key – be alert to when to insert follow-up or clarification questions of your own, or when to offer encouragement to those who are speaking.

Closing and Prayer

Once again, as the session closes, consider establishing a pattern of praying together, including both speech and silence. One suggestion: name and lift up the concerns and joys of the group and then close by saying aloud, *Lord, in your mercy, hear our prayers* or by praying together the Lord's Prayer.

The Session Guides

SESSION 1
JESUS BRINGS GOOD NEWS: A DIFFERENT REALITY

Reading Selections: Mark 1.1–8; Mark 2.1–12; Mark 2.18–22

Introduction

A good deal of Christian faith is a matter of learning to live by this different reality even when we can't see it. Sometimes, at decisive and climactic moments, the curtain is drawn back and we see, or hear, what's really going on; but most of the time we walk by faith, not by sight. One of the things Mark is saying to us, in the way he's written his gospel, is that when we look at the whole life of Jesus that's how we are to understand it. Look at this story, he says, look at this life and learn to see and hear in it the heavenly vision, the heavenly voice. Learn to hear these words addressed to yourself. Let them change you, mould you, make you somebody new, the person God wants you to be. Discover in this story the normally hidden heavenly dimension of God's world. (page 4)

Gathering

Welcome and then center the group with a brief prayer, closing by reading aloud, for example, a verse from Psalm 19: *Let the words of my mouth and the meditation of my heart be acceptable to you, O Lord, my rock and my redeemer* (Psalm 19.14, NRSV); or recite together Mark 1.15 from a specific translation.

Attending to the Word in the Text

Hear read aloud, one at a time, the selected scripture passages for this session. After hearing each selection, discuss the related question below.

Mark 1.1–8

The Gospel writer includes both John's announcement (1.4) and Jesus' announcement (1.15) in the opening chapter. How do both messages compare in meaning? How do both messages together convey what is new about Jesus' coming?

Mark 2.1–12

How does the text's location of Jesus 'at home' (2.1) give new meaning or fresh insight to Jesus' words and actions in the story?

Mark 2.18–22

What contemporary images – particularly from congregational life – would illustrate what Jesus says about mixing the old with the new?

Engaging the Word in Context

According to Wright, a key verse in the story of the healing of the paralytic is 2.10, where Jesus uses the phrase 'son of man' to signal how he understands his authority to forgive sin. How does Wright understand Jesus' authority? How do we understand Jesus' authority, and how does it inform the church's authority today?

Responding to the Word in the World

'Forgiveness is the most powerful thing in the world' (page 18). At the same time, Wright observes that it is so costly, we settle for less. To what extent do you agree or disagree with him? What ways have you found to bring healing and forgiveness to your community?

Closing and Prayer

Name and lift up the concerns and joys of the group, and then close by saying aloud, *Lord, in your mercy, hear our prayers.*

SESSION 2
JESUS ON THE MOVE: SIGNPOSTS SMALL AND SPECTACULAR

Reading Selections: Mark 4.1–20; Mark 4.35–41; Mark 5.1–20

Introduction

Part of the point of the gospel story, and of this whole section of Mark, is precisely that the life-giving power of God is breaking into, and working through, the ordinary details of life. . . . [And yet] just as Jesus wasn't coming to be a one-man liberation movement in the traditional revolutionary sense, so he wasn't coming to be a one-man emergency medical centre. He was indeed starting a revolution, and he was indeed bringing God's healing power, but his aim went deeper; these things were signs of the real revolution, the real healing, that God was to accomplish through his death and resurrection. Signposts are important, but they aren't the destination. (pages 46–47)

Gathering

Welcome and then center the group with a brief prayer, closing by reading aloud, for example, a verse from Psalm 143.8: *Let the morning bring me word of your unfailing love, for I have put my trust in you. Show me the way I should go, for to you I entrust my life* (NIV), or recite together Mark 1.15 from a specific translation.

Attending to the Word in the Text

Hear read aloud, one at a time, the selected scripture passages for this session. After hearing each selection, discuss the related question below.

Mark 4.1–20

According to Wright, a way to understand Jesus' parables, including the parable of the sower, is to see them functioning as a 'version of Jesus' entire ministry'. How do the various aspects of the parable of the sower (e.g.: the sower, the seed, the soils) reflect the radical, unexpected dimensions of Jesus' ministry? How does the parable serve as a sign of Jesus' announcement in Mark 1.15: 'The time is fulfilled! . . . God's kingdom is arriving! Turn back, and believe the good news!'(NIV)?

Mark 4.35–41

Taking a cue from the disciples' experience with Jesus in the boat, this story poses two basic questions of faith: Who is this Jesus, and do we trust him? What does the story reveal about how the disciples might have answered those two questions *before* the storm? In what ways might their answers have changed (or not) after they were safely back on shore?

Mark 5.1–20

Especially remarkable in this exorcism story are the details – the setting in a cemetery, the dialogue between Jesus and the demoniac, the community's reaction to what happens, the pigs. What do you think Mark intended the details to convey to his hearers?

Engaging the Word in Context

Wright suggests that the story of Jesus calming the storm is *our* story: 'If you sign on with Jesus for the kingdom of God, it will become your story whether you realize it, whether you like it, or not. Wind and storms will come your way.'

When or how has the story of Jesus calming the storm been *your* story?

Responding to the Word in the World

At the end of the story of Jesus and the demoniac, the newly healed man is instructed not to follow Jesus but to go back to his own people and 'tell them what the Lord has done for you'. How does this story inform our own discipleship today?

Closing and Prayer

Name and lift up the concerns and joys of the group and then close by saying aloud, *Lord, in your mercy, hear our prayers.*

SESSION 3
JESUS ON MISSION: PICNICS AND TRADITIONS

Reading Selections: Mark 6.7–13; Mark 6.30–44; Mark 7.1–13

Introduction

Jesus' sharing of his urgent mission with the Twelve was not, then, simply an example of a good leader choosing to delegate, to give his followers experience and get the work done more quickly – though no doubt that is all true as well. It was a deeply symbolic act of witness to the Israel of his day as to what time it was in God's urgent timetable. . . . If we are to make this passage our own today, therefore, it won't do either to suppose that we have to copy exactly Jesus' instructions to his followers, which were for a specific time, place and purpose, or to imagine that we can set the whole thing aside as irrelevant. . . . Learning to hear a passage like this and to respond obediently involves learning to listen to the prophetic call of God, and to the pain of the present world, and to live at the point of intersection between the two. (page 51)

Gathering

Welcome and then center the group with a brief prayer, closing by reading aloud, for example, a verse from Psalm 19: *Let the words of my mouth and the meditation of my heart be acceptable to you, O LORD, my rock and my redeemer* (Psalm 19.14, NRSV); or recite together Mark 1.15 from a specific translation.

Attending to the Word in the Text

Hear read aloud, one at a time, the selected scripture passages for this session. After hearing each selection, discuss the related question below.

Mark 6.7–13

Wright suggests that the mission Jesus sent out the Twelve to accomplish (i.e.: proclaiming repentance, casting out demons, healing the sick) was a 'deeply symbolic act of witness to the Israel of his day'. What does he mean by that? How does that witness *look* to the world of today?

Mark 6.30–44

Wright calls the feeding miracle a 'sign of new creation'. What does he mean by that? How might this notion of Jesus' breaking bread as a sign of new creation inform – or critique – the church's liturgical practice of breaking bread?

Mark 7.1–13

Enter this story by recasting the issue that brings Jesus and the Pharisees into debate in contemporary terms. What human traditions (similar to 'washings of cups, pots, and bronze dishes') are often misconstrued as practices ordained by God? How do they affect Christian faith and/or congregational life?

Engaging the Word in Context

Jesus' feeding the multitude was not a supernatural show of divine power, observes Wright; it was a sign pointing to the inbreaking of God's kingdom. And it included Jesus' command: 'You give them something to eat' (pages 58–59). Where are opportunities for 'prayer and faithful action' in the power of Jesus here and now?

Responding to the Word in the World

The wider issue for Jesus and the Pharisees was: who speaks for God today? Discuss Wright's comment about the Mark 7.1–13 passage in the context of the church today – what debates and challenges today are framed by the question of who speaks for God, Jesus (revealed by scripture) or the church (interpreter of scripture)?

Closing and Prayer

Name and lift up the concerns and joys of the group and then close by saying aloud, *Lord, in your mercy, hear our prayers.*

SESSION 4
JESUS IN CONVERSATION: INVITATIONS
AND CHALLENGES

Reading Selections: Mark 8.31—9.1; Mark 9.38-50; Mark 10.17-31

Introduction

Jesus is a prophet announcing the kingdom of God: the long-awaited moment when God would rule Israel, and ultimately the world, with the justice and mercy of which the scriptures had spoken and for which Israel had longed. What Jesus has been doing – notably, for Mark, the healings, the battles with evil, and the extraordinary feedings, stilling of storms and so on – are signs that this is indeed the moment when the true God is beginning to exercise this power. . . . He had been going around doing things that spoke powerfully but cryptically of a strange new agenda: God's healing energy sweeping through the land, bringing about a new state of affairs, arousing passionate opposition as well as passionate loyalty. And he'd been saying things, by way of explanation, which were often so cryptic that even his friends were puzzled by them. (pages 79-80)

Gathering

Welcome and then center the group with a brief prayer, closing by reading aloud, for example, a verse from Psalm 19: *Let the words of my mouth and the meditation of my heart be acceptable to you, O LORD, my rock and my redeemer* (Psalm 19.14, NRSV); or recite together Mark 1.15 from a specific translation.

Attending to the Word in the Text

Hear read aloud, one at a time, the selected Scripture passages for this session. After hearing each selection, discuss the related question below.

Mark 8.31—9.1

Peter's rebuke of Jesus in this passage comes not long after he proclaims Jesus to be the Messiah, revealing the beginnings of a confessional faith and yet one that remains conditional. Why does Jesus' declaration that God will win the world only through losing evoke such fear among the first disciples? In what ways does that vision evoke a similar response today?

Mark 9.38–50

The sayings here continue Jesus' conversation about true greatness that began a few verses earlier, beginning at 9.30. What particular challenges of discipleship do Jesus' warnings against sin address?

Mark 10.17–31

This story is actually two connected stories – Jesus' encounter with a rich man and Jesus' follow-up conversation about that encounter with his disciples. What similar misconceptions about God are held by both the rich man and the disciples? What is similar about Jesus' responses to both the rich man and to the disciples?

Engaging the Word in Context

In all three of the selected passages, Jesus identifies something in the way of those who would follow him: the risk of the cross, the distraction of sin or the burden of worldly possessions. To what extent are these three barriers still in the way of would-be followers today?

Responding to the Word in the World

'Following Jesus is, more or less, Mark's definition of what being a Christian means; and Jesus is not leading us on a pleasant afternoon hike, but on a walk into danger and risk' (page 82). Is what Wright saying good news for us today or not? How so?

Closing and Prayer

Name and lift up the concerns and joys of the group and then close by saying aloud, *Lord, in your mercy, hear our prayers.*

SESSION 5
JESUS GETS SERIOUS: WHIPS AND WARNINGS

Reading Selections: Mark 11.12–25; Mark 12.13–17; Mark 13.1–13

Introduction

If we take the New Testament seriously, it appears that those who follow Jesus, who are equipped with his spirit, are themselves given authority, under his direction, to act in his name in the world. Have we even begun to consider what this might mean? Where, to use picture language, are the traffic jams in our world waiting for people to step quietly forward and take charge? Where are the Temples that need to be challenged and warned? Where are the people who will know how to give wise answers to the question, Who do you think you are? (page 115)

Gathering

Welcome and then center the group with a brief prayer, closing by reading aloud, for example, a verse from Psalm 19: *Let the words of my mouth and the meditation of my heart be acceptable to you, O LORD, my rock and my redeemer* (Psalm 19.14, NRSV); or recite together Mark 1.15 from a specific translation.

Attending to the Word in the Text

Hear read aloud, one at a time, the selected scripture passages for this session. After hearing each selection, discuss the related question below.

Mark 11.12–25

Mark includes Jesus' cleansing the Temple and cursing a fig tree in the same narrative section. What features do the Temple and the fig tree share in common that help to explain Jesus' words and actions in this passage?

Mark 12.13–17

The question posed to Jesus in verse 15, suggests Wright, is a religious question, not a political one. What does he mean by that? And how is Jesus' response to the question also not a political one?

Mark 13.1–13

The main subject of Jesus' words in this passage is the fate of the Temple in Jerusalem, not the end of the world. How does having that perspective help make sense of Jesus' words? What 'end' does Jesus envision?

Engaging the Word in Context

The fig tree is a recurring image throughout scripture. The fig tree is the third tree mentioned in the Bible and is used by the prophets to signal both God's hope and God's judgment for the people of Israel. What do you think Jesus hoped to communicate to his followers through the image of the withered fig tree (11.20)? What warning does the image convey to contemporary followers?

193

Responding to the Word in the World

According to Wright, when Jesus declared, 'Give Caesar what belongs to Caesar – and give God what belongs to God!' he did *not* mean to define the religious and the sociopolitical as separate segments of life or make a statement on church and state. Then how do Jesus' words here inform the ways we practice our faith in the religious, social and political contexts of our lives?

Closing and Prayer

Name and lift up the concerns and joys of the group and then close by saying aloud, *Lord, in your mercy, hear our prayers.*

SESSION 6
JESUS AT THE END: PASSION AND PUZZLEMENT

*Reading Selections: Mark 14.1–11; Mark 15.16–32;
Mark 15.33–39; Mark 16.1–8*

Introduction

The narrative bumps along from one to the next like an old car on a road full of potholes. What is Mark trying to tell us?

Let's begin at the end, because what the centurion said links up with the theme we have observed from the very start of the gospel. The opening line speaks of Jesus the Messiah, the son of God. The voice at the baptism hails Jesus as God's beloved son; the voice at the transfiguration says the same to Peter, James and John. The parable of the wicked tenants spoke of the beloved son, sent by the father but killed by the workers. Caiaphas asked Jesus if he was the Messiah, God's son. The crowds mocked him in the same words.

And now at last, not the high priest, not a leading rabbi, not even a loyal disciple, but a battle-hardened thug in Roman uniform, used to killing humans the way one might kill flies, stands before this dying young Jew and says something which, in Mark's mind, sends a signal to the whole world that the kingdom has indeed come. (page 158)

Gathering

Welcome and then center the group with a brief prayer, closing by reading aloud, for example, a verse from Psalm 19: *Let the words of my mouth and the meditation of my heart be acceptable to you, O LORD, my rock and my redeemer* (Psalm 19.14, NRSV); or recite together Mark 1.15 from a specific translation.

Attending to the Word in the Text

Hear read aloud, one at a time, the selected scripture passages for this session. After hearing each selection, discuss the related question below.

Mark 14.1–11

Use this excerpt from Wright's commentary to discuss this passage:

> The contrast of reactions as Jesus goes to the cross invites Mark's readers to ponder their own position, feelings and attitudes. 'Were you there', asks the old song, 'when they crucified my Lord?' Yes, but the more important question is, What was going on inside you? Were you part of those who wanted to look the other way, because some people were so exuberant in their devotion? Were you, like Judas, hoping that, if Jesus was determined to die anyway, you at least might make something out of it? Were you glad to be rid of such a troublemaker? Or were you ready to give everything you had to honour this strange man, this unexpected Messiah, this para-doxical Passover-maker? (page 140)

Mark 15.16–32; 15.33–39

A feature of Mark's account of Jesus' crucifixion and death is the variety of sights and sounds that accompany the stark scene of Jesus hanging on the cross: soldiers gambling, bystanders shouting, bandits on either side taunting, a sponge of sour wine raised, a mock sign on display, religious leaders scoffing aloud, midday darkness, the Temple veil torn. Through it all, observes Wright, 'Jesus must stay on the cross.' Why? What is the good news here?

Mark 16.1–8

Wright believes that Mark's original ending is missing. What do you think? What message is conveyed by the account ending with verse 8?

Engaging the Word in Context

Mark's account of the crucifixion does not include any explanation of how or why the Temple veil is torn as Jesus takes his last breath. How does the gospel writer want us to understand it?

Responding to the Word in the World

'Christians are too used to the story of Jesus' death in general'. How do you respond to Wright's statement? Then, to close your study, accept his invitation: 'Find ways of making the story strange again' (page 157).

Closing and Prayer

Name and lift up the concerns and joys of the group, and then close by saying aloud, *Lord, in your mercy, hear our prayers.*